D1426084

GUIDE TO
ADIRONDACK TRAILS

HIGH PEAK REGION

TENTH EDITION
ADIRONDACK MOUNTAIN CLUB, INC.

Published by
The Adirondack Mountain Club, Inc.
Glens Falls, New York
1980

Copyright © 1980

by

ADIRONDACK MOUNTAIN CLUB

All Rights Reserved

First Edition	1934
Second Edition	1941
Third Edition	1945
Fourth Edition	1947
Fifth Edition	1950
Sixth Edition	1957
Seventh Edition	1962
Reprinted with minor revisions	April 1966
Reprinted with minor supplement	July 1968
Fourth Printing	1969
Fifth Printing	1971
Eighth Edition	1972
Reprinted with minor revisions	May 1973
Reprinted with minor revisions	June 1975
Ninth Edition	1977
Reprinted with revisions	1979
Tenth Edition	1980

Library of Congress Cataloging in Publication Data

Adirondack Mountain Club.
  Guide to Adirondack trails.

  Includes index.
  1. Hiking—New York (State)—Adirondack Park—Guide-
books. 2. Trails—New York (State)—Adirondack Park—
Guide-books. 3. Adirondack Park, N.Y.—Guide-books.
I. Title.
GV199.42.N652A342 1980   917.747′54   80–15403
ISBN 0–935272–11–9

Printed in the
UNITED STATES OF AMERICA

Dedication

ROBERT DENNISTON

1900–1980

The 10th Edition of the *Guide to Adirondack Trails* is dedicated to the memory of Bob Denniston, for many years a loyal and hard working member of the Adirondack Mountain Club. He served two terms as president and gave fourteen years of devoted service as treasurer. Bob loved the mountains and was an early Forty-Sixer; one result of his many ascents was a pamphlet giving trail times for the various peaks. Members like Bob enabled ADK to grow. We shall miss him.

Colden, MacIntyre and Indian Pass from N. Elba, Route 73
Photo by R. Meyer

PREFACE PAGE FOR THE HIKER

TRAVELING OFF TRAILS

As most hikers have come to realize, there is precious little wilderness left. Hence, it behooves all of us to help keep attractive the wild lands which still remain. The Adirondacks have comparatively little alpine terrain—above the timberline—and the alpine vegetation of moss, flowers and grass is being threatened by human presence. Hikers are urged to **stay on trails** above the timberline and to refrain from camping on vegetation. If we must leave a beaten trail, we should walk on rock or gravel that cannot be destroyed by wear.

In climbing the peaks without maintained trails, the "trailless peaks," as we have called them in the past, the same basic practice should be followed below the timberline. Most of these peaks have beaten paths where others have walked before. These are called "herd paths." By sticking to existing herd paths, hikers will avoid creating more of them and thus avoid the erosion and unsightly conditions produced by a network of informal trails.

Private Property

Of the six million acres in the Adirondack Park, 3.7 million acres (62%) are private lands, while 2.3 million acres (38%) are state owned. It is of the utmost importance that the rights of property owners be respected. Many of the trails described in the guide are located partly or wholly on private land. The owners of these lands have granted the public access to their properties with the understanding that no hikers will build fires, camp, hunt or fish as they pass through. Because a small minority has chosen to ignore these conditions, landowners have already closed some trails formerly available to the public. Respect private property within the park.

Safety in the Adirondacks

Although the Adirondacks are not as high as the Rockies and several other ranges, hikers must respect them. As a forest ranger has said, anything above 3500 feet is a different world where one mistake can be fatal. Midwinter temperatures and storms make it imperative to travel in groups of not less than four during this season and to wear proper clothing and footgear. Further details in this guide and other manuals will help you to choose the most practical outfits and to be prepared for emergencies. The months of April and May can also be very treacherous in the High Peak Region. In fact, there are dangers for the unwary or the uninformed at all seasons. Temperatures in winter above the tree line are like those at the Arctic Circle.

The cairns (conical piles of stones) on Marcy and Algonquin are not to be disturbed. They are there for your safety and well-being in case of storms or near-zero visibility.

As a result of decisions by the authorities, eight lean-tos were torn down in 1976—two at Indian Falls, the two Plateau lean-tos, plus Four Corners, Sno-Bird, Lake Tear and Lake Arnold lean-tos. There are also plans for eliminating some lean-to clusters at places like Marcy Dam and Lake Colden, thus encouraging campers to camp in small groups. To insure overnight protection, campers should carry tents.

We wish to note that the Duck Hole and Shattuck Clearing Ranger Stations have been eliminated. As of 1978, the State undertook a review of camping policies in the High Peaks. Camping is now restricted either to designated campsites or to areas 150 ft. away from a stream or trail. Camping above the 4000 ft. level in the High Peaks is prohibited except in winter and then only with special permission of the DEC. See Additional Information, Section A.

(Editor's Note: As ADK red trail markers need replacement, new orange ones are being used.)

PREFACE TO THE TENTH EDITION

This guidebook, which for some years included the entire Northville–Placid Trail and a section on Outlying Mountains and Trails, now deals with the High Peak Region of the Adirondack Mountains only. The "High Peaks," as they are familiarly called by hikers, include 46 mountains over 4000 feet (including nine alpine summits), spread over an area of some 12,000 square miles. Alpine summits have vegetation similar to that of the Alps in Europe. This vast natural sanctuary is located within a day's traveling distance for 55 million residents of the United States and Canada.

Much water has gone over the proverbial dam since the preparation of the 1977 Ninth Edition by the Map and Guidebook Committee of the Adirondack Mountain Club. Section B5, The Upper Ausable Lake Region, was completely done over for the 1979 reprinting of the guide. This was necessitated by the sale, on June 10, 1978 on the summit of Noonmark, of some 9,000 acres by the Adirondack Mountain Reserve of its high-level land to the State of New York. Details of this sale and for hiking in this region are found below in the corresponding section of the guide.

The Northville–Placid Trail section which appeared in previous editions of this guide is now available from the Adirondack Mountain Club as a separate volume. It deals with a separate area of the Adirondacks and is concerned with a different manner of hiking and camping. This is in keeping with the Club's publication of other regional guides covering areas throughout the Adirondack Park.

There is a third major change in the Tenth Edition. The section on the Trailless Peaks has been rewritten. The long introduction to this chapter that had been accumulating material with each new edition has been streamlined. The descriptions for taking the preferred "herd path" have been updated in some cases. Esther has been moved into this section now that the ski trails formerly used here have become overgrown and hardly discernible. The editor feels that the contents of this portion of the guide are more pertinent to the climber of the 1980s.

The first two editions of this guide were published in 1934 and 1941 under the chairmanship of Dr. Orra A. Phelps. Three more editions followed in 1945, 1947 and 1950 under the direction of A. T. Shorey. The Sixth and Seventh editions were the work of the late L. Morgan Porter, a remarkable and indefatigable man equally at home behind a trail-measuring wheel and an editorial desk. He measured and described many of the trails in this guide. The Eighth Edition, prepared under the chairmanship of Donald W. McLaughlin, came out in 1972 and was reprinted in 1973 and 1975. The Ninth Edition appeared in 1977 and was reprinted in 1979.

Special acknowledgment must be given to past ADK presidents Glenn Fish, Hank Germond and Franklin Clark, and to the present president, Almy Coggeshall, for their constant help and encouragement. Likewise, to Grant Cole and Carmen Elliott and the staff at ADK headquarters in Glens Falls, New York, and especially to Jim Goodwin, who has continued to act as co-editor for this edition and has kept updated the map that accompanies it. Special mention to Pat Quinn, Peg O'Brien, Tony Goodwin and Clint Miller for their aid and encouragement.

Lawrence E. Cotter, *Chairman*
Map and Guidebook Committee
Adirondack Mountain Club, Inc.

Hammond, New York
January 1980

CONTENTS

SECTION A

INTRODUCTION

THE ADIRONDACK PARK

The Adirondack Park was created by an act of the New York Legislature in 1892 to be situated within the counties of Hamilton, Herkimer, St. Lawrence, Franklin, Essex and Warren. Of these, Hamilton is the only one entirely within the park boundaries, known as the "blue line." Since then, the "blue line" has been expanded to include parts of the counties of Clinton, Saratoga, Fulton, Lewis and the northeast corner of Oneida. This area, including both state and private land, now comprises over 6 million acres (9375 square miles, about the size of Vermont and nearly three times the area of Yellowstone National Park). 2.3 million acres (38%) are state-owned, constitutionally protected Adirondack Forest Preserve and 3.7 million acres (62%) are private lands devoted principally to forestry, agriculture and recreation. There are 112,000 permanent and 90,000 seasonal residents.

The High Peak Region is situated in the northeastern section of the park, a mountain wilderness in which more than forty summits rise above 4000 ft. Mt. Marcy, the highest, is 5344 ft. and Algonquin, second highest, is 5114 ft. The principal towns in this area are Saranac Lake, Tupper Lake, Lake Placid, Wilmington, Keene, Keene Valley and Elizabethtown. These are readily found on any New York State road map.

Although an extensive network of highways surrounds the rugged High Peak Region, an area of 180,000 acres has remained unspoiled by public roads. To make this interesting area accessible to the average hiker, the New York State Department of Environmental Conservation (DEC), formerly the New York State Conservation Department (SCD), maintains and marks 241 mi. of hiking trails. The Adirondack Mountain Club (ADK) maintains 63 mi. and the Adirondack Trail Improvement Society (ATIS) 85 to 90 mi.

THE ADIRONDACK MOUNTAIN CLUB

The Adirondack Mountain Club was organized in 1922 for the purpose of bringing together in a working unit a large number of people interested in the mountains, trails, camping, and forest conservation. A permanent club headquarters was established, and with an increasing membership, club chapters were organized. The chapters are as follows: Adirondak Loj (Heart Lake), Albany, Algonquin (Plattsburgh), Black River (Watertown), Cold River (Long Lake, Hamilton Co.), Finger Lakes (Ithaca–Elmira), Genesee Valley (Rochester), Glens Falls, Hurricane Mountain (Keene), Iroquois (Utica), Keene Valley, Knickerbocker (New York), Lake Placid, Laurentian (Canton–Potsdam), Long Island, Mid-Hudson (Poughkeepsie), New York, Niagara Frontier (Buffalo), North Jersey (Bergen Co.), North Woods (Saranac Lake–Tupper Lake), Onondaga (Syracuse), Ramapo (Pearl River), Schenectady, Seneca (Canandaigua), Shatagee Woods (Malone), and Susquehanna (Oneonta). In addition, there is an extensive membership-at-large.

Members of the Adirondack Mountain Club have formulated the following creed that reflects the theme of the club and its membership:

"I subscribe, without reservation, to the following pledge: As a member of the Adirondack Mountain Club, I agree to support the objects and conservation policy of the club and to use the forests with care and consideration for those who follow. To this end, I will help maintain their wild character by leaving no trace of my own temporary occupancy and, by example, to encourage others to do the same. I will take particular care in the making and extinguishing of campfires. I will help others to experience and enjoy the values afforded by the New York State Forest Preserve in a manner consistent with its constitutionally protected wild forest character."

Most chapters do not have qualifying requirements, and a note to the Executive Director, Adirondack Mountain Club, 172 Ridge St., Glens Falls, New York, 12801, will bring you information on membership in a local chapter (e.g., names and addresses of persons to be contacted) or details on membership-at-large. Persons elected to a chapter, upon payment of their chapter dues, *ipso facto* become members of the club. Membership dues include a subscription to *Adirondac,* a bi-monthly magazine. An application for membership is in the back of this book.

MAPS

The map enclosed in the back of this book, "Trails of the Adirondack High Peak Region," is a composite of the U.S. Geological Survey Maps of Mt. Marcy, Santanoni and one-half of the Elizabethtown quadrangle joined in one unit and marked with existing trails, shelters and other detail. It is especially valuable because of the combination of contour lines and trail locations. Extra copies of the trail map are available from the Adirondack Mountain Club, 172 Ridge St., Glens Falls, New York, 12801.

U.S. Geological Survey Maps of areas not covered by the composite unit are recommended for those who are interested in more detailed topographical data. In addition to the three maps included in the composite unit, the High Peak Region is shown on the Saranac Lake, Lake Placid and Ausable Forks Quadrangles. These are available from the Washington Distribution Section, U.S. Geological Survey, 1200 South Eads Street, Arlington, Virginia, 22202, at some local mountaineering outfitters and at certain book and sporting goods stores.

A word or two about the topographic maps. The newer maps bear dates from the 1950s and while the topography is more accurate than that on the older maps, being based on photogrammetric plotting from aerial photographs, some of the brooks mentioned in connection with the trailless peaks have been omitted. However, by studying the contours in connection with the route descriptions, one can generally tell where the omitted brooks should be. These maps also have numerous errors in trails and show some trails that do not even exist and omit other trails that do exist.

TRAIL SIGNS AND MARKERS

With normal alertness to one's surroundings, trails in the Adirondacks are easy to follow. Where state maintained trails leave a highway or at trail junctions, DEC has erected board signs giving details of the trails ahead. Along these trails you will find DEC trail markers. Some trails are marked with red, some with blue and some with yellow DEC disks. Trails maintained by the ADK also have sign boards at junctions, and red and white and the newer orange trail markers are used. Trails that traverse the private park of the Adirondack Mountain Reserve are taken care of by the ATIS. Their signs have white painted carved lettering on a green board. The trails are mostly marked by ax blazes which require care in the following, but where the trail is quite indistinct, ATIS trail markers show the way. Do not remove trail markers. Porkies, bears, wind and weather do enough damage. The hikers after you want to find their way too.

DAMAGED SIGNS

Damaged or missing ADK trail markers or poorly marked trails maintained by the ADK should be reported to the Adirondack Mountain Club, 172 Ridge St., Glens Falls, New York, 12801. In case of the same situation applying to trails maintained by the Department of Environmental Conservation, report to the Department at Ray Brook, New York, 12977. ATIS trail problems should be reported to the Adirondack Trail Improvement Society, St. Huberts, New York, 12943.

Persons desiring to purchase an ADK trail marker as a souvenir should write to the Adirondack Mountain Club, 172 Ridge St., Glens Falls, New York, 12801. A good woodsman will not remove them from the trails.

Along some trails are "posted" signs. Although these trails traverse private land, the owner gave permission for hikers to pass through. He usually posts his land to hunting, fishing, camping and diverging from the trail. The public is urged to comply with the owner's request and not abuse the privilege.

DISTANCE AND TIME

Except where otherwise noted, all trails described in this guidebook have been measured with a professional surveyor's measuring wheel. This makes it possible to give accurate distances to the nearest 0.01 mi. Such detail may seen unnecessary since 0.01 mi. is only 52.8 ft., but it is very helpful in defining many short stretches of trail in addition to giving more accurate total distances.

The trail descriptions are given with cumulative mileage from the beginning of each trail. Distances are also noted to all intersections, lean-tos, etc. In addition, there is a mileage summary after each trail description, giving distances from the beginning to the principal points. These details make it relatively simple to figure total distance over any desired network of trails. To the inexperienced hiker, the trails will seem longer than these distances, but one soon learns that "sidewalk" miles and "mountain" miles, though measuring the same, are quite different in time and energy required.

Since the Klondike Notch Trail between JBL and South Meadow is used so much as a connecting trail, it has been described in both directions, from JBL in the Keene Valley section and from South Meadow under Heart Lake.

The time required for ascents or round trips has not been given because it is too variable. A conservative rule to follow is to allow an hour for every 1½ miles, plus half an hour for every 1000 ft. ascended, experience soon enabling each hiker to apply his own correction factor. Most experienced hikers will take less time than that given by the formula, but it is better to allow plenty of time. If heavy packs are carried, the pace may be slower. Time can be saved on easy descents, but steep, rough descents may require nearly as much time as the ascent. It is wise to plan half-day trips not over 6 mi. An all day trip may cover 10 to 15 mi.

WILDERNESS CAMPING

There is no hut system in the Adirondack Forest Preserve, nor are there any private hostelries. The only wilderness lodge available is JBL in the Johns Brook Valley owned by the Adirondack Mountain Club. It is a 3.5 mi. hike from the nearest road above Keene Valley. Bunk and meals may be obtained there during the summer months. Reservations are necessary.

To enable hikers to spend several days in the woods, DEC has erected a number of open camps, "lean-tos," along the trails. (A list of lean-tos located in the forest is contained in Section E.) No permit or fee is required for lean-to use. Since reservations cannot be made, it is best to take your own lightweight tent or tarp. There are many possibilities for tenting along the way. Any one lean-to may be used by the same party for up to three successive nights or ten nights in a season. Camping permits exceeding these limits may be obtained at DEC Regional Headquarters at Ray Brook (about midway between Lake Placid and Saranac Lake) or from local forest rangers. A small party does not have exclusive rights to a lean-to just because they were there first. Latecomers should be accommodated until the capacity of the lean-to is reached.

The average lean-to is adequate for about seven campers; at the more popular locations they are built to hold more people. These rustic, open shelters have a generous over-hanging roof. The back wall and the sides are built of logs; the front is open to the forest. Most lean-tos have wooden floors. There are no pots, blankets, stoves or any other equipment. An open stone fireplace in front, sometimes provided with a primitive grill, serves as a kitchen. Some lean-tos have picnic tables, usually donated in memory of a deserving outdoors personality. They are not to be used as firewood! It also shows poor taste and lack of consideration to carve initials on tables, lean-tos or trees. Nearby is a water supply. It may be a spring, a brook, or a lake. Spring water is usually safe; water from a brook is taken from above the lean-to and, if the previous campers were as meticulous as you to keep the brook clean, may be safe too. Water from a lake should be boiled or chemically purified in a pot or canteen. Purification tablets are available in most drugstores and camping supply houses. Keep water sources pure by not bathing, washing dishes or dumping refuse there. Keep your detergents at home. For cleaning of any kind, use biodegradable soap, spreading used water 150 ft. back from and downhill of any water source. A final concession to civilization is a pit toilet often a short distance off in the woods. Where none exists, dig a trench 6–10 in. down into mineral soil and cover up upon leaving the site. Nature will do the rest.

There are just two more important items. There are hanging at the side of the lean-to a rake and shovel, subtle hints for you to keep a clean camp and leave it clean and neat. Leave your camp the way you would like to find it.

—Leave dry firewood in a corner of the lean-to.

—Pack out cans, glass, aluminum foil and plastic.

—Burn papers and garbage.

—Leave nothing behind.

If you carry it in, carry it out!

CAMPFIRES

The New York State Constitution provides that the lands of the Forest Preserve shall be kept "forever wild" and its timber shall not be sold, removed or destroyed. For a camper this means that he may use for his fire (or any other purpose) only wood that is dead and lying on the ground.

Because of the increasing numbers of backpackers using the forest and frequent wet weather, it is increasingly difficult to find dead and down dry firewood. The carrying and use of a backpack stove is encouraged.

A fire permit is not required on state lands. A sensible small fire in a lean-to's fireplace is comparatively safe, but it has to be carefully extinguished "until dead and out" before leaving the site. If no lean-to is available and you camp in your own little lightweight tent, under a plastic tarp or in the open, extreme care is necessary when building a fire. The forest floor is made up of duff (pine needles, leaves, decayed root matter and a trace of actual soil), and is highly flammable. It may smoulder for weeks underground and then burst into flame. Remove all surface material down to the mineral soil (sand, clay, or rock) to a diameter of six feet. Find some rocks to line your fireplace, then build as small a fire as workable. When leaving camp, smother and douse your fire with plenty of water. If water is not available, don't build a fire. Feel to make sure it is cold and dead out. Leaving a fire smoldering not only endangers the forest and the wildlife therein but also constitutes a misdemeanor under the Conservation Law. Leave some kindling and firewood at a dry place at the lean-to in case the next campers arrive in a downpour or after dark.

EQUIPMENT

Whether you are camping in a lean-to or in your own packed-in shelter, you will have to bring in all your supplies: sleeping bag (down when dry is warmest for its weight but also more expensive than less efficient fillings), foam pad, cooking pot and fry pan, eating utensils and clean-up needs. Because of possible sudden rainy weather and often sparse firewood supply, it is best to carry and use a backpack stove (don't forget appropriate gas, matches and repair kits). Unless you are of herculean strength, keep the amount and weight of supplies to a minimum. It pays to figure out exact rations beforehand. There are many dehydrated and freeze-dried items in supermarkets and at camping supply outfitters which are easy to carry and prepare. Remember to keep all food well sealed and out of your sleeping quarters (tent or lean-to). Hang your food in a sturdy bag, at least 15 ft. up a tree and well out on a strong limb, and 100 ft. away from your campsite. Camp robbers like chipmunks, porcupines, raccoons, or an occasional bear are delightful to watch but you need your supplies more than they do. Make a check list of needed items so that you don't forget necessary things like matches, flashlight with extra batteries, toilet paper (wrapped in plastic to avoid dampness), sewing kit, map, extra wool socks, and first aid kit.

REFUSE

CARRY OUT ALL YOU CARRY IN. This is a very simple rule and important to follow in these days of increased use of our natural resources, which includes the "forever wild" area of the Forest Preserve. Avoid burning garbage, drippings or food containers in fireplace and do not bury garbage. It attracts animals and is an offense to the senses. Take along a sturdy plastic litterbag and carry everything out. Garbage can be minimized by serving only that which will most likely be eaten.

Our increasingly polluted habitat and the press of the expanding population make it necessary for man to employ vigilance in battle to preserve nature. The Adirondack Mountain Club is dedicated to enjoying the forest with care and consideration in order to maintain its wild and virgin nature. Many campers have already come to realize that they must help spread this conservation philosophy until the ever increasing number of campers are made aware of their responsibilities. Until such time, we must share the burden of careless and less concerned persons by carrying out more than we carry in.

> IF YOU CARRY IT IN, CARRY IT OUT!

CLOTHING

IT CAN BE HOT. When hiking or especially when climbing, you may be happy with shorts and a short-sleeved shirt as long as you have insect repellent for exposed body surfaces. If your hike includes a lot of sun or bushwhacking or rough terrain, a light-weight long pant and shirt may well be preferable.

IT CAN BE COLD. Mountain weather is unpredictable and variable, and one should be prepared for all eventualities. Temperatures in the Adirondacks have been known to dip to below freezing even in July and August. Generally speaking, summer months see warm days and cool nights. It is entirely possible to experience snow squalls in September and even late August, and also in May and even June. Real winter sets in from November through May. It is best to check the area weather before your trip. Even on a day hike in summer, some warm clothing is a must. Wool is still best. A windbreaker with hood and long trousers are needed above timberline, around the campsite in the evenings, and for bushwhacking in winter; also snowshoes (crampons if traversing icy summits), winter hiking boots, wool socks, warm jacket, wool hat and gloves or mittens.

IT CAN GET WET. A poncho large enough to cover you and your pack is essential. A rain suit for you and a rain cover for your pack is an alternative (but is usually too hot). It is a question of whether to get wet from the outside in or the inside out. A waterproof hiking boot (designed for winter or summer as the case may be) with a non-slip sole—trails sometimes resemble brooks or are often very muddy—is recommended. Two or more pairs of socks (the inner for absorption and the outer of wool or combination wool for warmth and cushion) make a boot more comfortable.

If your body loses more heat than it can produce, your body's inner core temperature begins to drop. If not halted, death follows usually within two hours. This can happen even in summer. This foe of hikers is called hypothermia. What causes hypothermia? Improper clothing, over-exhaustion, sweating, chilling, improper eating and drinking, and getting wet. The body adjusts to preserve normal temperatures in the vital organs. This effort drains the energy reserve and exhaustion sets in. If exposure continues until all energy reserves are expended, hypothermia takes over. Cold reaches the brain and the internal core temperature moves downward. First symptoms such as unnoticed loss of clothing and undue stumbling should be countered by immediately stopping, drinking hot, sweet liquids, and eating quick energy food, such as a candy bar, and re-warming with dry clothes.

Frostbite is not hypothermia, but is often a side effect. Frostbite is a cold injury to the extremities (nose, ears, chin and cheekbones, fingers and toes) that progresses from the outside in. The safe immediate treatment is to warm up the core temperature by drinking hot fluids and eating quick energy food.

FIRST AID

Everyone entering the woods should be prepared for emergencies. The amount of first aid equipment carried depends upon the size of the party and the length of the trip. For one day trips, sterile gauze compresses with adhesive tape (band-aid type) will care for small cuts, scratches, friction blisters or burns. A roll of two-inch bandage, plain gauze or elastic will take care of a sprained ankle or knee. Adhesive backed moleskin (available at drugstores) is best for preventing blisters. When a party is camping several days, more complete equipment should be carried, including band-aids, sterile folded gauze compresses in packages, several roller and triangular bandages, adhesive tape, burn ointment and a liquid antiseptic. A small amount of rubbing alcohol (50%) and a container of boric acid powder are often useful. Salt and soda also have first aid uses. Unless carried in a sewing kit, a pair of scissors and a few needles of assorted sizes will be found useful in more ways than one. Also take insect repellent, and for a lake environment or above timberline, sun lotion. If it is hot, salt tablets help prevent heat exhaustion. There are no known venomous snakes in the High Peak Area but peace of mind might dictate your carrying a snake bite kit.

The most common conditions needing treatment are blisters, fatigue, sprains, burns (including sunburn), scratches, cuts, hypothermia and frostbite.

ABBREVIATIONS

R and L are used for right and left with periods omitted; likewise, N, S, E and W are used without periods for north, south, east and west. Some compass directions are given in degrees for more detail, figuring from true N as 0 or 360° clockwise around the compass such that E is 90°, etc. In speaking of brooks, the right and left banks are determined when facing downstream. Likewise, the right fork of a brook is the fork on the right when facing downstream.

The following abbreviations are used in the text or on the maps:

ADK	Adirondack Mountain Club
AMR	Adirondack Mountain Reserve
ATIS	Adirondack Trail Improvement Society
BRL	Bouquet River Lodge
DEC	New York State Department of Environmental Conservation
JBL	Johns Brook Lodge
N-P	Northville–Placid
PBM	Permanent Bench Mark
SOA	Shore Owners Association
USGS	United States Geological Survey
ft.	Feet
mi.	Mile or miles
Mt.	Mount if before; mountain if after a name
yds.	Yards

GLOSSARY OF TERMS

Bivouac	Camping in the open under improvised shelter or none at all.
Bushwhacking	To make one's way through bushes or undergrowth.
Cairn	A pile of stones set up to mark a summit or route.

Chimney	A steep and narrow cleft or gully in the face of a cliff or mountain, usually by which it may be climbed.
Cobble	A small stony (cobblestones) peak on the side of a mountain.
Col	A pass between two adjacent peaks.
Corduroy	A road, trail or bridge formed by logs laid side by side transversely to facilitate crossing swampy places.
Couloir	A deep gorge; a gully on a mountainside.
Cripplebrush	Thick stunted growth at higher elevations.
Dike	A tabular body of igneous rock that has been injected while molten into a fissure. A parallel sided sheet of rock which cuts across (or transgresses) the principal structural planes of the country rock. It is not necessarily vertical. If the dike is softer than the country rock, it weathers away to form a depression such as a chimney or gorge. The Colden Dike is of this type. Often, however, a dike will erode more slowly than the country rock and appear as a wall jutting therefrom.
Duff	Partly decayed vegetable matter on the forest floor.
Lean-to	An open camp with overhanging roof on the open side.
Pass	A passageway through mountainous country, especially between two peaks, frequently difficult to traverse.
Pitch	A short steep ascent or descent.
Sag	A low point in a trail or ridge.
Tote Road	An inferior road used for hauling, such as a lumber road, often with corduroys.
Vlei	A marsh or swampy meadow (pronounced *vly*).

ADDITIONAL INFORMATION

The DEC stresses the following rules and regulations:

Camping is prohibited within 150 feet of any road, trail, spring, stream, pond or other body of water except at camping areas designated by the Department;

No person may camp on lands under the jurisdiction of the Department which are located at an elevation in excess of 4000 ft. above sea level in the Adirondack Park;

Except in an emergency, no open fires are permitted on lands under the jurisdiction of the Department which are located at an elevation in excess of 4000 ft. above sea level;

No group of 10 or more individuals may camp on State lands at any time except under permit; and

The erection of tents in open camps is prohibited.

For a complete listing of New York State DEC rules and regulations and other free circulars, contact the DEC, 50 Wolf Road, Albany, N.Y. 12233.

The following pamphlets are available by sending a self-addressed, stamped (#10) envelope for each, plus cost, to the Adirondack Mountain Club, 172 Ridge St., Glens Falls, New York 12801.

For the Day Hiker	15¢
For the Summer Backpacker	15¢
For the Winter Mountaineer	15¢
Hypothermia	15¢
Wilderness Tips	10¢
The Bear Facts	10¢
Biting Trail Bugs	10¢
Frostbite	10¢

On the last page of this volume is a list of books that can be ordered from the Adirondack Mountain Club.

MOUNT MARCY

Mt. Marcy, the highest peak in the Adirondacks, rises 5344 ft. above sea level. It was named in 1837 in honor of Governor William Learned Marcy by Ebenezer Emmons, Professor of Chemistry at Williams College and Geologist-in-Chief of the Second District of the Geological Survey of New York, who was the leader of the party that made the first recorded ascent on August 5, 1837. The Indian name for this peak is Tahawus (pronounced *Ta-ha-wus*), which means cloud-splitter. The last 800 ft. of its crest rises above timberline—an irregular rocky dome with alpine vegetation growing in the crevices and depressions where soil has accumulated. A copper bolt was set into the rock of the actual summit at the time of the Colvin Survey in 1875.

The extent of the view depends upon atmospheric conditions and the time of day. Clouds are seen resting on the top of Marcy many times when the sun is shining in the valleys. To be on top in a cloud is a common experience. Under such conditions, one should be very careful not to lose the trail or other distinct landmarks. When there is a party of people on top, they should stay together. The wind may be so violent that shouting to one another is of no avail. Experiences on mountain tops in adverse weather are adventures to those who enjoy the mountains, not just the views.

On a vertical rock wall just below the summit is a bronze plaque (see below) commemorating the first recorded ascent of this "High Peak of Essex."

The view from Marcy on a clear day is of an endless wilderness of irregular mountain tops and miles of unbroken forest. Only toward the N and far E are farm lands and villages visible. To the ESE near at hand is Haystack, the third highest Adirondack summit, with its long rocky crestline. Between Marcy and Haystack is the precipitous and wild Panther Gorge. From Haystack the Great Range runs NE toward Keene Valley. Prominent in this range, ENE from Marcy, is Gothics with its bare rock sides. Directly over Gothics is the col between Giant on the L and Rocky Peak Ridge on the R. Through this col on a clear day may be seen Camel's Hump in the Green Mountains of Vermont, about 54 mi. away. Directly to the R of Gothics is its third summit, Pyramid, beyond which a long low col leads over to Sawteeth.

To the NNE, across the Johns Brook Valley from the Great Range, the rock face of Big Slide stands out against a background of Porter and Cascade to the L. In the distance to the N the waters of Lake Placid shine below the regular cone of Whiteface. Nearer at hand, NNW, lies little Heart Lake at the foot of Mt. Jo. Slightly

1837—MARCY—1937
Also Known by the Indian Name
TAHAWUS
Meaning "Cloud-Splitter"

ON AUGUST 5, 1837 THE FIRST RECORDED ASCENT OF THIS MOUNTAIN WAS MADE AND ITS HEIGHT MEASURED. IT WAS NAMED MT. MARCY IN HONOR OF GOVERNOR WILLIAM LEARNED MARCY, WHO HAD APPOINTED A COMMISSION TO MAKE THE FIRST GEOLOGICAL SURVEY OF THE NORTHERN DISTRICT.

The following made the ascent:
    Prof. Ebenezer Emmons of Williams, and
    James Hall, state geologist;
    Prof. John Torrey, botanist;
    Professors Strong and Miller, geologists;
    William C. Redfield, engineer and meteorologist;
    C. C. Ingham, artist and Ebenezer Emmons, Jr.;
    Archibald MacIntyre and David Henderson,
    original explorers and early owners of this region;
    Harvey Holt and John Cheney, guides;
    and three unknown woodsmen.

Erected by the Adirondack Mountain Club in conjunction with the Conservation Department of New York State.

(Editor's note: The Conservation Department mentioned above is presently the Department of Environmental Conservation of New York State.)

W of NW, Colden, with its rock slides, stands out against the broad side of the MacIntyre Range, with Boundary directly above Colden, Iroquois to the L and Algonquin, second highest Adirondack summit, to the R. To the R of Algonquin is Wright Peak with the slide, and through the col between these two peaks may be seen Street.

Due W, about 0.75 mi. away, is Gray Peak, seventh highest peak and the highest trailless summit, and directly below Marcy to the SW is little Lake Tear of the Clouds, the highest lake source of the Hudson River. In line with Tear Lake stands Redfield, while near at hand, SSW, is Skylight, the fourth in order of height. Between Redfield and Skylight, and about 38 mi. away, may be seen Snowy, the highest peak in the southern Adirondacks, elevation 3899 ft. Slightly to the L of and behind Skylight is Allen with its two summits, while almost due S the Boreas Ponds gleam in a forest setting. The Boreas Mt. fire tower may be seen to the E of the ponds, and the long, low tree-covered ridge with the many bumps SE from Marcy is the Colvin–Pinnacle Ridge behind which lies Elk Lake.

There are four main approaches to Marcy: From Keene Valley, Elk Lake, Sanford Lake and Heart Lake. From Keene Valley there are two direct trails and the longer route via the Great Range. From Elk Lake there is one main trail which crosses the inlet of the Upper Ausable Lake. From Sanford Lake there are two main trails. One route follows the Opalescent River to Twin Brook lean-to, then branches into two trails that unite at Buckley Clearing before reaching the summit. The other route, easier but less scenic, starts at the Upper Works (former Tahawus Club) and follows Calamity Brook to Flowed Lands where it joins the trail from Twin Brook lean-to via Hanging Spear Falls. From Heart Lake there is one direct route, the Van Hoevenberg Trail and the indirect routes via Avalanche Pass and Lake Arnold. Marcy may also be approached by several trails from St. Huberts which eventually reach either the Range Trail or the Elk Lake Trail. By studying the map one can also plan his own approach to Marcy over a network of trails, all of which are described in detail in the following sections.

Summary of Principal Trails to Marcy

Miles

Keene Valley:

Phelps Trail via Slant Rock from Garden	9.05
Phelps Trail via Hopkins Trail from Garden	9.05
Great Range via Rooster Comb from Iron Bridge	13.31

Elk Lake:

Elk Lake–Marcy Trail from Elk Lake Dam	10.96

Sanford Lake:

Via Opalescent River and Twin Brook from Parking Lot	11.37
or Opalescent River and Flowed Lands from Parking Lot	13.74
Via Calamity Brook from Upper Works	10.11

Heart Lake:

Via Van Hoevenberg Trail from Adirondak Loj	7.46
Via Avalanche Pass and Lake Colden from Adirondak Loj	10.80
Via Lake Arnold from Adirondak Loj	8.95

SECTION B1

KEENE VALLEY REGION

The village of Keene Valley has for many years been a favorite resort for those who love the mountains. Boarding houses and tourists' accommodations are plentiful. The stores carry camping equipment and sporting goods as well as food supplies. There are good garages for repair and for car storage. In this region, trails start for many major peaks including Marcy, the Great Range, Big Slide and Porter, as well as many lesser summits providing attractive short trips.

Of chief importance are the various trails to Mt. Marcy. The most direct route is via the Phelps Trail on the N side of Johns Brook to Johns Brook Lodge, thence to Bushnell Falls, and then by either the Phelps Trail via Slant Rock, or the Hopkins Trail. JBL may also be reached by the ADK-maintained trail on the S side of Johns Brook. A trail connecting Rooster Comb with the

Trails Described	Year Measured	Total Miles
Johns Brook Lodge via Phelps Trail	1954	3.52
Johns Brook Lodge via Crossover and Southside Trails	1961	3.55
Marcy via Phelps Trail from JBL	1954	5.53
Marcy via Hopkins Trail from JBL	1954	5.53
Lower Wolf Jaw via Woodsfall Trail	1954*	2.52
Short Job	1954	0.74
Gothics via Orebed Brook Trail	1954*	3.45
High Water Routes from JBL	1954	
ADK Range Trail to Upper Wolf Jaw, Armstrong and Gothics	1953	4.73

Trails Described	Year Measured	Total Miles
State Range Trail to Saddleback, Basin and Marcy	1954*	7.32
Shorey Short Cut from Range Trail to Phelps Trail	1954	1.11
Haystack from Range Trail	1953	0.55
Marcy from Keene via the Great Range		13.31
Johns Brook Lodge to South Meadow via Klondike Notch Trail	1955	5.27
Big Slide via Slide Mt. Brook Trail from Phelps Trail	1968	2.35
Big Slide via Klondike Notch Trail	1968	2.70
Big Slide via The Brothers from the Garden	1953*	3.85
Porter from Keene Valley Airport via Ridge Trail	1952	4.54
Porter from Road near the Garden	1954	3.84
Rooster Comb from Route 73	1953	1.85
Lower Wolf Jaw via Rooster Comb and Hedgehog	1953**	4.95
Baxter and Nubble from Beede Farm	1961	1.45
Baxter from Upham Road	1953	1.70
Baxter from Spruce Hill	1961	1.09
Spread Eagle and Hopkins from Paved Road	1954	2.92
Hopkins via Direct Trail from Lumber Road	1954	2.65

* Partly based on measurements made in previous years.
** Partly remeasured in 1961.

W.A. White Trail from St. Huberts makes possible a complete traverse of the Range from Keene Valley to Mt. Marcy. Intermediate points on the Range Trail may also be reached from JBL.

Keene Valley may be reached by automobile from the Northway, Interstate 87, at milepost 104, and/or U.S. Route 9 by taking the Chapel Pond road, Route 73, 10 mi. S of Elizabethtown or from U.S. Route 9N by turning S on 73, 10 mi. W of Elizabethtown. Busses from New York and Lake Placid pass through Keene Valley. Airline service is available from New York and Albany to the Saranac Lake/Lake Placid Airport, 15 mi. W of Lake Placid Village.

Of the 64 mi. of trails described in this section, 39.2 mi. are maintained by the ADK or some of its chapters, the rest being maintained by DEC, except the ATIS trail to Haystack from the Range Trail.

Johns Brook Lodge and Mt. Marcy via Phelps Trail

This route to Marcy was established by Edward Phelps, son of Old Mountain Phelps, the famous Keene Valley guide. The DEC recreation circular, *Trails to Marcy,* calls it the Johns Brook Trail. It is through the woods N of Johns Brook, reaching the brook about 0.45 mi. below JBL. Above the Lodge, it continues along the L (N) bank of the stream, crossing it above Bushnell Falls and after gradual climbing reaches Slant Rock, a famous campsite. Beyond this, it enters a ravine between Haystack and Marcy where the climbing is quite steep. At the head of the ravine it turns W and climbs a shoulder of Marcy, joining the Van Hoevenberg Trail from Heart Lake 0.58 mi. below the summit.

From the center of Keene Valley at DEC sign, "Trail to the High Peaks," follow yellow markers W along paved road. At 0.60 mi. the road turns R over Johns Brook on an iron bridge and begins a steady climb of about 390 ft., becoming a dirt road as it approaches its end at a small clearing known as the Garden (PBM 1523 ft.) at 1.60 mi., where cars may be parked. This is private land and no camping is permitted here. Parking is limited to the capacity of the parking lot. Winter climbers are advised to leave their cars in Keene Valley.

Leaving the far end of the Garden (0 mi.), the trail, marked with yellow DEC disks, follows high above the L bank of Johns Brook most of the way to JBL, crossing many tributaries affording drinking water. The route is also posted with blue half-mile markers.* The grade is steady but not difficult. At 0.03 mi. the trail

---

* Half-mile markers are yellow numbers on a blue field for contrast with DEC yellow trail markers.

crosses the first small brook and starts climbing through a fine stand of white birch, the grade moderating at about 0.30 mi. At 0.51 mi. the Crossover Trail, with red ADK markers, enters on the L from the Southside Trail (see below). Twin Mt. Brook is crossed at 0.60 mi. and Bear Brook at 0.87 mi. Bear Brook lean-to (1962) is L of trail just beyond the brook. Deer Brook lean-to (1952) is reached at 1.27 mi. Just beyond, the trail descends abruptly to cross double bridges over Deer Brook in the ravine at 1.30 mi. and climbs the opposite bank.

At 1.43 mi. there are three large boulders, one making a natural shelter for a fireplace. After crossing a small brook at 1.50 mi., the grade, easy up to this point, starts a steady uphill pull. Wagon Wheel Brook is crossed on a log bridge at 1.84 mi. and the grade moderates. PBM 2134 ft. on a granite boulder on L side of trail is passed at 1.96 mi., and the 2.00 mi. marker is at the top of a small grade. The trail now continues at an easy grade, crossing several small brooks and detouring away from the telephone line for a short distance. Johns Brook is heard at 2.88 mi. where there is a glimpse of Lower Wolf Jaw. (An alternate trail bears R at 2.89 mi. to avoid a swampy section, rejoining the main trail at the spring house.) The trail descends a short distance at 2.94 mi., crosses a swampy section on corduroys, passes a spring house with flowing water and reaches a trail junction and the ranger's camp at 3.07 mi. where all hikers should register. (Painted BM 2215 ft.). Here a blue-marked trail enters on the L. This leads across Johns Brook on a suspension bridge to the Orebed Brook Trail, the Wolf Jaws Trail and the Southside Trail. (See below.)

Continuing with yellow markers past the ranger's cabin, a side trail on L at 3.14 mi. leads a few yards to the Howard Memorial lean-to. A second side trail from the lean-to rejoins the main trail at 3.18 mi. where Slide Mt. Brook is crossed on a bridge. At 3.21 mi., the trail to Big Slide Mt. branches R (ADK markers), and the bridge across Johns Brook to the ADK Winter and Grace Camps is reached at 3.25 mi. Black Brook is crossed on a bridge at 3.40 mi., and the signpost at JBL is reached at 3.52 mi. (PBM 2316 ft. is a few steps down the blue trail toward Johns Brook.) The Phelps Trail to Marcy continues upstream, past the lodge, with yellow markers. (See below.) Johns Brook Lodge is owned and operated by the ADK and offers accommodations to hikers. For further information, see Section E5.

Distances: Garden to Crossover Trail, 0.51 mi.; to Deer Brook lean-to, 1.27 mi.; to ranger station, 3.07 mi.; to Howard lean-to, 3.14 mi.; to Big Slide Trail, 3.21 mi.; to JBL, 3.52 mi. (5.12 mi. from Keene Valley, Route 73.) Ascent, 793 ft. from the Garden; 1276 ft. from Keene Valley.

Southside Trail to Johns Brook Lodge

This route follows an old tote road along the S side of Johns Brook and connects with trails in the vicinity of JBL. Most of the way, it follows closely the R (S) bank of Johns Brook giving the traveler many different views of this characteristic mountain stream. It used to be maintained by DEC and started at the iron bridge 0.60 mi. W of the center of Keene Valley. Due to bad washouts along the R bank of Johns Brook, the trail was abandoned in 1942 by DEC but was later reopened and is now maintained by the Keene Valley Chapter of the ADK. However, the original section between the iron bridge and the Crossover Trail has not been reopened due to the washouts. While DEC has bulldozed a route (1961) around the washouts so that supplies may be more easily taken to the ranger's cabin in the winter, in order to follow the ADK-marked trail it is necessary to start at the Garden and follow the Phelps Trail to the Crossover Trail. (See above.) Future washouts and lumbering may cause rerouting of the reopened part of the trail at any time.

Leaving the Garden (0 mi.), follow the Phelps Trail to the Crossover Trail at 0.51 mi. and turn L, following red ADK markers. The trail descends steeply along a hogback and crosses Johns Brook at 0.69 mi. The brook is crossed on large boulders which may present some difficulty in times of high water. On the far side of the brook the trail crosses the route of the old Southside Trail tote road, now mostly indiscernible, and enters the woods away from the brook to avoid a bad washout. (On returning to the Garden via this trail, the brook crossing must be watched for carefully as it is not well marked.) Turning R and in a few yards joining the bulldozed route from the iron bridge at 0.75 mi., the trail swings

R across a tributary and immediately turns sharply to the L as it rejoins the old tote road at 0.81 mi.

Continuing at 0.81 mi. the route is now plain and few markers are necessary as the old tote road departs from and rejoins the bulldozed route at intervals over short stretches. Several large, interesting boulders are passed, followed by a stretch of corduroy, and at 1.51 mi. an unmarked trail leads R across Johns Brook to a private camp. At 1.55 mi. the bulldozed route swings L and follows an old high water route well above the rock ledges along the edge of the brook. The trail continues along the old tote road to the R, descends into the brook bed under the ledges at 1.85 mi., the route being marked with paint on the rocks, and leaves the brook bed at 1.95 mi. At 2.03 mi. the trail swings L away from the brook to get around a rock face and cross a tributary, returning immediately to the tote road. A few yards after crossing a small brook, the bulldozed high water rejoins the old tote road at 2.13 mi., the two routes coinciding the rest of the way to the suspension bridge near the ranger's cabin.

A side trail on the R at 2.19 mi. leads to flat rocks and Tenderfoot Pool in Johns Brook, a favorite swimming hole. The trail, for the most part having followed close to the brook, soon veers slightly away from it, crosses two small brooks, then a larger brook at 2.53 mi. and Wolf Jaws Brook at 2.73 mi., the bulldozed route descending to the L into the ravine to cross the brook and swinging R to climb the far bank and rejoin the old route. The ADK trail to Wolf Jaws lean-to and Wolf Jaws Notch enters on the L at 2.87 mi., and the DEC blue-marked Orebed Brook Trail to the Range Trail at the col between Gothics and Saddleback enters on the L at 3.03 mi. End of ADK markers. (See High Water Routes from JBL.)

Continuing straight ahead, the trail, now with blue DEC markers, crosses Johns Brook on a suspension bridge at 3.04 mi. and reaches the ranger's cabin at 3.10 mi. where it joins the yellow-marked Phelps Trail from the Garden. From here, the route to JBL is the same as described above for the Phelps Trail.

Distances: Garden to Crossover Trail, 0.51 mi.; to Southside Trail, 0.75 mi.; to Wolf Jaws Notch Trail, 2.87 mi.; to Orebed Brook Trail, 3.03 mi.; to ranger station, 3.10 mi.; to JBL, 3.55 mi. (5.15 mi. from Keene Valley, Route 73).

Mt. Marcy via Phelps Trail and Slant Rock from Johns Brook Lodge

This trail coming from Keene Valley via the N side of Johns Brook (see above) continues with yellow markers past JBL. Leaving the JBL signpost (0 mi.) a lean-to (1960), 30 yds. off trail on L, is passed at 0.12 mi. Passing the lean-to, the trail follows up the L bank of Johns Brook through second growth at an easy grade, sometimes close to the brook, sometimes back a short way from the brook, crossing several small tributaries. It enters the brook bed for a short distance at 0.65 mi. and reaches Hogback lean-to at 0.94 mi. After crossing Hogback Brook at 0.96 mi., the trail climbs steeply up the hogback through conifers high above the two streams. The grade slackens at 0.99 mi. and levels off at 1.04 mi. after which the grade is easy to moderate with the trail high above Johns Brook, which is heard but not seen. A lookout over the brook is reached at 1.32 mi., and at 1.51 mi. a side trail on the L leads down the steep bank 0.07 mi. to Bushnell Falls in a deep ravine. These falls were a favorite spot of Reverend Horace Bushnell of Hartford, Connecticut, and were named in his honor by the Keene Valley guides, Dr. Bushnell having been a very well-liked summer resident of the valley.

Just beyond this side trail there is another trail junction and a lean-to at 1.53 mi. (The yellow trail straight ahead is the Hopkins Trail to Marcy, 4.00 mi., which joins the Van Hoevenberg Trail from Heart Lake in 2.80 mi., 0.38 mi. N of former Plateau lean-to.) The Phelps Trail, now marked with red disks, turns L down the bank at an angle and crosses Johns Brook on the rocks at 1.63 mi. to the R bank just above the confluence with Chicken Coop Brook, where two more lean-tos are located. The original Bushnell Falls lean-to is a few yards downstream to the L across Chicken Coop Brook, the second lean-to being located 55 yds. upstream at 1.67 mi. (In times of high water, cross Johns Brook on foot bridge 125 yds. upstream and follow down trail to the upstream lean-to.)

From the Bushnell Falls lean-tos the trail swings away from Johns Brook and climbs at a moderate grade through spruce and balsam, entering a bad blowdown area at about 2.30 mi. as the grade becomes easier. A large tributary from the L is crossed in a ravine at 2.84 mi. From here, the trail is fairly level with more hurricane damage in evidence as it meets and crosses Johns Brook again at 3.27 mi. and comes to Slant Rock at 3.29 mi. This is a famous camping spot, the huge rock forming a natural shelter. On the R of the trail is the Slant Rock lean-to. Following up the L bank of the brook brings one to a trail junction at 3.41 mi. Here across the brook is the site of the old Slant Rock lean-to which may offer a good campsite. (The yellow trail turning L across the brook is the Shorey Short Cut leading 1.11 mi. to the Range Trail. (See description of Haystack from the Range Trail, Section B1.)

Continuing up the L bank of the brook, the red trail starts climbing again with several fairly steep sections. Johns Brook is crossed again at 3.83 mi., the trail becoming wet and rocky at about 4.10 mi., and the top of the divide between Johns Brook and Panther Gorge is approached at 4.26 mi. Here the Range Trail, with blue markers, enters on the L. (See below.) The Phelps Trail, with red markers, continues to climb steeply up a rocky washed out brook bed, gaining 860 ft. in 0.69 mi. The grade moderates at 4.68 mi. and the Van Hoevenberg Trail with blue markers comes in on the R from Heart Lake at 4.95 mi. (See Heart Lake Region, Section B6.)

Now following the blue markers to the L, the trail makes a short climb, coming out on bare rocks, then crosses a wet sag at 5.09 mi. and climbs again to come out on the first rocky shoulder of Marcy at 5.19 mi. From this point, the trail is level for a short distance and then climbs up the bare rock cone to the summit at 5.53 mi. Over the bare rocks the trail is marked partly with small rock cairns and with paint blazes. In fog or rain great care is needed in following this part of the trail. Down the W side of Marcy toward Gray Peak, water can sometimes be found. It takes about 25 minutes to make the round trip to the spring. Descending toward Tear Lake, on the yellow trail, water can also be found to the R of the trail in the col at Schofield Cobble, 0.22 mi. below the summit of Marcy.

Distances: JBL to 1960 lean-to, 0.12 mi.; to Hogback lean-to, 0.94 mi.; to Hopkins Trail and first of three Bushnell Falls lean-tos, 1.53 mi.; to Slant Rock lean-to, 3.29 mi.; Shorey Short Cut, 3.41 mi.; to Range Trail, 4.26 mi.; to Van Hoevenberg Trail, 4.95

mi.; to summit of Marcy, 5.53 mi. (9.05 mi. from Garden, 10.65 mi. from Keene Valley.) Ascent, 3028 ft. from JBL; 3821 ft. from Garden; 4300 ft. from Keene Valley, Route 73. Elevation, 5344 ft. Order of height, 1.

Mt. Marcy via Hopkins Trail

This trail was laid out by Arthur S. Hopkins, former Director of Lands and Forests, as a short cut for his survey crew. It leads from the Phelps Trail (see above) at Bushnell Falls, 1.53 mi. SW of JBL, to the Van Hoevenberg Trail (see Heart Lake Region, Section B6.) The distance to Marcy is the same as via Slant Rock, but there is less steep climbing. However, it is very wet and soggy near its junction with the Van Hoevenberg Trail.

Leaving the Phelps Trail at Bushnell Falls junction (0 mi.) and continuing straight ahead with yellow markers, the trail follows up the L bank of Johns Brook, remaining high above the deep ravine as it climbs at an easy grade through splendid spruce and white birch. It descends into a small ravine and crosses a brook from R at 0.43 mi. Climbing is steeper from the brook, but the trail levels off at 0.51 mi. through a fine stand of spruce with partial views of Saddleback. Another good sized brook from R is crossed at 0.88 mi. with a steep climb up the opposite bank, after which the grades are easy to moderate. A blowdown area is reached at about 1.00 mi. with views of Basin. The trail is near the L bank of the L fork of Johns Brook at 1.47 mi., and a heavy blowdown area is reached at 1.65 mi. The climbing now gets steeper as the trail ascends the ravine with Little Marcy on the L and Table Top on the R. More hurricane damage and steep climbing is encountered at 1.85 mi. The trail is close to the L fork of the brook several times, finally crossing it at 2.10 mi. and following up a smaller tributary. The grade moderates at 2.15 mi., soon recrosses the L fork and levels off at 2.37 mi. through a very wet and soggy section among the thick spruce. After passing a swampy meadow on the L at 2.50 mi. the trail joins the Van Hoevenberg Trail, with blue DEC markers, and the alternate ADK trail with red ADK markers at 2.80 mi., 0.38 mi. N of former Plateau lean-to. Ascent from Bushnell Falls junction, 1600 ft. (Turn R for Indian

Falls, 1.73 mi.; Marcy Dam, 3.76 mi. and Adirondak Loj at Heart Lake, 6.01 mi.)

Turning L with the blue markers, the route to Marcy, now a wide-cut ski trail and well-worn, descends slightly through a very muddy section. Then a gradual climb starts at 2.92 mi. up a brook bed to the site of former Plateau lean-to at 3.18 mi. Here the dome of Marcy is in sight. The trail dips a little to cross a tiny stream which may be the last sure water. It then ascends through thick, stunted spruces and rejoins the Phelps Trail, with red markers, which comes in on the L at 3.42 mi. Turning R the route from here to the summit of Marcy is the same as for the Phelps Trail. (See above.)

Distances: JBL to Bushnell Falls Trail junction, 1.53 mi.; to Van Hoevenberg Trail, 4.33 mi.; to former Plateau lean-to, 4.71 mi.; to Phelps Trail, 4.95 mi.; to summit of Marcy, 5.53 mi. (9.05 mi. from Garden, 10.65 mi. from Keene Valley.)

Lower Wolf Jaw via Woodsfall Trail

This is an ADK-maintained trail providing the most direct route from JBL to Wolf Jaws lean-to, both Wolf Jaws and the lower end of the Range.

Leaving the signpost at JBL (0 mi.), with ADK red markers, descend and cross Johns Brook at 0.02 mi., turning R on the far bank. (See below for High Water Routes.) The trail leads up two steep pitches over a hogback and down to Orebed Brook at 0.24 mi. and then climbs steeply to a junction of five trails at 0.32 mi. (Blue markers L lead to suspension bridge.) ADK trail heading 110° leads to Short Job and trail 200° is Orebed Brook Trail to the Range Trail at the col between Gothics and Saddleback. Taking ADK trail heading 170° known as the Woodsfall Trail, the climbing is at an easy grade as the trail crosses several small brooks. At 0.54 mi. the trail swings L toward the E and follows up R bank of small brook at 0.65 mi. Soon leaving the brook it heads SE, the grade slackening at about 0.74 mi., and reaches height of land at 0.88 mi. Descending gradually, the trail joins an old tote road heading E which it follows for awhile, then crosses two brooks at 1.08 mi. and 1.12 mi. and joins the red ADK trail from the Johns

Brook Southside Trail near the Wolf Jaws lean-to at 1.13 mi. (0.88 mi. to Southside Trail).

Turning R the trail with ADK markers heads 160° and climbs gradually up the course of Wolf Jaws Brook but for the most part is back away from the brook's L bank. A tributary from the R is crossed at 1.58 mi. and a smaller tributary at 1.69 mi. after which the grade becomes steeper. The trail is close to the brook at 1.76 mi., and, at 1.81 mi., a side trail on L leads to the brook (last sure water). The climbing continues steadily, the junction with the ADK Range Trail in Wolf Jaws col being reached at 2.03 mi. Turn R for Upper Wolf Jaw, Armstrong and Gothics, L for Lower Wolf Jaw.

Turning L a spring may sometimes be found in about 20 yds., and the cut-off to the Wedge Brook Trail (see St. Huberts Region, Section B2) branches R at 2.06 mi. From here the climb to the summit is quite steep with occasional breathers. The Wedge Brook Trail enters on the R at 2.22 mi., and the summit of Lower Wolf Jaw is reached at 2.52 mi. Good views from lookout on L. (See Lower Wolf Jaw via Rooster Comb, Section B1.) The trail straight ahead is the W. A. White Trail from St. Huberts (see St. Huberts Region, Section B2). It connects with ADK trails over Hedgehog and Rooster Comb to Keene Valley.

Distances: JBL to Orebed Brook Trail, 0.32 mi.; to junction near Wolf Jaws lean-to, 1.13 mi.; to Wolf Jaws Notch and Range Trail, 2.03 mi.; to Lower Wolf Jaw, 2.52 mi. Ascent, 2000 ft. from JBL. Elevation, 4175 ft. Order of height, 30.

Short Job

Take Orebed Brook Trail with blue markers from JBL to junction of five trails at 0.32 mi. (See Lower Wolf Jaw via Woodsfall Trail; also High Water Routes.) At junction, take trail with ADK markers heading 110°. From the junction the grade is gradual, becoming steeper at 0.57 mi. with a steep pitch and sharp L turn at 0.63 mi. The grade is now easier as the first lookout toward the Range is reached on the summit at 0.69 mi. The trail continues with a slight descent to a lookout over the Johns Brook Valley at 0.74 mi.

Distances: JBL to Orebed Brook Trail, 0.32 mi.; to summit of Short Job, 0.69 mi.; to lookout, 0.74 mi.

Gothics via Orebed Brook Trail

The most direct route from JBL to the range at the col between Gothics and Saddleback is via parts of the Woodsfall Trail and the Orebed Brook Trail. Leaving the signpost at JBL (0 mi.), with red ADK markers, follow the Woodsfall Trail (see above for Woodsfall Trail and below for High Water Routes) to junction of five trails at 0.32 mi. (Blue markers L lead to suspension bridge. ADK trail heading 110° leads to Short Job. ADK trail heading 170° is Woodsfall Trail to Wolf Jaws Notch.)

Turning R, with blue markers, the Orebed Brook Trail, heading 200°, follows an old tote road at an easy grade and at 0.48 mi. is high above the R bank of Orebed Brook which is heard in the ravine below. The trail continues along the tote road and becomes a footpath at 0.95 mi. It then descends slightly and follows up the R bank of a tributary, which it crosses at 1.01 mi. Orebed Brook lean-to (1964), situated high on the L bank of the tributary, is reached by a side trail L at 1.03 mi. The trail continues up the course of Orebed Brook which is heard but not seen. A large boulder with trees growing on top (Slant Rock Junior) is passed on the R at 1.30 mi. After crossing two more brooks from the L, the trail descends and crosses a large brook from L at 1.52 mi. The climbing is now steady at a fair grade and becomes steeper at 1.94 mi. as the trail passes a campsite with fireplace at 2.29 mi. and crosses Orebed Brook at 2.31 mi. The grade becomes much steeper at 2.41 mi., and the first of several ladders is reached at 2.47 mi. Shortly past the first ladder, there is a side trail to the bare rock slide on the R offering views. A small brook, flowing from a spring in the col, is crossed at 2.72 mi. The trail levels off, recrosses the brook and passes a side trail on the R. (This trail leads to the site of the old Gothics lean-to which burned down in 1969.) The junction with the Range Trail in the col between Gothics and Saddleback is reached at 2.80 mi. (Short trail S from col leads to blowdown area with views of slides on Gothics and mountains to the S.)

Turning L with ADK markers the trail climbs quite steeply up the SW ridge of Gothics. The first of two cables fastened to the bare granite is reached at 2.95 mi. and the second at 3.00 mi. The SW summit of Gothics is reached at 3.10 mi. from which views are obtained. The trail descends into a saddle and then climbs gradually up the summit ridge. The trail from Lower Ausable Lake enters on R at 3.35 mi. The summit is reached at 3.45 mi. See ADK Range Trail below for notes on views.

Distances: JBL to Orebed Brook Trail, 0.32 mi.; to Orebed Brook lean-to 1.03 mi.; to campsite, 2.29 mi.; to Range Trail, 2.80 mi.; to summit of Gothics, 3.45 mi. Ascent from JBL, 2360 ft. Elevation, 4736 ft. Order of height, 10.

High Water Routes to Orebed Brook Trail and Wolf Jaws Notch from JBL

When high water makes it difficult to cross Johns Brook on the red ADK trail from JBL, access to the trails on the other side may be had by use of the suspension bridge below the ranger station.

Take Phelps Trail, yellow disks, downstream from JBL signpost (0 mi.) to junction at ranger station at 0.45 mi. where yellow trail swings L. The trail straight ahead with the blue markers leads to the suspension bridge at 0.51 mi. and junction with Orebed Brook Trail at 0.52 mi. (Straight ahead is the Southside Trail to Keene Valley.) Turning R, the blue trail climbs a short distance and soon turns R on a tote road which it follows at an easy grade to the junction with the regular trail at 0.99 mi. This route is 0.67 mi. longer than the direct route from JBL.

Continuing straight ahead on the Southside Trail at the far end of the suspension bridge (ADK markers), the trail to Wolf Jaws Notch branches R at 0.68 mi. from JBL. This ADK-marked trail climbs steadily at a fair grade and comes out on the L bank of Wolf Jaws Brook at 0.90 mi. At. 0.95 mi. the grade moderates, and the trail swings away from the brook. It crosses a tributary flowing from the R at 1.35 mi. and joins the regular marked Woodsfall Trail entering on the R from JBL at 1.56 mi. Wolf Jaws lean-to is about 50 yds. past the junction on the L. This route is 0.43 mi. longer than the direct route from JBL.

ADK Range Trail to Upper Wolf Jaw, Armstrong and Gothics

The ADK maintains the Range Trail from the summit of Lower Wolf Jaw over Upper Wolf Jaw, Armstrong and Gothics to the col between Gothics and Saddleback at the junction with the Orebed Brook Trail. It is marked with red ADK markers. See St. Huberts Region for naming of Saddleback and Gothics. Armstrong was named for Thomas Armstrong, a prominent lumberman of Plattsburgh, who, with his partner Almon Thomas, in 1866 acquired title to Township 48, Totten and Crossfield Purchase. In 1887 they sold it to the Adirondack Mountain Reserve, which still owns the part around the Ausable Lakes between the Great Range and the mountains to the SE.

Leaving Wolf Jaws Notch (0 mi.) and heading SW, the trail soon makes a steep winding ascent up the ridge, passing a lookout point back toward Lower Wolf Jaw at 0.25 mi. and reaching the lesser summit of Upper Wolf Jaw (elevation, 4080 ft.) at 0.45 mi. From here the trail swings W and makes an easy descent of 130 ft. to a col at 0.75 mi. The climbing now becomes steep, moderating at 0.90 mi. and reaching a trail junction at 1.00 mi. A short spur trail to the R leads about 20 yds. to the summit of Upper Wolf Jaw. Here there are good views of the Green Mts., Dix, Nipple Top, Colvin, Blake, Sawteeth, Armstrong, Saddleback, Basin, Haystack, Marcy and the MacIntyre Range. Ascent from JBL, 2000 ft. Elevation, 4185 ft. Order of height, 29.

Straight ahead from the junction the trail heads S and then W as it descends 270 ft. to a fern-filled col at 1.20 mi. It then makes a steep, winding ascent to about 1.30 mi. and drops into a sag at 1.45 mi. where a spring is sometimes found on the R. The trail now climbs steeply over a slight rise and drops into another col with ferns at foot of slide at 1.50 mi. From here the trail heads S and climbs very steeply up the summit ridge of Armstrong, moderating at 1.70 mi. and reaching the summit of Armstrong at 1.80 mi. A rock ledge just off trail to R offers good views of the Johns Brook Valley. By bushwhacking about 20 yds. S another lookout is reached offering a 270° view from Giant in the E almost around to Big Slide in the N. Total ascent from JBL, 2500 ft. Elevation, 4400 ft. Order of height, 22.

Continuing S the trail descends about 100 ft., some steep, some easy, to a col at 2.05 mi. and then climbs to the S summit of Armstrong at 2.15 mi., after which it heads W and descends gradually 130 ft. to the main col at 2.25 mi. where the ATIS trail from St. Huberts enters on the L. Shortly before reaching the junction there is an impressive view of the Gothics slides.

Continuing with ADK markers, the trail is level for a stretch and then starts climbing the NE ridge of Gothics at 2.35 mi. Good views are obtained as the trail makes its way through scrub spruce and balsam, sometimes steep, sometimes easy, to the bare rock summit of Gothics at 2.70 mi. (NYS Land Survey Station 287 placed here by Verplanck Colvin in 1896.) The view is unobstructed in all directions with about 30 major peaks discernible. The boathouse and a small part of the Lower Ausable Lake can be seen, but the Upper Ausable Lake is not visible from the summit. However, it may be seen from a point a short distance down the trail to the Lower Ausable Lake via Pyramid. Total ascent from JBL, 3000 ft. Elevation, 4736 ft. Order of height, 10.

The trail continues along the rocky ridge line, descending gradually into a saddle where the trail to Pyramid, Sawteeth and Lower Ausable Lake is encountered on the L at 2.82 mi. (See below.) The Range Trail continues climbing, reaching the SW summit at 3.05 mi. From here the descent to the Gothics-Saddleback col is quite steep, two cables being attached over the bare granite in the steepest places. In the col at 3.35 mi. the ADK trail joins the State Range Trail up Orebed Brook from JBL, blue markers.

Distances: JBL via Woodsfall Trail to Wolf Jaws Notch, 2.03 mi.; to Upper Wolf Jaw, 3.03 mi.; to Armstrong, 3.83 mi.; to ATIS trail to St. Huberts, 4.28 mi.; to Gothics, 4.73 mi.; to Pyramid–Lower Ausable Lake Trail, 4.85 mi.; to Orebed Brook Trail junction, 5.38 mi.

State Range Trail to Saddleback, Basin and Marcy

The Range Trail from the Gothics-Saddleback col over Saddleback, Basin and a shoulder of Haystack to the Phelps Trail, at the head of Panther Gorge, is maintained by DEC and is marked with blue DEC markers.

Leaving the trail junction in the Gothics-Saddleback col (0 mi.), the trail starts a steady climb at a fair grade up Saddleback, giving excellent views of the slides and cables on Gothics. After climbing 480 ft., the E summit is reached at 0.34 mi. where there is a fine lookout on the R. The trail is then level for a short stretch, descends gradually into the saddle at 0.45 mi. and comes to a steep pitch leading up to the main (W) summit of Saddleback at 0.56 mi. where there are excellent views of Basin, Marcy, Haystack, Colden, the MacIntyre Range, The Colvin–Pinnacle Ridge, Macomb, Boreas and the Upper Ausable Lake. Ascent from JBL via Orebed Brook Trail, 2200 ft. Elevation, 4515 ft. Order of height, 17.

The trail turns sharp R at the summit of Saddleback along the bare ledge and at 0.59 mi. descends precipitously down over the ledges where caution is needed. The bottom of the rock climb is reached at 0.65 mi. where the trail enters the scrub, still descending steeply. The grade moderates at 0.68 mi., and the col is reached at 0.77 mi. The trail now starts gradually up the fern-covered ridge of Basin, but the grade becomes progressively steeper and at 1.02 mi. the trail has been rerouted to the L. The trail reaches the top of a chimney at 1.06 mi. and continues climbing. At 1.13 mi. the grade levels off through the scrub conifers on the shoulder of Basin where views may be had back at the precipitous descent from Saddleback. After descending gradually through ferns to a saddle, the trail starts steeply up again at 1.31 mi. and comes out on a ledge at 1.42 mi. where there are excellent views over the Johns Brook Valley. From here, the trail swings L through the scrub and up over the rocks to the bare summit of Basin at 1.48 mi. Here in the rock is embedded the Colvin bolt, placed here during the Adirondack survey in 1876. The view is unobstructed in all directions with Gothics to the E, Marcy to the W, and Haystack to the SW being the most prominent peaks, with the Upper Ausable Lake lying to the S and the valley to the SE forming an almost perfect basin. Total ascent from JBL, about 2870 ft. Elevation, 4827 ft. Order of height, 9.

Leaving the summit of Basin the trail makes a steep descent to the SW over the bare rocks to 1.53 mi. and then descends gradually along the fern-covered, wooded ridge. At 1.68 mi. the trail heads steeply down again, bears R around top of slide at 1.73 mi. and comes to a ladder at 1.75 mi. leading down the rock face. A second ladder is reached at 1.81 mi. shortly after which the grade levels off and becomes easy, giving one's knees a slight respite. But at 2.00 mi. the trail gets steeper, reaching a trail junction at 2.12 mi. (Yellow trail to R is the Shorey Short Cut to the Phelps Trail near Slant Rock lean-to. See below.) The Range Trail continues the steep descent, crosses Haystack Brook at 2.17 mi. and climbs steeply up a rocky and eroded trail to a trail junction and the site of the former Sno-Bird lean-to at 2.27 mi. (Trail L down brook is ATIS trail leading 3.35 mi. to the Warden's camp on the Upper Ausable Lake.)

Continuing with the blue markers, the Range Trail passes in front of the former lean-to, crosses the brook at 2.32 mi. and climbs steeply up a rocky trail. It enters a brook bed at 2.47 mi. and continues a wet and rocky climb to a trail junction at 2.72 mi. (Trail L, marked with cairns and paint blazes, leads 0.55 mi. over Little Haystack to the summit of Haystack. See below.) Swinging R the Range Trail levels off through a slight sag and comes to a steep pitch leading up to the top of the ridge at 2.82 mi. A bare spot to the R, offering views, is passed at 2.84 mi. after which the trail starts down at a moderate grade, getting steeper at 3.08 mi. At 3.16 mi. the trail makes an exceedingly steep, rocky descent and joins the red-marked Phelps Trail from JBL via Slant Rock at 3.25 mi. Turning L with the red markers, the route from here to Marcy is the same as from the Phelps Trail. (See below.)

Distances: JBL via Orebed Brook Trail to Gothics–Saddleback col, 2.80 mi.; to Saddleback, 3.36 mi.; to Basin, 4.28 mi.; to Shorey Short Cut, 4.92 mi.; to the site of the former Sno-Bird lean-to, 5.07 mi; to Haystack Trail, 5.52 mi.; to Phelps Trail, 6.05 mi.; to Van Hoevenberg Trail, 6.74 mi.; to the summit of Mt. Marcy, 7.32 mi.

Shorey Short Cut from Range Trail to Phelps Trail

This trail was cut by A. T. Shorey, former Chairman of the Guidebook Committee, when he was with the Conservation Department. It connects the Range Trail between Haystack and Basin with the Phelps Trail near Slant Rock lean-to. Leaving the Range Trail (0 mi.), 0.15 mi. N of the former Sno-Bird lean-to close to Haystack Brook, the trail with yellow markers climbs easily at first and then at a not too difficult grade, passing a lookout at 0.19 mi., a big boulder on the L at 0.25 mi. and comes to the height of land on a shoulder of Haystack at 0.31 mi. The blowdowns here have opened up a view of Basin. The trail now descends continuously at a moderate grade, comes to a slight upgrade at 0.45 mi. and then descends steadily through more hurricane damage. A fairly steep pitch is descended at 0.66 mi. and another at 0.73 mi. The trail crosses Johns Brook and joins the Phelps Trail at 1.11 mi., 0.12 mi. above Slant Rock lean-to.

Distance: Range Trail to Phelps Trail, 1.11 mi.

Mt. Haystack from Range Trail

This third highest peak of the Adirondacks lies 1.25 mi. ESE of Marcy and was named by Old Mountain Phelps in August 1849 when he made the first recorded ascent of this mountain with Almeron Oliver and George Estey. Phelps remarked to his companions that the mountain was a great stack of rock but that he would call it Haystack.

The trail turns S from the Range Trail 0.45 mi. SE of the former site of Sno-Bird lean-to and is marked with cairns and paint blazes. Leaving the trail junction (0 mi.), the trail climbs steeply up the bare rock cone of Little Haystack and reaches its summit at 0.15 mi. Elevation, 4700 ft. This little peak offers a magnificent closeup view of Marcy. Between Marcy and Little Marcy on the R, a glimpse of Wright Peak may be had. The trail descends steeply about 100 ft. into the spruce-filled col at 0.20 mi. and then climbs at an easier grade up the bare N ridge of Haystack, reaching the summit at 0.55 mi. The view from the summit is considered to be one of the finest in the Adirondacks with about 27 major peaks discernible. By descending a short way down the W side toward Marcy, one can get a better closeup of the precipitous cliffs and depth of Panther Gorge which lies between Haystack and Marcy. There is a trail S from the summit to Bartlett Ridge, 0.75 mi.;

thence L to either Marcy Landing, 3.60 mi. or to the Warden's camp, 3.45 mi. on Upper Ausable Lake; or R to Panther Gorge lean-to on Elk Lake–Marcy Trail, 1.35 mi. (See Lower Ausable Lake Region, Section B3.)

Distances: Range Trail to Little Haystack, 0.15 mi.; to summit of Haystack, 0.55 mi. (4.35 mi. from Upper Ausable Lake via the site of the former Sno-Bird lean-to, 5.34 mi. from JBL via Phelps Trail, 5.67 mi. via Shorey Trail). Elevation, 4960 ft. Order of height, 3.

Mt. Marcy from Keene Valley via the Great Range

For those who wish to traverse the entire Range to Marcy from Keene Valley, reference should be had to the following trail descriptions in the Keene Valley Section: Lower Wolf Jaw via Rooster Comb and Hedgehog (see below); ADK Range Trail to Upper Wolf Jaw, Armstrong and Gothics (see above); State Range Trail to Saddleback, Basin and Marcy (see above); Mt. Marcy via Phelps Trail and Slant Rock from JBL (see above). This is a very rugged route and should be attempted only by those in the best of physical condition, the total climb to Marcy being about 9000 ft. Return to Keene Valley via the Phelps or Hopkins Trails. If making a continuous trip with heavy packs, allow at least two or three nights in the lean-tos. It is better to base at JBL and do the Range in a series of day trips, traveling light.

Summary of Distances: Iron Bridge, 0.60 mi. W of Keene Valley to:

Point	Distance Miles	Approx. Total Ascent, Ft.
Rooster Comb	1.75	1640
Hedgehog	3.10	2530
W. A. White Trail	3.50	
Lower Wolf Jaw	4.95	3670
Wolf Jaws Notch	5.44	
Upper Wolf Jaw	6.44	4510
Armstrong	7.24	5030

| | *Distance* | *Approx. Total* |
Point	*Miles*	*Ascent, Ft.*
ATIS Trail to St. Huberts	7.69	
Gothics	8.14	5530
Orebed Brook Trail	8.79	
Saddleback	9.35	6130
Basin	10.27	6800
Shorey Short Cut	10.91	
Site of former Sno-Bird Lean-to	11.06	
Haystack Trail	11.51	7630
Phelps Trail	12.04	
Van Hoevenberg Trail	12.73	8440
Marcy	13.31	9000

Klondike Notch Trail to South Meadow

This route leads from Johns Brook Lodge through Klondike Notch in a NW direction to South Meadow, and provides access to Adirondak Loj and the Heart Lake camping area with the least amount of climbing. Klondike Notch between Table Top and Big Slide Mts. has, apparently due to a cartographer's error, also been called Railroad Notch. This latter name more rightfully belongs to the notch between Big Slide and Porter Mts. where the grades are less and which years ago was surveyed for a railroad.

Leaving the JBL signpost (0 mi.), the trail heads across the back yard and crosses Black Brook at 0.06 mi. It is marked with red DEC disks. Climbing up along the L bank of the brook, the trail is quite soggy for a stretch swinging away from the brook at 0.37 mi. but still following its general course into the notch. The grades are easy to moderate with a steeper pitch here and there. A birch tree, bent over by a large blowdown, forms an arch over the trail at 0.78 mi., and trail junction is reached at 1.28 mi. (Painted BM, 3031.5 ft. on spruce tree. Trail R is the red-marked ADK trail over Yard Mt. to Big Slide Mt., 2.70 mi. Ascent 1208 ft. See below.)

Continuing with DEC markers at moderate grades, with occasional steeper pitches, the trail makes a slight descent at 1.36 mi.

to cross a level, swampy area, then continues climbing through the spruce forest, heavily damaged by hurricanes, and reaches the height of land in Klondike Notch at 1.72 mi. having gained 866 ft. elevation over JBL. (PBM, 3182 ft. just off trail to L.) Dropping down into a small sag and crossing another divide at 1.75 mi., the trail descends through a conifer forest at easy to moderates grades, with a few steeper pitches, and crosses Klondike Brook at 2.62 mi. where the brook makes a R angle turn. Upstream a few yards is a sign indicating a route to Phelps Mt. Following down the L bank of the brook on a tote road, Klondike Dam lean-to is reached at 2.69 mi. (Chiseled square BM, painted 2831.9 ft. near SE corner of lean-to.)

Passing in front of the lean-to the trail, now a tote road, makes a short climb above the brook, levels off at 2.84 mi. and crosses a fairly large brook flowing over bare granite at 3.10 mi. Continuing fairely level with a few moderate pitches up and down, several small brooks are crossed flowing from the L. At 3.70 mi. the trail starts down at a steady grade, swings R away from the tote road at 3.78 mi. and soon rejoins it in an eroded section shortly before turning R at 3.89 mi. and leveling off on a switchback toward the E. Swinging way around to the L and descending at 3.93 mi., a reference BM in the trail is reached at 3.94 mi. (PBM, 2567 ft. is located just off the trail to the R in a dim tote road.)

Now descending at moderate grades, there are some level stretches and rocky sections as the tote road continues toward the NW. Becoming grassy, the tote road finally levels off at 5.02 mi. and swings toward the W. An unmarked trail from the Cascade Lakes enters on the R at 5.10 mi., and the brink of the L bank of South Meadow Brook is reached at 5.16 mi. opposite an old, broken dam. Turning R the trail crosses the brook on a bridge (1954) a short distance upstream, turns downstream and reaches the signpost on the South Meadow Road at 5.27 mi. Continuing W on the dirt road, it is slightly over a mile to the Heart Lake Road and another mile SW to Adirondak Loj.

Distances: JBL to ADK Big Slide Trail, 1.28 mi.; to height of land in Klondike Notch, 1.72 mi.; to Klondike Dam lean-to, 2.69 mi.; to South Meadow Road, 5.27 mi.; to Adirondak Loj, 7.30 mi. Descent from height of land to South Meadow, 1127 ft.

Big Slide Mt. via Slide Mt. Brook Trail

This trail starts from the Phelps Trail on N side of Johns Brook 0.31 mi. NE of Johns Brook Lodge. Coming from Keene Valley the junction is just past Slide Mt. Brook, 0.14 mi. SW of the ranger's camp.

Leaving the Phelps Trail (0 mi.), the route is marked with red ADK markers and paint blazes and heads NW up the R bank of Slide Mt. Brook. The trail crosses to the L bank at 0.22 mi. following red arrows. The trail continues up the brook, crossing to the R bank at 0.30 mi., back to the L bank at 0.35 mi., and soon reaches the bottom of a bare rock slide. Climbing this slide to the top at 0.45 mi., views are obtained back toward Gothics and the Range. The trail returns to the brook at 0.50 mi., enters the woods again on the L bank and returns to the brook again at 0.68 mi. From here, the trail is in and out of the brook several times, meeting a tributary at 0.88 mi. Following up the R bank of the tributary, it leaves the brook at 0.97 mi. (last sure water).

The general course of the trail is now N, climbing at an easy grade through second growth. As the climbing continues, one can look directly up at the bare rock slide which occurred in 1830 and from which the mountain takes its name. The grade steepens at 1.85 mi., and water can sometimes be found in a spring at 1.95 mi. The climbing is now quite steep through berry bushes and open spots affording views of the Range. At 2.05 mi. the climbing is now quite steep through berry bushes and open spots affording views of the Range. At 2.05 mi. the trail from the Garden over the Brothers enters on the R (see below) marked with red ADK markers. (Distance to Garden, 3.55 mi.)

Continuing on the Big Slide Trail, the climbing becomes very steep at 2.10 mi., but trees furnish footing and handholds over the ledges, the final steep assault commencing at 2.20 mi. The top of the mountain is wooded, but the trail leads to several lookouts on the S ledges, the first lookout being reached at 2.30 mi. The summit is reached at 2.35 mi. where magnificent views are obtained of Giant, Dix Peak, the Great Range, Mt.Colden and the MacIntyre Mts. E, S and W the view is unbroken, but to the N and Whiteface Mt., the view is partly hidden by the spruce and balsam. The trail straight ahead is the Big Slide Trail from the Klondike Notch Trail. (See below.)

Distances: Phelps Trail to trail over The Brothers, 2.06 mi.; to summit of Big Slide, 2.35 mi. (2.66 mi. from Johns Brook Lodge; 5.56 mi. from the Garden.) Ascent, 2000 ft. from Phelps Trail. Elevation, 4240 ft. Order of height, 27.

Big Slide Mt. via Klondike Notch Trail

The trail starts from the Klondike Notch Trail (see below) at 1.28 mi. NW of Johns Brook Lodge, branching R, and is marked with red ADK markers. Coming from South Meadow, the junction is 0.44 mi. past the height of land in Klondike Notch.

Leaving the Klondike Notch Trail (0 mi.), the Big Slide Trail starts climbing steadily, heading NE and then swinging back toward the NW and becoming quite steep as it ascends the SW spur of Big Slide, known as Yard Mt. Water can sometimes be found at a rock face at 0.65 mi. and at 0.80 mi. A view toward Marcy and the Range is afforded at 0.90 mi., and then the trail goes through the "lemon squeezer" at 1.20 mi., reaching the summit of Yard (4018 ft.) at 1.25 mi. (not included in the 46 peaks).

From Yard the trail proceeds NW and then NE along the ridge toward Big Slide. At 1.40 mi. there is a vista of Big Slide profile. The trail now climbs easily through the woods to the summit of Big Slide at 2.70 mi. where magnificent views are obtained. (See above).

Distances: Klondike Notch Trail to Yard, 1.25 mi.; to summit of Big Slide, 2.70 mi. (3.98 mi. from Johns Brook Lodge; 6.69 mi. from South Meadow). Ascent, 1208 ft. from Klondike Notch Trail; 1924 ft. from Johns Brook Lodge. Elevation, 4240 ft. Order of height, 27.

Big Slide Mt. via The Brothers

A trail was constructed between Second Brother (also known as Upper Twin) and the summit of Big Slide in June 1951 by the Keene Valley Chapter of the ADK. Together with the original Brothers Trail, this trail offers a spectacular approach to Big Slide, nearly a quarter of which is over open ledges that offer extensive views. It goes over the Third Brother and joins the traditional route up Slide Mt. Brook from the Phelps Trail 0.03 mi. below the summit of Big Slide. Combined with these two trails, it makes possible an interesting day's trip from the Garden above Keene Valley.

Follow the Phelps Trail (see Section B1) 1.60 mi. W from the center of Keene Valley Village to the Garden. Leaving the R side of the Garden (0 mi.) the trail, marked with red ADK markers, climbs steeply for about 100 yds. and then moderates to an easy, steady grade through a stand of white birch, following above the L bank of Juliet Brook. At 0.25 mi. the ravine of the brook is visible.

At 0.40 mi. the Brothers Trail turns L down a slight grade, crosses Juliet Brook (sometimes dry) and starts climbing again at 0.45 mi. The grade becomes very steep at 0.60 mi., the trail emerging on a bare rock slide at 0.75 mi., affording views of Hurricane to the NE, Giant to the E, the Range to the S, and Johns Brook Valley and Marcy to the SW. A short, steep rock climb is reached at 1.20 mi., after which the trail is mostly in the open over bare rocks, reaching the flat rock summit of First Brother (Lower Twin) at 1.45 mi. Elevation, 2940 ft. The trail then makes a slight dip and climbs to the summit of Second Brother (Upper Twin) at 1.70 mi., the summit and lookout being 20 yds. off the trail to the R. Elevation, 3120 ft. Ascent from Garden, 1600 ft.

Beyond Second Brother the trail enters the woods, descending slightly, and then starts climbing again at 1.90 mi. A sag through white birch and ferns is reached at 2.00 mi. and a brook bed crossed at 2.05 mi. Climbing now becomes steady at a moderate grade through white birch, passing a lookout back toward Keene Valley at 2.20 mi. and reaching the summit of Third Brother at 2.50 mi., where a spectacular view of the slide on Big Slide is obtained. Other views include Noonmark, Dix Peak, Nipple Top, the Range and the two Haystacks. Elevation, 3681 ft. Ascent from the Garden, 2160 ft.

Leaving Third Brother the trail descends gradually into a beautiful spruce and balsam forest with many ferns. A natural rock shelter is passed on the L at 2.65 mi., and the bottom of the col

is reached at 3.10 mi. where a brook is crossed and recrossed
times dry). From here the trail climbs steadily at a moderate
through conifers and joins the Slide Brook Trail from Johns Brook
at 3.55 mi. just below the Big Slide summit cliffs. Turning R on
the Slide Brook Trail, the climbing becomes very steep and the
summit of Big Slide is reached at 3.85 mi. where magnificent views
are obtained. (See above.)

Distances: Garden to First Brother, 1.45 mi.; to Second
Brother, 1.70 mi.; to Slide Brook Trail from Johns Brook, 3.55 mi.;
to summit of Big Slide, 3.85 mi. Total ascent from the Garden,
2800 ft. Elevation, 4240 ft. Order of height, 27.

Porter Mt. from Keene Valley Airport via Ridge Trail

Porter Mt., once known as West Mt., was named by the residents of Keene Valley for Dr. Noah Porter, President of Yale University from 1871 to 1886, who made the first recorded ascent
of the mountain in 1875 with Ed Phelps, Keene Valley guide and
son of Old Mountain Phelps.

From Keene Valley at the sign "Trail to High Peaks," proceed
N on Route 73 2.00 mi. to sign "Porter" and a dirt road on L.
(PBM, 990 ft. on R.) Follow dirt road about 100 yds. and turn R
into airfield. Leaving dirt road (0 mi.), follow auto track to SW
edge of field at 0.10 mi. Park cars here. Taking L fork the trail,
marked with red ADK markers, enters the woods and climbs gradually. It ascends a small hill, crosses a level stretch of pine needles,
descends to a swampy area, which it crosses, and turns L into a
good tote road which it follows a short distance. At 1.00 mi. it
turns sharp R into another tote road and follows up a brook which
it crosses at 1.15 mi. After crossing brook bed at 1.25 mi., the
trail becomes steep and soon emerges on steep rock ledges and
reaches the NE shoulder of Blueberry Mt. at 1.75 mi. Trail now
ascends gradually over bare rocks, up and down, and reaches large
boulder on Blueberry Mt. at 2.40 mi. Good views to the E and S.

After descending to col at 2.60 mi., the trail winds through a
spruce forest and then climbs very steeply up a ravine between
two ridges, crossing several small brooks and reaching a grassy

summit at 3.10 mi. The ascent continues over a long ridge. At 4.10 mi. the ADK trail from Keene Valley near the Garden comes in on the L. (See below.)

Continuing straight ahead along the ridge at easy grades, the E summit is reached at 4.42 mi. and the main summit of Porter at 4.54 mi. where there are views in all directions, over 20 major peaks being visible. The trail continues with red DEC markers, descending into a col and then climbing over the shoulder of Cascade Mt. It is 0.95 mi. to the summit of Cascade and 2.80 mi. to Route 73 near upper end of Cascade lakes, 3.30 mi. if one wishes to go over Cascade en route since trail divides, making it necessary to retrace steps. (See Cascade–Keene–Hurricane Region, Section B7.)

Distances: Dirt road at Keene Valley Airport to Blueberry Mt., 2.40 mi.; to ADK trail from road near Garden, 4.10 mi.; to summit of Porter, 4.54 mi. Total ascent, 3275 ft. Elevation, 4059 ft. Order of height, 38.

Porter Mt. from Road near The Garden

For beginning of this trail take road W toward the Garden from Route 73 in Keene Valley. Leave cars at the Garden and retrace steps 0.25 mi. to a dirt road marked by a sign. Leaving this junction (0 mi.), follow the road 0.15 mi. at which point the road turns L and the Porter Trail leads straight ahead, then turns R, crosses Slide Brook at 0.24 mi. and starts to climb, rounding off at 0.34 mi. and then starting up again at about 0.45 mi. Taking the R fork at 0.62 mi., the trail continues to climb, reaching the site of a former sugar camp at 0.88 mi. where the trail intersects a jeep road coming in from a real estate development. Turning L, the trail to Porter crosses the jeep road and climbs at times steeply to an area at 1.26 mi. where it levels off. Avoid trail L to Hi–Vue Camp (private) just beyond this junction. Steady climbing starts again at 1.29 mi., and at 1.38 mi. the trail turns sharp L up over ledges, levels off at a bare spot and descends slightly into sag at 1.46 mi. The trail joins a skid road near a cabin at 1.50 mi. and leaves it at 1.52 mi., turning R and climbing up over ledges. The trail levels off at about 1.58 mi. and then continues up and down over bare ledges with little gain in elevation, coming to a bare promontory known as Little Porter at 1.76 mi. where there are excellent views.

The trail now makes a descent over bare rocks to 1.78 mi. and then heads NW through a grassy area with white birch and cherry at a fairly level or slight grade. It crosses a brook from L at 2.10 mi., follows up its L bank and swings away from it at 2.15 mi. where it starts climbing at a moderate grade. A brook from R is crossed at 2.31 mi., followed by a slight descent at 2.36 mi. Steady climbing starts again at 2.46 mi., moderating at 2.61 mi. and becoming easy at 2.69 mi. The trail leaves the grassy area and enters conifers and white birch at 2.73 mi. where it starts a gradual downgrade and crosses another brook from the R at 2.85 mi. Now climbing at a moderate grade the trail levels off at 3.00 mi. and crosses two more brooks from R at 3.07 mi. and 3.11 mi. The climbing continues through the white birch, finally pitching up onto a grassy area where it meets the trail from the airport at 3.40 mi. Turning L, the trail continues on the level or at easy grades along the ridge to the E summit at 3.72 mi. and the main summit of Porter at 3.84 mi.

Distances: Road junction near Garden to sugar camp, 0.88 mi.; to Thomas Ridge Trail, 1.26 mi.; to Little Porter, 1.76 mi.; to trail from airport, 3.40 mi.; to summit of Porter, 3.84 mi. Ascent, 2700 ft. Elevation, 4059 ft. Order of height, 38.

Rooster Comb from Route 73

There are two trails to Rooster Comb of about equal grade and length, one starting from Route 73 S of Keene Valley, the other starting from the iron bridge over Johns Brook W of Keene Valley.

The trail leaves a side road branching W from Highway 73, 0.75 mi. S of trail sign to High Peaks in Keene Valley. There is a red fire hydrant just S of the road. Starting at highway (0 mi.) bear R across field at 0.10 mi. where road veers L. Red ADK markers start here. The trail crosses an unmarked trail at 0.20 mi. and soon starts climbing at a steady grade through hemlocks and then hardwoods, reaching brink of L bank of Rushing Brook at 0.35

mi. It then swings away from the brook following course of a small tributary. The grade moderates at 0.75 mi., starts climbing at 0.85 mi. where the brook is heard on the L and becomes easy again at 1.00 mi., continuing to the junction with the ATIS trail on L at 1.20 mi. (This trail leads 0.65 mi. to Snow Mt. and connects with the trail from Deer Brook and the W. A. White Trail from St. Huberts. Distance to W. A. White Trail, 1.29 mi.; to St. Huberts, 2.24 mi. See St. Huberts Region, Section B2.)

The trail now climbs more steeply through white birch up L bank of brook bed, the grade moderating at 1.30 mi. and continuing to the junction, near two large boulders, with the red ADK trail to Hedgehog and Lower Wolf Jaw on the L at 1.60 mi. (See below.) Continuing straight ahead, the trail veers R and climbs very steeply around a cliff, the "Comb," and scrambles over rock ledges to the summit at 1.85 mi., which is approached from the N by swinging along the top of the cliff. Many vantage points will be found by exploring the top of the "Comb." Marcy dominates the view at the head of the Johns Brook Valley with the Range on the L and Big Slide, the Brothers and Porter on the R.

Distances: Route 73 to ATIS trail to Snow Mt., 1.20 mi.; to ADK trail to Hedgehog and the Range, 1.60 mi.; to Rooster Comb, 1.85 mi. Ascent, 1720 ft. Elevation, 2762 ft.

Lower Wolf Jaw via Rooster Comb and Hedgehog

A trail was cut in 1953 from just below the cliffs on Rooster Comb, over the summit of Hedgehog, to the W. A. White Trail S of Hedgehog. This makes possible a traverse of the entire Great Range which now starts at Rooster Comb.

This route starts at the iron bridge over Johns Brook on the road to the Garden, 0.60 mi. W of the High Peaks trail sign on Route 73 in Keene Valley. Passing through the stone gate on the L (0 mi.) just before reaching the bridge, the trail bears L following the dirt road, passes through another gate and then takes a R fork at 0.10 mi. It is marked with red ADK markers. At 0.23 mi. it bears L and climbs a moderate grade toward the SW, then swinging W. The grade eases at 0.36 mi. and a small clearing is reached at 0.45 mi. where several tote roads converge. (The tote road straight ahead on the extreme R heading 315° is the bulldozed route leading

1.07 mi. to the junction of the Southside and ADK Crossover Trails. See above.) Here the trail swings L along the edge of the clearing about 25 yds. to a dirt road, turns L on dirt road and at 0.50 mi. turns R on a lumber road. (The dirt road straight ahead leads back to the iron bridge, but it is about 65 yds. longer than the marked route.)

The lumber road is not an attractive climb, being a rather steep and eroded bull-dozed route up the mountain with occasional easy stretches. However, the messy part is short, the foot trail turning R at 0.79 mi., continuing to the end of the lumbered area at about 1.00. The climbing now becomes fairly steep and continues at a steady grade until the trail levels off for a short distance at 1.50 mi. where a height of land is visible through the conifers on the R. (Bushwhacking a few yards, to R a view of Porter and the Brothers may be had.) The climbing continues steep to bare ledges at 1.65 mi. where there is a view of Porter, the Brothers and Big Slide with Marcy looming high above at the head of Johns Brook Valley. The summit of Rooster Comb is reached at 1.75 mi. Ascent, 1640 ft. Elevation, 2762 ft. The top of the "Comb," although partially wooded, is bounded by cliffs on three sides offering many vantage points for fine views.

Turning sharp L at the summit, the trail heads back toward the N and then swings R again as it descends very steeply over rock ledges and through hardwoods to the foot of the cliff and a trail junction near two large boulders at 2.00 mi. (Trail straight ahead is the Rooster Comb Trail from Route 73 and connects with the ATIS trail to Snow Mt. and St. Huberts. See above.)

Turning R, still with ADK markers, the trail starts climbing with alternate steep and moderate grades. The grade gets steeper at about 2.10 mi. and the trail climbs through conifers along the foot of a rock face. A height of land is reached at 2.40 mi. and the trail then dips into a slight sag with easy going. Climbing becomes steeper again at 2.60 mi., and the summit of N Hedgehog is reached at 2.70 mi. Both this and the main summit are wooded, offering no views. The trail descends gradually through the conifers, crosses a brook bed and starts climbing at 2.95 mi., reaching the summit of Hedgehog at 3.10 mi. Total ascent, 2530 ft. Elevation, 3369 ft.

From Hedgehog the trail descends toward the W and SW

through conifers to a brook at 3.50 mi. (May be dry in late summer.) A few yards beyond the brook the W. A. White Trail from St. Huberts enters on the L. (See St. Huberts Region, Section B2.) Turning R on the W. A. White Trail, marked with ATIS markers, the trail climbs steadily through hardwoods and then conifers to the crest of a ridge at 3.90 mi. The grade is easier up the ridge with occasional views S through the trees. A slight sag is reached at 4.00 mi. and the climbing becomes steeper at 4.25 mi., the Wolf's "Chin" being reached at 4.50 mi. Elevation, 4000 ft. Do not mistake this for the Lower Jaw. The trail now descends steeply to a col at 4.60 mi., becomes fairly level and then starts an exceedingly steep climb at 4.70 mi. The grade moderates at 4.80 mi. as the trail passes a lookout toward Giant, Nipple Top and Dix on the L at 4.90 mi. and reaches the summit of Lower Wolf Jaw at 4.95 mi. Good views from lookout on R include the Range, the MacIntyres, Table Top, Phelps, Big Slide, Whiteface, Cascade, Porter, the Johns Brook Valley and Santanoni in the distance W. Total ascent, 3670 ft. Elevation, 4175 ft. Order of height, 30.

The trail straight ahead with ADK markers descends steeply into Wolf Jaws Notch. (This section was part of the original W. A. White Trail but is now maintained by the ADK). At 5.25 mi. the ATIS-maintained Wedge Brook Trail enters on the L from St. Huberts, and a cut-off from this trail enters on the L shortly before the trail junction in the col is reached at 5.44 mi. Trail R leads 0.90 mi. to Wolf Jaws lean-to and 2.03 mi. to JBL. Trail straight ahead is the ADK Range Trail over Upper Wolf Jaw, Armstrong and Gothics.

Distances: Johns Brook bridge to Rooster Comb, 1.75 mi.; to junction with Hedgehog Trail, 2.00 mi.; to N Hedgehog, 2.70 mi.; to Hedgehog, 3.10 mi.; to W. A. White Trail, 3.50 mi.; to Wolf's Chin, 4.50 mi.; to summit of Lower Wolf Jaw, 4.95 mi.; to Wolf Jaws Notch, 5.44 mi.

Baxter Mt. from Beede Farm

There are three trails to the summit of Baxter, the steepest starting near the late Mrs. Upham's cottage, "Lone Pine," the other two, one from the Beede farm and one from Spruce Hill, joining just before the steep climb to the SE summit. For a round trip, ascending the trail from the Beede farm and descending via Upham Road is suggested.

Turn E on Beede Road 0.40 mi. N of Johns Brook bridge on Route 73. Cross E branch Ausable River on iron bridge at 0.15 mi. and tributary at 0.30 mi. from Route 73. Paved road turns L at 0.40 mi. where dirt road straight ahead over bridge leads to trail for Hopkins and Spread Eagle. (See below.) Continuing on paved road, pass dirt road on L at 0.60 mi. leading to Upham cottage. The triangle at the junction can be used for parking a couple of cars if making the round trip. The paved road soon becomes a dirt road and climbs to the abandoned Beede farm on the L at 1.00 mi. where there is a sign "Baxter." Cars may be parked near the farmhouse.

Leaving the farmhouse (0 mi.), the trail, marked with red ADK markers, passes a barn and follows a path across a bushy former pasture, climbing gradually. It enters heavy woods at 0.20 mi. and continues on a tote road at an easy grade. The tote road runs out at 0.67 mi. where the trail becomes quite rocky and the grade a little steeper. It levels off in a pass at about 0.92 mi. and comes to a trail junction at 1.03 mi. (Trail R is the ADK-marked trail to Spruce Hill, 0.67 mi. See below.)

Continuing straight ahead the trail starts a steep climb, the grade moderating at 1.12 mi. as the trail swings to the NW. The climbing continues among pine trees and blueberry bushes with stretches of bare rock to the level SE summit at 1.29 mi. Many side trails on L lead to lookouts on rock ledges. The trail descends slightly into a col at 1.37 mi. and climbs over bare rocks at a moderate grade to the NW summit of Baxter at 1.45 mi. Excellent views to the S and W from nearby rock ledges.

Distances: Beede farm to Spruce Hill Trail, 1.03 mi.; to NW summit of Baxter, 1.45 mi. Ascent, 1150 ft. from Beede farm. Elevation, both summits, 2440 ft.

Baxter Mt. from Upham Road

Proceed as above in the description of the trail to Baxter Mt. from Beede Farm by turning onto Beede road from Route 73 and going on the paved road 0.60 mi. to the third driveway on the L beyond road for Hopkins and Spread Eagle. Leaving junction (0 mi.), follow dirt road toward the Upham cottage, "Lone Pine," and turn R into the woods at 0.20 mi. just before reaching the cottage. Red ADK markers designate the turn. The trail climbs through the woods, swinging to the L, and joins a tote road at 0.25 mi. Just before the tote road, a trail turns R to Beede Ledge. Turning sharp R on the tote road, the trail proceeds at an easy grade through hardwoods, crosses a small hogback, and descends to a brook bed at 0.90 mi. where there is a spring on the R. The climbing now becomes very steep and the footing made insecure by pine needles. At 1.30 mi. the trail reaches the crest of a shoulder and descends gradually through red pines and hardwoods. A steep pitch up is reached at 1.50 mi. after which there is a gradual ascent through red pines and over bare rocks to the NW summit of Baxter at 1.70 mi.

Distances: Junction of paved road and Upham Road to summit of Baxter, 1.70 mi. Round trip from junction, 3.55 mi. Ascent from junction, 1300 ft. Elevation, 2440 ft.

Baxter Mt. from Spruce Hill

This trail starts 40 yds. SE of the road leading to the Mountain House at the top of Spruce Hill on Route 9N and is marked with a sign. Leaving the highway (0 mi.), the trail heads W across a field on an old tote road following ADK markers. It swings SE at 0.08 mi. amid scattered white pines and enters denser woods at about 0.19 mi. as the tote road gives way to a footpath. The grade, having been easy to moderate, steepens at 0.29 mi. After an easy stretch, the grade steepens again at 0.39 mi. as the trail swings W and back to the SW. Swinging S at 0.51 mi. the grade becomes easy at 0.58 mi., soon heads SW again, reaches a height of land at 0.65 mi. and continues pretty much on the level to the junction with the trail from the Beede farm at 0.67 mi. Turning R the route is the same as that from the Beede farm. (See above.)

Distances: Spruce Hill Road to Beede farm trail, 0.67 mi.; to summit of Baxter, 1.09 mi. Ascent, 770 ft. from Spruce Hill Road. Elevation, 2440 ft.

Spread Eagle and Hopkins

These two summits in the Giant Range just E of Keene Valley offer an opportunity for a half day's climb with rewarding views. Hopkins was named for Rev. Erastus Hopkins of Troy, New York who later served several terms in the Massachusetts Legislature while a resident of Northampton. It was he who suggested to Old Mountain Phelps the name of "Resagone," meaning "the King's great saw," for the mountain we now call "Sawteeth."

Follow Route to Baxter from Route 73, 0.40 mi. to road junction at bridge (see above), near which cars should be parked. After steep climbing, the road turns R to a private cottage at 0.43 mi. Continue straight ahead on jeep road. At 0.64 mi. the jeep road turns R and, after a level stretch, the trail leaves the jeep road and turns L, climbing to where it joins a gravel road through a real estate development. The gravel road is followed, ignoring a L fork at 0.89 mi. and a R fork at 0.91 mi. At 1.51 mi. a trail branches L from the gravel road and crosses a brook. This is the direct trail to Hopkins, 1.14 mi. without going over Spread Eagle. It is very steep at the upper end and is therefore easier for the return route. (See below).

The route to Spread Eagle continues up the road to where at 1.75 mi. the road turns R to a cottage site. Here, the Spread Eagle Trail leads straight ahead, angling W and SW at a moderate grade. There is a steep pitch shortly before reaching side trail on R at 2.05 mi. This leads a few yards to lookout with views to W over Keene Valley. The climbing gets steep again at 2.07 mi., levels off at 2.19 mi., and after crossing an open ledge and climbing a moderate pitch, the trail continues at an easy grade to the summit of Spread Eagle at 2.31 mi. Views to S and W. Elevation, 2840 ft.

The trail now descends about 100 ft. over ledges, gradually at first and then steeper, and reaches the bottom of the col at 2.39 mi. Now climbing again the top of a bare ledge is reached at 2.50 mi. where there is a view from Dix in the S to Big Slide in the W. Then descending slightly, the trail soon starts steadily up again and levels off at 2.65 mi. The grade becomes moderate at 2.73 mi. and steeper just before reaching a junction at 2.83

mi. (Trail on L is direct route to Hopkins from lumber road.) Keep R and climbing, a steep pitch is reached at 2.85 mi., then easy going followed by another steep pitch at 2.89 mi. Here the trail leaves the woods and climbs up over the bare rocks to the summit of Hopkins at 2.92 mi. where there are unobstructed views in all directions except to the NE. This is a good spot in the blueberry season. (Trail E with painted arrows is Mossy Cascade Trail (ATIS-maintained) to St. Huberts, and connects with trail via Green Mt. to the Giant. See St. Huberts Region, Section B2.)

Distances: Junction of paved and dirt roads at bridge to upper end of passable road, 0.64 mi.; to gravel road, 1.28 mi.; to direct trail to Hopkins, 1.51 mi.; to Spread Eagle, 2.31 mi.; to direct trail from lumber road, 2.83 mi.; to Hopkins, 2.92 mi. Ascent from paved road, 2250 ft. Elevation, 3183 ft.

Hopkins via Direct Trail from Lumber Road

Proceed as above to junction of trail and lumber road at 1.51 mi. Turning L and crossing the brook the trail follows an old tote road through a hardwood forest climbing steadily at a moderate to average grade. After crossing a yellow-blazed property line at 1.88 mi. the trail approaches a brook on the L at 1.94 mi., follows up its L bank and crosses it at 1.99 mi. A brook bed is crossed at 2.17 mi., and after climbing steadily through ferns, the trail levels off for a short respite at 2.36 mi. The ascent becomes very steep at 2.40 mi. as the trail climbs straight up the mountain through conifers, leveling off at 2.53 mi. and joining the trail over Spread Eagle, which enters on the R at 2.56 mi. Turning L the route to the summit is the same as described above, the summit being reached at 2.65 mi.

Distances: Junction of paved and dirt roads at bridge to junction of lumber road and direct trail to Hopkins, 1.51 mi.; to upper junction with trail over Spread Eagle, 2.56 mi.; to summit of Hopkins, 2.65 mi. Ascent from paved road, 2150 ft. Elevation, 3183 ft.

SECTION B2

ST. HUBERTS REGION

St. Huberts is on the Chapel Pond Road (Route 73) 2.5 mi S of Keene Valley Village. In this region, trails start for the Lower Ausable Lake and many summits, including the Great Range, Snow, Sawteeth, Colvin, Nipple Top, Bear Den, Noonmark, Dix, Round, Giant, and Hopkins.

A half mile from the highway at the top of the hill is the Ausable Club which administers the Adirondack Mountain Reserve (AMR). (PBM 1352 is located in a granite boulder near tennis court S of main Club entrance.)

The approaches to the Ausable Lakes and to many peaks in this region cross this privately-owned Adirondack Mountain Reserve, which includes all the lower land from the Clubhouse to beyond the Elk Lake–Marcy Trail some 10 mi. to the SW. The State of New York has acquired permanent rights of way for foot travel by the public along many trails within the Reserve, including the road to the Lower Ausable Lake; but off-trail travel, including rock climbing and bushwhacking along the shores of the Lower Ausable Lake, is not allowed. In addition, hunting, fishing, the building of fires, camping, boating, swimming, and the bringing of pets into the Reserve are strictly prohibited.

These restrictions, of course, do not apply to the use of the trails not crossing Adirondack Mountain Reserve property. Hence, all trails E of Route 73, as well as approaches to Dix, Noonmark, and Round Mountain via Round Pond, as well as to Wolf Jaws and Snow Mountain, once private property is passed, are unrestricted save for regulations universally enforced on State land throughout the Adirondack Park.

Those using trails in the Adirondack Mountain Reserve are required to park their cars a short distance SW of Route 73 opposite the parking lot for the Giant–Roaring Brook Trail (0.55 mi. S of the main road to the Ausable Club and about 3 mi. S of the High Peaks sign in Keene Valley Village.) This parking area is about 0.50 mi. from the Ausable Club building, reached by hiking along what is called the southerly road to the Ausable Club. It is gravel as far as the golf course on the R and then macadam.

Except for the Dix Trail from Round Pond, which is now maintained by the Adirondack Forty–Sixers, and the Ranney Trail to Hopkins maintained by the ADK, all trails described in Section B2 are maintained by the Adirondack Trail Improvement Society (ATIS). In caring for its 95 miles of trail, all but 25 miles of which are on State land, it employs a professional trail crew, supplemented by volunteers.

Trails Described	Year Measured	Total Miles
Road to Lower Ausable Lake from Clubhouse	1953	3.50
East River Trail to Bridge at Lower Ausable Dam	1961	3.32
Ladies Mile	1954	0.88
West River Trail to Bridge at Lower Ausable Lake Dam	1953*	3.79
Cathedral Rocks and Bear Run	1954	1.92
Lost Lookout to Lower Ausable Lake from Gothics Trail	1953	1.45
Rainbow Falls from Bridge at Lower Ausable Lake Dam	1953	0.20
W. A. White Trail to Lower Wolf Jaw from Gate	1953**	4.36
Wedge Brook Trail to Lower Wolf Jaw	1953	2.15
Wedge Brook Trail to Wolf Jaws Notch	1953	1.85
Gothics from Lake Road	1953	3.35
Alfred E. Weld Trail to Gothics from Lower Ausable Lake via Pyramid	1970	2.74
Sawteeth from Lower Ausable Lake Bridge	1953	3.00
Sawteeth via the Pyramid–Gothics Trail	1970	2.18

Trails Described	Year Measured	Total Miles
Indian Head from Boathouse	1960	0.61
Indian Head from Colvin Trail	1953	0.70
Fish Hawk Cliffs and Colvin Trail from Indian Head	1960	0.68
Colvin from Lake Road via Gill Brook	1953	3.52
Nipple Top via Elk Pass from Lake Road	1954	3.52
Henry Goddard Leach Trail to Nipple Top via Bear Den and Dial from Lake Road	1954	5.88
Dix Peak from St. Huberts	1954	6.70
Noonmark via Stimson Trail from Club Road	1954	2.06
Noonmark via Round Pond and the Felix Adler Trail	1954	3.36
Round Mt. via S. Burns Weston Trail	1954	2.27
Round Mt. from Dix Trail and Club Road	1954	2.38
Giant via Roaring Brook Trail	1963	3.60
Giant's Washbowl and Nubble	1954	1.43
Giant from Chapel Pond via Giant Ridge Trail	1954***	2.94
Mossy Cascade Trail to Hopkins	1954	3.10
Ranney Trail to Hopkins	1961	2.65
Giant from Hopkins via Green Mt.	1961	3.02
Snow Mt. via W. A. White Trail	1953	2.19
Snow Mt. via Deer Brook	1953	1.75
Snow Mt. via Rooster Comb Trail	1953	1.85

* Lake Road to second crossover remeasured 1961.
** Lake Road to ADK trail from Rooster Comb and Hedgehog remeasured 1961.
*** Partly remeasured 1961.

Road to Lower Ausable Lake

This private road, known as the Lake Road, runs SW from the main Club building past the private cottages, 3.5 mi. to the boathouse at the foot of the Lower Ausable Lake. A quarter mile from the Club is the locked gate, beyond which private vehicles are not permitted. However, a narrow opening provides foot passage. The Club operates a bus over this road which makes frequent, scheduled runs during the day when the Club is open during the summer season. This service is available to the public after Club members have been accommodated, the fare being $1.00 one way. Inquire at the Club office for reservations.

From the gate this road leads through a splendid forest with easy grades, gaining about 700 ft. in elevation between the gate and the height of land near the foot of the lake. Several trails branch from this road 90 yds. before reaching the gate; the W. A. White Trail for the Range leads R across the Ausable River (E branch) and connects with the West River Trail.

Leaving the gate (0 mi.), the "Ladies Mile" branches R at 45 yds., and a bridge leads across a brook to this same trail at 0.25 mi. A side trail on R at 0.30 mi. is the start of the East River Trail. At 0.73 mi. the Henry Goodard Leach Trail to Nipple Top via Bear Den and Dial turns S, and at 0.86 mi. a bridge on R leads across Gill Brook to a tote road which connects with the East River Trail. Continuing on the road, Gill Brook is crossed at 1.10 mi., and at 1.75 mi. a trail leads W to the River Trails and Gothics. At 1.78 mi. the trail up Gill Brook to Colvin and Nipple Top branches L. The shorter regular trail to Colvin turns L at 2.50 mi., and at 3.10 mi. the height of land near the foot of the lake is reached where the trail to Indian Head veers L. At 3.15 mi. a side road on the R leads 0.05 mi. down to a footbridge connecting the East and West River Trails just below the dam. Continuing downhill, the Lake Road reaches the boathouse at 3.25 mi. (PBM 1971 ft.)

Distances: Gate to East River Trail, 0.30 mi.; to Nipple Top Trail via Bear Den, 0.73 mi.; to trail for Gothics, 1.75 mi.; to trail up Gill Brook, 1.78 mi.; to shorter Colvin Trail, 2.50 mi.; to Indian Head Trail, 3.10 mi.; to boathouse, 3.25 mi. (3.50 mi. from clubhouse.) Mileage markers on road show distances from clubhouse.

East River Trail

This trail turns R from the Lake Road 0.30 mi. past the gate. It may be reached via the "Ladies Mile," which branches R 45 yds. beyond the gate. It follows up the R (or E) bank of the Ausable

River (E branch) for 3.32 mi. to the dam at the foot of the Lower
Ausable Lake, where a bridge leads across the river to the West
River Trail and the trail to Rainbow Falls, Sawteeth, and Gothics.
Shortly past the dam, it rejoins the road 0.10 mi. from the boat-
house.

Leaving the road (0 mi.), the trail veers gradually away from
the road and reaches a tote road at 0.13 mi. The tote road leads
L 45 yds. back to Lake Road. Turning R, a crossover to the West
River Trail is reached at 0.16 mi. Here the "Ladies Mile" enters
on the R (see below) and the East River Trail turns L. Following
up the Ausable on a level trail, a choice of routes marked "steep"
and "easy" is reached at 0.45 mi. just before coming to a steep
pitch up. Going R and ascending the pitch, the easier but slightly
longer route soon re-enters on the L just before descending to
cross Gill Brook on a bridge at 0.50 mi. at its confluence with
the Ausable. Then following up the L bank of Gill Brook the trail
swings away at 0.60 mi. and reaches another tote road at 0.65
mi. (To the L this tote road leads 0.13 mi. to the Lake Road at
the bridge over Gill Brook, 0.86 mi. from the Gate. To the R the
tote road leads up a slight grade and then follows up the R bank
of the Ausable past a gravel bank 0.29 mi. to a bridge over the
river. Crossing the bridge a trail makes a short steep ascent by
traverses and joins the West River Trail in another 80 yds.)

Crossing the tote road instead of turning R as formerly, the
East River Trail continues on the level and then begins a gradual
ascent passing several rock formations on the L. The trail then
crosses a small brook at 0.82 mi., the grade becoming steeper up
a small valley and leveling off at 0.91 mi. After a steep pitch at
1.14 mi., the trail passes through a magnificent forest of large hemlocks very high above the gorge of the river with a view of a
slide on the opposite bank at 1.46 mi. A lookout over the gorge
is reached at 1.64 mi. where the almost vertical rock wall is visible
on the other side. After passing some falls at 1.85 mi., the trail
continues at an easy grade not far from the R bank of the river,
and crosses the aqueduct pipe line shortly before reaching a junction at 2.22 mi. Here the trail to Gothics from the Lake Road
enters on the L. Both trails continue straight ahead, the Gothics

Trail branching R at 2.27 mi., crossing the Ausable on a bridge and reaching the West River Trail at Beaver Meadow Falls in 115 yds.

The East River Trail continues straight ahead on the R bank past a dam (head of aqueduct and beginning of Beaver Meadow) and swings to the L away from the river to get around the meadow. Approaching the head of the meadow, fast water is reached again at about 2.80 mi. Continuing along the R bank of the river, a rock face is passed on the L at 3.06 mi., and the bridge and dam at the foot of the Lower Lake are reached at 3.32 mi. The bridge connects with the West River Trail and the trail to Rainbow Falls, Sawteeth, and Gothics via Pyramid. (See below.) The East River Trail climbs up to the Lake Road at 3.38 mi. which it follows downhill to the PBM (1971 ft.) at the boathouse at 3.48 mi.

Distances: Lake Road to first Ausable crossover, 0.16 mi.; to tote road leading to second crossover, 0.65 mi.; to crossover at Beaver Meadow Falls and trail to Gothics, 2.27 mi.; to Lower Lake bridge and dam, 3.32 mi.; to boathouse, 3.48 mi. (3.78 mi. from the gate.)

Ladies Mile

This is a short jaunt through the woods, mostly on the level, affording a round trip of about a mile. It branches R from the Lake Road 45 yds. past the gate. Leaving the road (0 mi.), it descends a short flight of steps, crosses a bridge, turns L and continues to a tote road at 0.08 mi. where the trail forks. (The tote road L leads across a bridge about 80 yds. back to the Lake Road.) The E fork of the trail goes directly across the tote road; the W fork turns R along the road 30 yds. before swinging L and rejoins the E fork just before reaching the crossover between the East and West River Trails.

Crossing the tote road the E fork follows up the L bank of a brook, crosses a small bridge and reaches a junction at 0.25 mi. Here a footbridge leads L over the brook 30 yds. to the Lake Road. Continuing past the bridge, the trail continues along the L bank of a branch of the brook and rejoins the W fork of the trail at 0.40 mi. The East River Trail and crossover to the West River Trail are reached at 0.44 mi. The W fork of the trail offers an alternative return along the R bank of the Ausable River, the distance being about the same. This route comes out on the brink of the river offering a good view of the rock-filled stream. Another return route is via the crossover and West River Trail. (See below.)

West River Trail

This trail may be reached by turning R from the Lake Road 90 yds. before the gate where there is a sign, "Wolf Jaws via W. A. White Trail." It follows up the L (or W) bank of the Ausable River (E branch) for 3.75 mi. to the dam at the foot of the Lower Ausable Lake. Here it crosses the river on a bridge and joins the East River Trail. Much of the way is through virgin timber, and there are several fine waterfalls and cascades along the way.

Leaving the road (0 mi.), the trail starts in a private driveway and descends slightly to the river. Turning upstream along the R bank, the trail then crosses the river on a bridge and comes immediately to a trail junction at 0.16 mi. (Trail R is the W. A. White Trail via Maghee Clearing to Lower Wolf Jaw and the Range. It also connects with trails to Snow Mt., Hedgehog Mt. and the Rooster Comb. See below.) Turning L the West River Trail at first heads back a bit from the river, then comes out on the brink of the river bank where there is a view of Giant through the trees and reaches a trail junction at 0.62 mi. where there is a bridge providing a crossover to the East River Trail and the Ladies Mile. (Trail R leads to Cathedral Rocks. See below.)

Continuing straight ahead along the L bank, the trail, after a few minutes walk, swings away from the river following an old course through a beautiful stand of hemlock, and crosses Pyramid Brook on a bridge at 1.08 mi. About 25 yds. further the trail from Cathedral Rocks re-enters on the R. The trail soon starts climbing above the river and comes to a trail junction at 1.29 mi. (Trail L descends steeply by traverses and in 80 yds. crosses the river on a bridge to a tote road on the R bank. Following downstream, the tote road swings away from the river, crosses the East River

Trail 0.29 mi. from the bridge and continues another 0.13 mi. to the Lake Road at the bridge over Gill Brook.) Continuing straight ahead, the grade becomes easy at 1.40 mi. where there is a lookout down to the gorge of the river, now far below the trail. The grade becomes steeper at 1.60 mi. and levels off again at 1.70 mi. where there are views of Noonmark, Bear Den, Dial and the long shoulder of Nipple Top. Here the trail is still higher above the river. Wedge Brook is crossed on a bridge at 2.04 mi. where the Wedge Brook Trail to Lower Wolf Jaw and the Range enters on the R. (Distance to Lower Wolf Jaw, 2.15 mi.)

The trail swings L beyond the bridge and follows down the R bank of Wedge Brook, crossing some small tributaries near falls in the Ausable at 2.30 mi. (trail now almost on level with river) and reaches Beaver Meadow Falls on R at 2.74 mi. These beautiful falls of bridal veil-like appearance are well worth the trip alone. The trail crosses the brook at the foot of the falls and comes to a junction. (Trail L leads 115 yds. across river on bridge to East River Trail and another 0.50 mi. to the Lake Road. Trail R up ladder is trail to Lost Lookout (0.60 mi.), Armstrong (2.60 mi.), Gothics (2.80 mi.) and the Range.)

Continuing straight ahead the West River Trail follows close to the bank of Beaver Meadows and is wet in spots. At 3.20 mi. it follows along at the foot of vertical rock face on the R. This is approximately at the upper end of the meadow where the river becomes fast water again. The Lost Lookout Trail re-enters on the R at 3.74 mi., and the bridge and dam at the foot of the Lower Lake are reached at 3.79 mi. Trail straight ahead is trail to Rainbow Falls (0.20 mi.), Sawteeth Mt. (3.00 mi.), and Gothics (2.54 mi.). Turning R at the far end of the bridge (L is the East River Trail), the Lake Road is reached at 3.84 mi. and the boathouse at 3.94 mi. (PBM 1971 ft.)

Distances: Lake Road to departure from W. A. White Trail, 0.16 mi.; to crossover to East River Trail and trail to Cathedral Rocks, 0.62 mi.; to Pyramid Brook and reentry of Cathedral Rocks Trail, 1.08 mi.; to second crossover, 1.29 mi.; to Wedge Brook and trail to Wolf Jaws, 2.04 mi.; to Beaver Meadow Falls crossover and trail to Gothics, 2.74 mi.; to Lower Lake bridge and dam, 3.79 mi.; to boathouse, 3.94 mi.

Cathedral Rocks and Bear Run

This "off the beaten path" trail provides a short round trip excursion from the West River Trail and leads to some interesting rock formations and a waterfall. It climbs about 500 ft. above the valley, leaving the West River Trail at Pyramid Brook, and then descends, rejoining the West River Trail 0.46 mi. nearer St. Huberts.

Take West River Trail to Pyramid Brook at 1.08 mi. Trail to Cathedral Rocks is about 25 yds. past the brook. (This junction may also be reached via the East River Trail by turning R on the tote road at 0.65 mi. and using crossover to West River Trail. This joins the West River Trail at the 1.29 mi. point.) Leaving West River Trail (0 mi.), the trail climbs steadily up the R bank of Pyramid Brook, crossing to the L bank at old blowdown at 0.18 mi. It then makes a steep climb up L bank to waterfall at 0.22 mi. Leaving course of brook, the trail climbs to top of rock overlooking brook at 0.25 mi. where grade moderates. A junction is reached at 0.30 mi. (Trail R leads to Cathedral Rocks, avoiding climb to Bear Run. It soon descends a short way, continues somewhat on the level and then climbs steadily to a junction in 0.26 mi. with the main trail descending from Bear Run.)

Taking L trail to Bear Run past large boulder, the grade becomes steep again up over switchbacks and under a rocky overhang. Beyond the overhang, the trail swings R as the grade moderates and reaches a lookout at 0.38 mi. where there are views of Giant, Rocky Peak Ridge, Noonmark, and Round Mt. The trail is now fairly level but ascends a steep pitch at 0.45 mi., crosses a red-blazed property line at 0.51 mi. and reaches a very large, vertical rock face on the L (Bear Run) at 0.57 mi. Following along at foot of rock face, the trail reaches a height of land at 0.59 mi. and descends to a junction at the foot of the rock face at 0.64 mi. Side trail on L leads to lookout. Continuing R, the trail descends steadily, crossing and recrossing a small brook several times, and reaching a junction at 0.83 mi. (Trail R is the trail described above, 0.26 mi. long, bypassing Bear Run and leading back to Pyramid Brook.)

Turning L the trail is fairly level; then descending slightly the first and largest of several rock faces on the L (Cathedral Rocks) is reached at 0.86 mi. The trail follows along the foot of the rock face, which is about 100 yds. long, going downgrade gradually. More outcroppings of the rock face are passed at 1.07 and 1.13 mi., after which the trail starts a steady descent. It levels off at 1.18 mi. and starts down again at 1.25 mi. After crossing and recrossing a brook three times in the next 0.10 mi., the trail follows down the L bank at easy grades, finally crossing the brook again at 1.61 mi. and rejoining the West River Trail at 1.66 mi. This junction is the 0.62 mi. point on the West River Trail at the crossover bridge to the East River Trail and the Ladies Mile.

Distances: West River Trail junction near Pyramid Brook to waterfall, 0.22 mi.; to lower end of bypass trail, 0.30 mi.; to lookout, 0.38 mi.; to Bear Run, 0.57 mi.; to upper end of bypass trail, 0.83 mi.; to first of Cathedral Rocks, 0.86 mi.; to West River Trail at 0.62; point, 1.66 mi.

Lost Lookout

The trail to this scenic spot parallels the West River Trail (see above) from Beaver Meadow Falls to just before the bridge at the foot of the Lower Lake. It climbs about 500 ft. above the valley on a shoulder of Armstrong to two lookout points offering exceptional views of the lake and the mountains to the S and E.

Reach Beaver Meadow Falls by either the West or East River Trails or by the Gothics Trail (see below) from the Lake Road. Leaving Beaver Meadow Falls (0 mi.), the trail coincides with the Gothics Trail, ascending the ladder and climbing steeply along the R bank of the brook. At 0.25 mi. the trail to Lost Lookout branches L and heads SW. It climbs steadily to the first lookout at 0.60 mi. and levels off as it follows edge of cliff with views through the trees and then descends slightly to the second lookout at 0.70 mi. Shortly beyond this lookout, the trail starts a steady descent but the grade soon moderates. A brook bed is crossed at 1.20 mi., and a lookout on the R to Rainbow Falls is reached at 1.50 mi. The trail now descends steeply for 0.10 mi., joins the West River Trail at 1.65 mi. and reaches the bridge and dam at the foot of the Lower Lake at 1.70 mi. Crossing the bridge and turning R, the boathouse is reached at 1.85 mi.

Distances: Lake Road via Gothics Trail to Beaver Meadow Falls, 0.55 mi.; to Lost Lookout Trail, 0.80 mi.; to first lookout, 1.15 mi.; to West River Trail near Lower Lake, 2.20 mi.; to boathouse, 2.40 mi.

Rainbow Falls

From W end of bridge at foot of Lower Lake follow Sawteeth Trail to junction at 0.10 mi. Turning R the trail follows up R bank of brook into gorge to a big pool near Rainbow Falls. By clambering about 50 yds. more over large rocks, the foot of the falls can be reached. Distance from bridge, 0.20 mi.

W. A. White Trail to Lower Wolf Jaw

This trail, named after one of the founders of the ATIS and the designer of the Range Trail from Gothics to Haystack, turns R from the Lake Road 90 yds. before reaching the gate.

Leaving the road (0 mi.), the trail starts in a private driveway and descends slightly to the river. Turning upstream along the R bank, the trail crosses the river on a bridge and comes immediately to a trail junction at 0.16 mi. (Trail L is the West River Trail to Beaver Meadow Falls and the Lower Lake. See above.) Turning R, the W.A. White Trail continues N at an easy grade through a hardwood forest, crosses a brook on a bridge at 0.29 mi. and passes some large boulders shortly before joining tote road at 0.64 mi. (Tote road may be followed R 0.40 mi. to old Keene Valley Road near iron bridge.) Turning L with tote road, the trail climbs at a fair grade, branches R when the tote road swings L and passes an excellent spring on R at 0.81 mi. just before entering the Maghee Clearing (many ferns, good view of Giant.) The trail crosses a small knoll in the clearing at 0.86 mi., descends gradually, re-enters the woods, crosses a brook bed and ascends a moderate grade to a trail junction at 0.95 mi. (Trail straight ahead connects with trails for Deer Brook, Snow Mt. and the Rooster Comb.)

The W. A. White Trail turns L on a rerouted section and ascends a steep pitch, joining the old route at 1.05 mi. Continuing on a moderate grade the trail zigzags up a steep pitch at 1.19 mi. after which the grade moderates again. There is a short, easy stretch just before coming to a side trail on L at 1.54 mi. leading 25 yds. to a lookout. A sharp switchback to the R is reached at 1.57 mi. where the trail makes a pitch up away from an older route continuing straight ahead. After a short level stretch, the trail continues climbing at a moderate grade up through the hardwoods and comes to the first ledge at 1.75 mi. where there are excellent views, the Ausable Club being visible directly below with Green, Giant, Rocky Peak, Round, Noonmark, Dix, Dial, Nipple Top and Colvin in the background. Then making a short descent and turning L to climb along a small rock face, a second and higher ledge is reached at a height of land at 1.81 mi. where Hurricane now comes into view with the other peaks mentioned above.

The trail now descends gradually, becomes fairly level and then swings R at a moderate pitch up at 1.94 mi. After descending an easy grade at 2.02 mi., the trail continues to climb at easy to moderate grades along with level stretches, crossing several brook beds as it slabs along the E spur of the Lower Wolf Jaw. A trail junction is reached at 2.91 mi. where the red-marked ADK trail from Keene Valley via Rooster Comb and Hedgehog enters on the R. (A few yds. down this trail water may often be found. See Keene Valley Region, Sect. B1.)

Continuing straight ahead, the W. A. White Trail swings toward the SW and climbs steadily through hardwoods and then conifers to the crest of a ridge at 3.31 mi. The grade is easier up the ridge with occasional views S through the trees. A slight sag is reached at 3.41 mi. and the climbing becomes steeper at 3.66 mi., the Wolf's "Chin" being reached at 3.91 mi. This is not the summit of Lower Wolf Jaw. The trail now descends steeply to a col at 4.01 mi., becomes fairly level and then ascends an exceedingly steep pitch at 4.11 mi. The grade moderates at 4.21 mi. as the trail passes a lookout toward Giant, Nipple Top and Dix on the L at 4.31 mi. and reaches the summit of Lower Wolf Jaw at 4.36 mi. Good views from lookout on R include the Range, the MacIntyres, Table Top, Phelps, Big Slide, Whiteface, Cascade, Porter, the Johns Brook Valley and Santanoni in the distant W. Total ascent, 3000 ft. Elevation, 4175 ft. Order of height, 30.

The trail straight ahead with ADK markers descends steeply into Wolf Jaws Notch. (This section was part of the original W. A. White Trail but is now maintained by the ADK.) At 4.66 mi. the ATIS-maintained Wedge Brook Trail enters on the L from St. Huberts, and a cut-off from this trail enters on the L shortly before the trail junction in the col is reached at 4.85 mi. Trail R with ADK markers leads 0.90 mi. to Wolf Jaws lean-to and 2.03 mi. to JBL. Trail straight ahead is the ADK Range Trail over Upper Wolf Jaw, Armstrong and Gothics.

Distances: Lake Road to departure from West River Trail, 0.16 mi.; to Snow Rooster Comb Trail, 0.95 mi.; to rock ledges, 1.75 mi. and 1.81 mi.; to ADK trail from Keene Valley, 2.91 mi.; to Wolf's Chin, 3.91 mi.; to summit of Lower Wolf Jaw, 4.36 mi.; to Wolf Jaws Notch, 4.85 mi.

Wedge Brook Trail to Wolf Jaws

Arthur Wyant, a well-known artist who first came to Keene Valley in 1869, is credited with conferring the name, Wolf Jaws, suggested by the deep col between the two peaks. The spot on Noonmark from which Wyant painted a view of these peaks is supposed to offer the best representation of a wolf's jaw.

The trail branches R (NW) from the West River Trail where the latter trail crosses Wedge Brook, 2.04 mi. from the gate. Leaving the West River Trail (0 mi.), the trail climbs fairly steeply along the R bank of Wedge Brook, crosses a small tributary flowing from the L at 0.05 mi. and recrosses it at 0.15 mi. The trail is now back from the main brook and the grade is relatively easy. A brook bed is crossed on a log bridge at 0.45 mi., and after crossing a few more small brook beds, a clearing with many nettles is reached at 1.15 mi. Shortly beyond this clearing the climbing becomes steep again, and as the climb progresses up the headwall of the ravine, the bare rock slides of Lower Wolf Jaw are visible on the R. At 1.55 mi. the cutoff trail to Wolf Jaws Notch branches L. This trail climbs for another 0.10 mi. and then descends gradually along the foot of a rock wall to the notch where it joins the ADK Range

Trail at 1.85 mi. From there it is another 1.00 mi. to the summit
of Upper Wolf Jaw; 0.49 mi. to summit of Lower Wolf Jaw; and
2.03 mi. to JBL. (See Keene Valley Region, Sect. B1.)

Taking the R fork at 1.55 mi., the trail continues climbing
and joins the ADK Range Trail at 1.85 mi. at a point 0.19 mi.
above the notch. Turning R with ADK markers the trail climbs
steeply to the summit of Lower Wolf Jaw at 2.15 mi. Good views
from lookout on L. Trail straight ahead is the W. A. White Trail
from St. Huberts (see above), and connects with ADK trails over
Hedgehog and Rooster Comb to Keene Valley. (See Keene Valley
Region, Sect. B1.)

Distances: West River Trail to Wolf Jaws Notch cutoff trail,
1.55 mi.; to Wolf Jaws Notch, 1.85 mi.; to Upper Wolf Jaw, 2.85
mi. (4.89 mi. from the gate.) Ascent, 2400 ft. (2900 ft. from the
gate.) Elevation, 4185 ft. Order of height, 29. West River Trail to
ADK Range Trail on Lower Wolf Jaw, 1.85 mi.; to Lower Wolf
Jaw, 2.15 mi. (4.19 mi. from the gate.) Ascent, 2350 ft. (2850 ft.
from the gate.) Elevation, 4175 ft. Order of height, 30.

Gothics from Lake Road

The arched peaks of this triple-crested mountain, with their
great slides and bare rock, suggested Gothic architecture to Fred
Perkins and Old Mountain Phelps that day in 1857 when they
sat on the top of Tahawus and christened four mountains with
characteristic names. They were Skylight, Basin, Saddleback and
Gothics.

The trail to Gothics starts at the Lake Road near the 2.00
mi. sign (1.75 mi. from the gate.) Turning W from the road (0
mi.), the trail climbs at an easy grade, crosses a good brook at
0.30 mi. and joins the East River Trail at height of land at 0.45
mi. Turning L on the East River Trail, the crossover to the W
side branches R at 0.50 mi. This leads across the Ausable River
on a bridge to the West River Trail and Beaver Meadow Falls at
0.55 mi. Here the trail ascends a ladder and climbs steeply along
R bank of the brook, the grade moderating at 0.65 mi. The Lost
Lookout Trail branches L at 0.80 mi.

Continuing straight ahead, the general course of the trail is westerly as it climbs at an easy grade up the SE spur of Armstrong. Several small brooks are crossed (may be dry in summer), the grade getting steeper again at 2.50 mi. as the trail nears the top of the ridge. A vertical rock wall on the L is passed at 2.60 mi. as the grade slackens. At 2.80 mi. a very steep rock slide is traversed on a crude log bridge, a cable providing a handhold. This is no place for people who get dizzy but the view is fine, especially down. From here the trail leads down a ladder and descends slightly into the col between Armstrong and Gothics at 2.90 mi. Here it joins the ADK Range Trail from JBL via Upper Wolf Jaw. (To the R this trail leads to Armstrong, 0.45 mi.; Upper Wolf Jaw, 1.25 mi.; Wolf Jaws Notch, 2.25 mi.; JBL, 4.28 mi. See Keene Valley Region, Sect. B1.)

Going L on the Range Trail, marked with ADK markers, the trail is level for a stretch and then starts climbing the NE ridge of Gothics at 3.00 mi. Good views are obtained as the trail makes its way through scrub spruce and balsam, sometimes steep, sometimes easy, to the bare rock summit at 3.35 mi. (NYS Land Survey Station 287 placed here by Verplanck Colvin in 1896.) The view is unobstructed in all directions with about 30 major peaks discernible. The boathouse and a small part of the Lower Ausable Lake can be seen, but the Upper Ausable Lake is not visible from the summit. However, by continuing 0.12 mi. on the ADK trail to the junction with the ATIS trail, and then following the ATIS trail 0.31 mi. to the rocky peak of Pyramid (the third peak of the mountain), the entire Upper Lake is visible to the S.

Distances: Lake Road to East River Trail, 0.45 mi.; to West River Trail at Beaver Meadow Falls, 0.55 mi.; to Lost Lookout Trail, 0.80 mi.; to ADK Range Trail, 2.90 mi.; to summit of Gothics, 3.35 mi. Ascent from Lake Road, 3050 ft. Elevation, 4736 ft. Order of height, 10.

Alfred E. Weld Trail to Gothics from Lower Ausable Lake via Pyramid

This approach to Gothics was laid out by Jim Goodwin and opened in 1966. It is the shortest route to the summit and offers the added interest of Pyramid, the sharp southern peak of Gothics, but has some very steep climbing in its upper sections.

The trail, marked with orange ATIS markers, starts at the W end of the bridge below the dam on Lower Ausable Lake. It coincides with the old trail to Sawteeth from which it turns R at 0.02 mi., and at 0.12 mi. the trail to base of Rainbow Falls, 0.10 mi., diverges R. Beyond this junction a steady ascent begins through hardwood forest with numerous steep pitches. At 0.28 mi. there is a side trail R leading a short distance to an outlook over Rainbow Falls. Swinging L with an easing of the grade, the trail crosses a brook from the L at 0.40 mi. Beyond this, it continues at an easy grade with level stretches, becoming steeper at 0.51 mi., with an even steeper pitch from 0.62 mi. to 0.67 mi. After this, the grade eases as the trail slabs the hillside high above the brook on the R. At 0.80 mi. the climbing becomes stiffer, easing off at 0.92 mi. when the trail descends to cross a small brook with a view of the mountains across the ravine. A small brook is crossed at 1.05 mi., followed by a steep, rocky pitch at 1.10 mi. A good brook is crossed at 1.28 mi., and the trail follows up the L bank with a steep climb at 1.37 mi. The brook is recrossed at 1.45 mi., and there are steep pitches at 1.51 mi. and 1.60 mi. before arriving in the col between Sawteeth and Pyramid at 1.68 mi. (Elevation, 3640 ft.)

At this point there is a junction. The trail L leads 0.50 mi. to Sawteeth, and the Gothics Trail turns R. At first, the grade is easy until 1.84 mi. where there is a steep pitch easing off at 1.91 mi., followed by an extremely steep one at 1.95 mi. The climb continues extremely stiff, with very short breathers, until the trail levels off below the rocky summit of Pyramid at 2.25 mi. At 2.31 mi. there is a side trail leading a few yards to the summit of Pyramid (elevation, 4520 ft.) from which there is a sweeping view of the Range. From the junction, the trail continues toward Gothics, descending steeply at 2.35 mi. and reaching the bottom of the col at 2.45 mi. It then ascends at moderate to steep grades with a stiff pitch at 2.54 mi., rounding off at 2.57 mi. before meeting the ADK-maintained Range Trail at 2.62 mi. Turning R, it reaches the summit of Gothics at 2.74 mi.

Distances: Bridge at Lower Lake to trail to foot of Rainbow Falls, 0.12 mi.; to outlook at top of Rainbow Falls, 0.28 mi.; to col between Pyramid and Sawteeth, 1.68 mi.; to junction with side trail to summit of Pyramid, 2.31 mi.; to junction with Range Trail, 2.62 mi.; to summit of Gothics, 2.74 mi. Approximate total ascent from Lower Ausable Lake, 2870 ft. Elevation, 4763 ft. Order of height, 10.

Sawteeth from Lower Ausable Lake

The striking, serrated profile of this mountain on the W side of Lower Ausable Lake appears like the teeth of a giant saw and suggested the name "Sawteeth" to the inhabitants of Keene Flats during the middle of the nineteenth century. It has also been called "Resagonia," a corruption of the name of a mountain in the Italian Alps called "Resagone," meaning "the King's great saw."

The older trail starts at the W end of the bridge below the dam at the foot of the Lower Lake, follows along the lake shore and climbs gradually to a lookout high above the lake. It then climbs by a zigzag route up the steep ridge of the mountain, offering spectacular views during the ascent.

When the trail to Gothics via Pyramid was cut in 1966, an extension was added to the summit of Sawteeth from the col between the mountain and Pyramid. (See below.) This permits the climber to ascend Sawteeth via the old "scenic" trail from Lower Ausable Lake and return via the more direct route.

Leaving the W end of the bridge (0 mi.), a branch is reached at 0.02 mi. To the R is the new (1966) trail to Gothics via Pyramid (see above) and the cutoff to the foot of Rainbow Falls. Keeping L, the Sawteeth Trail stays close to the shore of the lake, reaching it at 0.30 mi. After following along the rocky shore, it starts a gradual traversing climb at 0.60 mi. and reaches a spectacular lookout 250 ft. above the lake at 1.00 mi.

The trail now turns away from the lake and starts a steep climb up the mountain. A side trail to a second lookout (60 yds. off trail to L) is reached at 1.05 mi. after which "St Bernard" rock is passed on the L at 1.10 mi. (Turn around to see the St. Bernard.) After several zigzags the trail passes by the foot of the first of three vertical rock faces on the R at 1.20 mi. as conifers start to put in an appearance among the hardwoods. While heading SW, the second vertical rock face is passed at 1.30 mi. After a small zigzag a steep climb leads to a lookout at 1.40 mi. Easy going here. Again heading SW, the third vertical rock face is passed at 1.50 mi. The trail continues its steep zigzag ascent, the grade moderating at 1.70 mi., now heading NE, and reaches a height of land at 1.80 mi. Lookout Rock, a climb of a few yds. off the trail on the R, offers a precipitous view of the Lower Lake, 1600 ft. below, with fine views of Giant, Rocky Peak Ridge, Dial, Nipple Top, Colvin and Blake.

Leaving Lookout Rock, the trail descends slightly into a sag, crosses a low ridge at 1.90 mi. and starts a steady, but not difficult, climb through a conifer forest in a NW direction. A good spring is almost always found running on the L at 1.95 mi. The grade continues to a col and a series of cliffs on the R at 2.20 mi. The climbing now becomes very steep and difficult for the next 0.25 mi. as the trail ascends the cliffs by a series of ledges. The climbing becomes easy again at 2.45 mi. where there is a lookout back at Dix over Nipple Top and Colvin. In the distance through the Colvin–Blake col, may be seen the pointed summit of Hoffman Mt. in the Blue Ridge.

After a short, steep pitch the grade again becomes easy, and the SE summit (4060 ft.) is reached at 2.60 mi. This summit is completely wooded and the views are obstructed. Continuing NW, the trail descends 140 ft. into fern-filled Rifle Notch at 2.75 mi., the grade being easy and then fairly steep for 0.10 mi. By going SW through the ferns, a view of the Upper Lake and Allen Mt. may be obtained. The trail makes a steep pitch out of the notch and then ascends at an easy grade. The trail from the Upper Lake enters on the L at 2.95 mi., and a large boulder beside the trail indicates the NW summit (4100 ft.) at 3.00 mi. About 20 yds. N from this boulder there is a lookout offering views of Haystack, Marcy, Basin, Saddleback, Gothics, Pyramid and Armstrong. Another side trail leads E about 20 yds. to a lookout toward Giant.

Distances: Bridge at Lower Lake to lookout over lake, 1.00 mi.; to Lookout Rock, 1.80 mi.; to SE summit, 2.60 mi.; to Rifle Notch, 2.75 mi.; to NW summit, 3.00 mi. Total ascent from Lower Lake, 2275 ft. Elevation, 4100 ft. Order of height, 35.

Sawteeth via The Pyramid–Gothics Trail

The Pyramid–Gothics Trail is followed from the bridge below the dam on Lower Ausable Lake to the col at 1.68 mi. Turning

L, the trail to Sawteeth takes a southerly direction nearly on the level until 0.14 mi. when it begins to ascend. At 0.16 mi. it ascends a cleft in a rocky ledge, becoming very steep with poor footing. Beyond this point, it climbs steadily up the shoulder of the mountain rounding off at 0.38 mi. as it reaches the flat summit. At 0.50 mi. it reaches a junction at the summit. A few yds. to the R is a ledge giving a fine view of the Range and especially the bold, rocky southwestern side of Pyramid. The trail to the L is the old trail which continues E and eventually returns to Lower Ausable Lake. The actual summit is said to be marked by a large boulder beside the trail a few yds. E of the junction.

Distances: From junction in col to summit of Sawteeth, 0.50 mi.; total distance from W end of bridge below dam at Lower Ausable Lake, 2.18 mi. Total ascent from Lower Lake, 2135 ft. Ascent from col, 460 ft. Elevation, 4100 ft. Order of height, 35.

Indian Head

This is a rocky peak 750 ft. above the Lower Lake which lies directly below it. It offers excellent views of both lakes, Nipple Top, Colvin, Sawteeth, Gothics, Armstrong and both Wolf Jaws. Allen is just visible over the Bartlett Ridge. There are three trails to the summit.

1. From the boathouse (0 mi.) a trail climbs very steeply to a junction in about 60 yds. (Trail L leads 110 yds. on level to height of land on Lake Road, 0.15 mi. from the boathouse.) Continuing straight ahead, the trail levels off but soon climbs steeply again. At 0.29 mi. a large overhanging rock makes a natural shelter a few yds. to L of trail. The grade soon moderates, but a steep pitch is ascended just before reaching the junction with the trails from Gill Brook and Fish Hawk Cliffs at 0.57 mi. Turning R it is then mostly level to the large, bare lookout overlooking the lake. Distance from boathouse, 0.61 mi.

2. Another trail branches R from the Colvin Trail (see below) at a point 0.17 mi. above the junction with the trail from the lake road up Gill Brook. This is 0.65 mi. from the road via the shorter trail and 1.32 mi. via trail up Gill Brook. Leaving the Colvin Trail (0 mi.), this trail crosses a brook to L bank at 0.05 mi., climbs

steadily and reaches a very steep pitch at 0.30 mi. At 0.40 mi. a trail leads about 60 yds. R to lookout affording view of Giant, Dial, Nipple Top and Wolf Jaws. The trail levels off through the conifers at about 0.50 mi., descends slightly and joins the trail from the boathouse on the R at 0.66 mi. The trail from Fish Hawk Cliffs enters on the L at this point. Continuing straight ahead, the lookout over the lake is reached at 0.70 mi.

3. A third approach to Indian Head may be made from the Colvin Trail via Fish Hawk Cliffs. (See below.)

Fish Hawk Cliffs

This outlook over the Lower Lake lies to the S of Indian Head and at a somewhat lower elevation. If offers a good view of the profile from which Indian Head received its name. It may be reached from either the Colvin Trail or Indian Head, the shortest route being via the Indian Head Trail from the boathouse. Except for the first very steep descent from the Indian Head Trail, the grades are mostly easy or pretty much on the level.

Starting (0 mi.) from the trail junction 0.04 mi. N of the Indian Head, the trail zigzags down a very steep pitch and crosses the headwaters of a brook in a col at 0.09 mi. Then climbing gradually at 0.15 mi. the turnout on R to Fish Hawk Cliffs is reached at 0.23 mi. It is then but 25 yds. to the lookout over the lake. Continuing to the L at the junction, the trail follows along pretty much at grade, heading NE then NNE and crossing a brook at 0.45 mi. Continuing toward the E, the junction with the trail to Colvin and Nipple Top is reached at 0.68 mi. This point is 0.64 mi. above the junction of the two trails from the Lake Road.

Distances: Indian Head Trail to Fish Hawk Cliffs, 0.24 mi.; to Colvin–Nipple Top Trail, 0.68 mi.

Mt. Colvin from Lake Road

This mountain was named for Verplanck Colvin in 1873 by Rev. T. L. Cuyler, a member of Colvin's survey party who thought the peak was nameless. A few years earlier, however, Old Mountain Phelps has named it "Sabele" (also spelled "Sebille" and "Sabael") for the Indian credited by some to have discovered the ore at the MacIntyre Ironworks.* Colvin was Superintendent of the Adirondack Survey and the most prominent character in Adirondack Mountain history. Besides making the first positive measurement of Mt. Marcy in 1865 with level and rod, he was also largely responsible for the inauguration of the Adirondack Park and State Forest Preserve. It is, therefore, highly fitting that his name attached to the mountain has endured.

There are two approaches to Colvin from the road. The shorter route turns L from the road 2.75 mi. from the Ausable Club (2.50 mi. from the gate), climbs at an easy grade through hardwoods for 0.48 mi. and joins the trail up Gill Brook. The other route is the more picturesque trail up Gill Brook which turns L from the road near the 2.00 mi. sign about 60 yds. S of the trail to Gothics.

Leaving the road (0 mi.), this trail follows up the L bank of Gill Brook at an easy grade, crosses two small tributaries and enters the brook for a short distance at 0.25 mi. At 0.50 mi. a large chockstone in a gorge has created a waterfall. The trail follows the granite ledges in the brook at 0.60 mi. and again at 0.90 mi., meeting the shorter trail on the R at 1.15 mi. where there is a small waterfall. Continuing up the L bank of the brook, soon after crossing a tributary, a junction is reached at 1.32 mi. Last sure water. (Trail R leads 0.70 mi. to lookout on Indian Head and another 0.61 mi. to the boathouse on the Lower Lake. See above.)

Continuing straight ahead, the Colvin Trail swings away from the brook and climbs high above it as it makes its way up the NE shoulder of the mountain. Another junction is reached at 1.79 mi. (Trail R leads 0.46 mi. to Fish Hawk Cliffs and another 0.24 mi. to trail junction just N of the Indian Head.) Continuing on the Colvin Trail, the climbing is steady with several steep pitches before the trail levels off through a stand of conifers at 2.07 mi. Steady climbing starts again at 2.33 mi. and a junction is reached

---

* A letter from David Henderson to Archibald MacIntyre dated Oct. 14, 1826 (Published by Arthur H. Masten in his book "The Story of Adirondac") points out that the Indian who showed him the iron ore and led him through Indian Pass to the ore deposits was not the old Indian who reputedly discovered an ore bed near Elba (apparently Sabele), but rather a young Indian called Lewis Elija.

at 2.47 mi. (Trail L leads to Elk Pass and Nipple Top. See below.) Turning R, there is a steep climb from the junction, moderating at 2.57 mi. followed by a steep pitch. Spotty hurricane damage is evident at 2.75 mi. as the grade becomes gradual again. Another short, steep climb is reached at 2.95 mi., and a rock shelter on the R is passed at 3.25 mi., followed by another steep ascent. The trail drops into a small sag and them climbs steeply at 3.40 mi. A second sag is reached at 3.47 mi., followed by a steep pitch to the summit at 3.52 mi. (NYS Land Survey Station 289, placed here by Verplanck Colvin in 1896.) From the lookout just off the summit Lower Ausable Lake is seen directly below with splendid views of the Range and Sawteeth directly across the lake. About 100 yds. S on the trail toward Blake Peak (see Upper Ausable Lake Region, Sect. B3), another lookout offers a view over the Upper Ausable Lake to North River Mt., Cheney Cobble and Allen.

Distances: Lake Road at Gill Brook to shorter trail from road, 1.15 mi.; to Indian Head Trail, 1.32 mi.; to Fish Hawk Cliffs Trail, 1.79 mi.; to Nipple Top Trail, 2.47 mi.; to summit of Colvin, 3.52 mi. Ascent from road, 2330 ft. Elevation, 4057 ft. Order of height, 39. Colvin to junction with trail to S end of Lower Lake, 0.80 mi.; to Blake Peak, 1.35 mi.

Nipple Top via Elk Pass

One must see this mountain from Elk Lake to appreciate its characteristic name. At one time it was called "Dial," a name probably given by Prof. Emmons or some of his companions in 1837, but with the assistance of Old Mountain Phelps, the present name has survived, the name "Dial" being transferred to the neighboring mountain to the N.

There are two approaches to Elk Pass and Nipple Top from the Lake Road, being the same as those used for Colvin. (See above.) Leaving the road (0 mi.) via the shorter route (2.50 mi. from the gate), the trail climbs at an easy grade through hardwoods and joins the trail up Gill Brook at 0.48 mi. Turning R up the L bank of the brook soon after crossing a tributary, a junction is reached at 0.65 mi. (Trail R leads 0.70 mi. to lookout on Indian Head and another 0.61 mi. to the boathouse on the Lower Lake. See above.)

Continuing straight ahead, the Nipple Top Trail swings away from the brook and climbs high above it as it makes its way up the NE shoulder of Colvin. The climbing is steady with easy to moderate grades, getting steeper at 0.88 mi. Another junction is reached at 1.12 mi. (Trail R leads 0.46 mi. to Fish Hawk Cliffs and another 0.24 mi. to trail junction just N of the Indian Head.) Continuing on the Nipple Top Trail, several steep pitches are encountered before the trail levels off through a stand of conifers at 1.40 mi. Steady climbing starts again at 1.66 mi. and a junction is reached at 1.80 mi. (Trail R leads 1.05 mi. to summit of Colvin. See above.)

Turning L for Nipple Top, the climbing is much easier with moderate grades, becoming steeper at about 2.00 mi. A steep pitch is reached at 2.05 mi. after which the trail levels off near a vertical rock face on R at 2.09 mi. The trail starts descending at a gradual grade at 2.25 mi. and reaches a small pond on the L at 2.31 mi. After crossing a small hogback, a side trail leads to a second pond on the R at 2.38 mi. The trail crosses the outlet of this pond and then the combined outlet of both ponds, flowing S toward Elk Lake, at 2.41 mi. The trail now circles back around the first pond in a N and NE direction across wet ground before swinging E to climb the mountain. The grade is moderate at first, becoming more difficult at 2.53 mi. with occasional steep pitches. The grade becomes continuously steep at 2.76 mi., rounds off through many ferns at 2.95 mi. and gets steeper again at 3.00 mi. After a steep pitch at 3.20 mi., the junction with the trail along the ridge from Bear Den and Dial is reached at 3.27 mi. (See below.) Turning R, the grade is easy up the ridge, reaching a height of land at 3.41 mi. from where the summit is visible ahead. After dropping into a sag at 3.45 mi., the summit of Nipple Top is reached at 3.52 mi. The view of Dix to the E is quite impressive, with the Great Range visible over Colvin to the W and NW. The view of Elk Lake to the S is partially blocked by the scrub growth.

Distances: Lake Road at Colvin–Nipple Top Trail to trail up Gill Brook, 0.48 mi.; to Indian Head Trail, 0.65 mi.; to Fish Hawk Cliffs Trail, 1.12 mi.; to departure from Colvin Trail, 1.80 mi.; to outlet of ponds in Elk Pass, 2.41 mi.; to Bear Den–Dial Trail, 3.27 mi.; to summit of Nipple Top, 3.52 mi. Ascent from road, 2760 ft. Elevation, 4620 ft. Order of height, 13.

Henry Goddard Leach Trail to Nipple Top via Bear Den and Dial

A third approach to Nipple Top from the Lake Road is the Henry Goddard Leach Trail. It starts shortly before reaching the 1.00 mi. sign (0.73 mi. from the gate) and leads 5.88 mi. over Bear Den and Dial to the summit. This is 2.36 mi. longer than the route via Elk Pass (see above) but makes possible a good one-day circuit. This trail, due to its low maintenance priority, has been spotted with paint blazes to aid in following it.

Leaving the road (0 mi.), the trail heads S and then SE climbing at a moderate grade, soon becoming steeper as it ascends a hogback high above a ravine on the L at about 0.12 mi. A steep pitch is reached at 0.31 mi., moderating at 0.36 mi. Then climbing steadily, at moderate to fairly steep grades, the trail comes out on the W shoulder of Noonmark at 1.28 mi., having gained about 1600 ft., where there are good views at the N lookout. The trail now descends slightly into a sag and crosses the blazed property line of the park at 1.31 mi. Climbing gradually, a side trail to another lookout on the R is reached at 1.64 mi. After passing the S lookout at 1.66 mi., the trail descends steadily, heading about 200° then swinging toward 270° at 1.74 mi. on a fairly level traverse. Again descending steadily, the trail turns abruptly L at 1.84 mi. and heads 140° as it continues the descent at a moderate grade into the col at 1.98 mi., having lost about 320 ft. in altitude. Water can sometimes be found here at the headwaters of a N tributary of Gravestone Brook.

The trail now ascends a steep pitch out of the col and heads SW, climbing steadily through a lumbered area with white birch and other second growth. Occasional bare spots offer views back toward Noonmark. The summit of Bear Den is reached in a small clearing at 2.49 mi., but the views are obstructed. Total ascent, 2280 ft. Elevation, 3423 ft.

Leaving Bear Den, the trail descends at a moderate grade in a SW direction, the grade becoming easy at 2.60 mi. A bare rock is reached at 2.76 mi. where there is a view ahead toward Dial and Nipple Top. Descending moderately, the trail passes through a col and makes a slight ascent to a rock at a height of land on a shoulder of Bear Den at 2.84 mi. Continuing at an easy downgrade for a short distance, the trail soon descends steadily into the main col between Bear Den and Dial at 2.98 mi., having lost about 220 ft. in altitude. Then climbing easily, a bare spot offering a view of Dial is reached at 3.01 mi., after which the trail drops into a sag at 3.06 mi. Now heading S, the grade is easy at first but gets progressively steeper as the trail climbs 780 ft. up the long ridge of Dial. The grade becomes quite steep at about 3.63 mi., and the wooded summit of Dial (N Dial) is reached at 3.77 mi. A large rock on the R offers good views to the NW. Total ascent, 3060 ft. Elevation, 3980 ft. (This summit is indicated as "Dial" on the old USGS topog map, Mt. Marcy quadrangle, and has accordingly been marked with a green and white ATIS sign. It is undoubtedly the peak Old Mountain Phelps had in mind when the name "Dial" was transferred from Nipple Top to the neighboring mountain to the N, since it is the predominant peak seen when climbing from the direction of Keene Valley. However, when detailed wheel measurements of the trail were laid out on the advance print of the new survey, it was discovered that this summit is slightly less than 4000 ft. and that the next summit, 0.51 mi. nearer Nipple Top, is slightly over 4000 ft. and could conceivably be considered as the true summit of Dial. To avoid confusion and to keep Dial numbered among the 4000 footers, the two summits are referred to as the N and S summits of Dial.)*

From N Dial the trail descends easily toward the S, becoming steeper and swinging SW at 3.90 mi. The col between the N and S summits is reached at 3.97 mi. with a loss in altitude of 160 ft. Continuing SW, the trail climbs at easy grades through ferns to the wooded S summit of Dial at 4.28 mi. Total ascent, 3260 ft. Elevation, 4020 ft. Order of height, 41.

Leaving the S summit, the trail descends to the W at easy to moderate grades, losing about 100 ft. in altitude, and reaches a

---

* When the 1953 USGS Marcy map was published both N and S Dial were given as 4020 ft.

col at 4.44 mi. Climbing out of the col, the trail soon heads S, then SW and later S as it climbs at easy to moderate grades up the conifer and fern-covered ridge to Nipple Top, reaching a bare spot on a height of land at 5.40 mi. (Good views of the Dix Range.) Continuing with fairly level going along the ridge, the trail makes a slight descent just before reaching a trail junction at 5.63 mi. where the trail from Elk Pass enters on the R. (See above.) Continuing straight ahead, the grade is easy up the ridge, reaching a height of land at 5.77 mi. from which the summit is visible ahead. After dropping into a sag at 5.81 mi., the summit of Nipple Top is reached at 5.88 mi. (See above for views.)

Distances: Lake Road to N lookout on shoulder of Noonmark, 1.28 mi.; to S lookout, 1.66 mi.; to Bear Den, 2.49 mi.; to N summit of Dial, 3.77 mi.; to S summit of Dial, 4.28 mi.; to trail from Elk Pass, 5.63 mi.; to summit of Nipple Top, 5.88 mi. Total ascent from road about 4000 ft. Elevation, 4620 ft. Order of height, 13.

Dix Peak from St. Huberts

This mountain, the sixth highest summit of the Adirondacks, was named by Prof. Emmons in 1837 for John Adams Dix, Secretary of State in Gov. Marcy's administration. In 1872 he was elected Governor of New York. He also served as a U.S. Senator, Secretary of the Treasury and a Major General during the Civil War.

The trail, maintained by the ATIS as far as its junction with the trail from Route 73 via Round Pond, starts at the top of the hill on the southerly approach to the Ausable Club near the edge of the golf course and 0.40 mi. from Route 73. Cars should be parked just off Route 73 at the parking lot found to the W of the main highway and 3 mi. S of Keene Valley. Hike up the hill for just over 0.30 mi. to the beginning of the trail, turn L, and leaving the road (0 mi.), the trail heads S following dirt road. Avoid private driveway on R at 0.13 mi. At 0.21 mi. the trail continues straight ahead as the road turns L near a barn. Now a footpath, the trail crosses a tributary brook from R at 0.43 mi. and climbs high above main brook in ravine on L. A side trail on L at 0.51 mi. descends to the brook. (Last sure water if climbing Noonmark. See below.)

At 0.56 mi. the Stimson Trail branches R and leads 1.50 mi. to summit of Noonmark.

Continuing straight ahead, the Dix Trail climbs steadily up the ravine on an old tote road with the brook below on the L, leveling off at 1.17 mi. and crossing a tributary from R at 1.29 mi. Now climbing steadily again the trail is quite rocky. The grade eases up at 1.56 mi. and a trail junction is reached at the height of land between Round Mountain and Noonmark at 1.61 mi. (Here the Weston Trail branches L and leads 0.77 mi. to summit of Round Mt.) Continuing straight ahead the trail descends at an easy grade and crosses a brook flowing S at 1.86 mi. and then a tributary. Continuing easy grade on tote road down R bank of brook (tributary of N Fork Bouquet River), a junction is reached at 2.21 mi., having descended about 110 ft. from the col. (Trail L with DEC markers leads 2.33 mi. to the Chapel Pond Road via Round Pond. Trail R maintained by the ATIS leads 1.03 mi. up the SE shoulder of Noonmark and joins Stimson Trail at the summit.)

The trail to Dix now marked with blue DEC markers continues straight ahead, following the R bank of the brook at a very slight grade, soon skirts a swamp and reaches the N fork of the Bouquet River at 2.56 mi. Now following up the L bank of the river, the grade being practically level, the trail crosses a tributary at 2.69 mi. and passes a large rock on the L at 2.74 mi. The trail is now quite grassy as it follows up the course of the river through a partially overgrown meadow offering a view of Dix and Nipple Top. Many blue gentians may be found along the way. At 3.00 mi., the trail is close to the river as it passes through an old lumber clearing. The alders give way to denser woods as the trail swings away from the river to go around a swamp, but it is still grassy and wet. A small brook is crossed at 3.39 mi., and Gravestone Brook, a large tributary from the R, is reached at 3.53 mi. Crossing this brook, the trail makes a short climb to drier ground, levels off at 3.67 mi. and descends gradually to the L bank of the river at 3.85 mi. where the outlet of Dial Pond flows in from the R. The trail soon swings away from the river but rejoins it when it reaches the Bouquet River lean-to at 4.10 mi., having gained only about 100 ft. elevation since leaving the trail from Round Pond.

Leaving the lean-to, the trail crosses the river on the stones and follows up the R bank, and it gradually gets further away from the river although following up its general course. The grade is slight at first but get progressively steeper. The trail comes close to the river at 4.37 mi. near some small cascades and swings away again at 4.45 mi. The climbing is easy to moderate, but the trail is very rocky. After crossing a small brook, a fair-sized tributary is reached at 4.94 mi. Climbing is now steeper with occasional breathers. The trail follows up the R bank of the tributary and crosses it at 5.10 mi. Leaving this brook, the trail crosses other small ones and comes to the R bank of another brook near a fork at 5.38 mi. as the hardwoods give way to the conifers. Crossing the brook, the trail climbs between the two forks and crosses the branch on the R (the brook's L fork) at 5.44 mi. and recrosses it at 5.48 mi. It again crosses this branch at 5.58 mi. at the foot of a long slide where the brook comes gliding down over the bare rocks. About 45 ft. N of the slide on the L bank of the brook in a granite boulder is located a PBM, 3240 ft.

After crossing the brook the real climbing starts, gaining about 1600 ft. in a little over a mile. The trail climbs through the conifers on the L (W) side of the slide and remains fairly close to the slide at first, being only 25 yds. away at 5.65 mi. where it is an easy bushwhack between them (about halfway up the slide). While the slide may be climbed with caution to its top, the trail is much further away and the down timber makes bushwhacking more difficult. The grade is now steep, becoming very steep and rough at 5.94 mi. It eases off a bit at 6.09 mi. but continues a steady ascent up the ridge through ferns and bunchberries. At 6.28 mi., the red trail from Elk Lake via Hunters Pass enters on the R. (See Elk Lake Region, Sec. B4.) BM 4371.4 ft. is painted on a rock a few yds. down the red trail. The climbing continues steadily up the ridge through the scrub spruce, getting steeper at 6.36 mi. and rounding off at 6.53 mi. as the long, bare crest of the summit is approached. A Coast and Geodetic Survey Triangulation Station is passed on the L at 6.65 mi., and the Colvin bolt on the summit, placed here in 1873 by Verplanck Colvin, is reached at 6.70 mi. The views are unobstructed in all directions. Elk Lake, with its many islands, lies to the SW, Lake Champlain and the Green Mts.

to the E, and to the NW one looks over Nipple Top to the high peaks of the Great Range.

Distances: Ausable Club Road to Stimson Trail from Noonmark, 0.56 mi.; to Weston Trail for Round Mt. at height of land, 1.61 mi.; to blue trail from Round Pond, 2.21 mi.; to Gravestone Brook, 3.53 mi.; to Bouquet River lean-to, 4.10 mi.; to foot of slide, 5.58 mi.; to Elk Lake Trail, 6.28 mi.; to summit of Dix, 6.70 mi. Ascent from Club Road, 3600 ft. Elevation, 4875 ft. Order of height, 6.

Noonmark via Stimson Trail

This prominent peak when viewed from Keene Valley has somewhat the appearance that Nipple Top has from Elk Lake. Lying practically due S of the village, it "marks noon" when the sun is directly over the summit.

This trail, scouted by and named for Henry L. Stimson, Secretary of State in President Hoover's cabinet, starts at the top of the hill 0.40 mi. W of Route 73 on the southern approach to the Ausable Club and the parking lot located on Route 73 that is found 3 mi. S of the High Peaks sign in Keene Valley. Cars should be parked in the area for the start of the Roaring Brook Trail to Giant. Hike up the hill to the sign and, leaving the road (0 mi.) the trail heads S and, at the start, is the same as the trail to Dix marked with ATIS markers. (See above.) The brook at 0.43 mi. and side trail into ravine at 0.51 mi. offer the last sure water.

At 0.56 mi. the Stimson Trail turns R from the Dix trail, makes a steep zigzag climb, and levels off at 0.62 mi. heading S through a hardwood forest. Steady climbing starts again at 0.74 mi. where the trail swings W and then S again. An interesting rock face is passed on the L at 0.90 mi., soon after which the grade moderates, only to become very steep at 0.97 mi. Swinging W at 1.04 mi. the grade slackens, then levels off and heads NW and then W. A steep pitch up rocks is reached at 1.12 mi. where the trail turns L. Then heading SW and S the trail comes out on bare rocks at 1.16 mi. where there are good views of Keene Valley and the Range.

Continuing S through scrub spruce and birch, the climbing is fairly easy with some steeper parts. A second outlook is reached at 1.45 mi. and a third bare spot, from which the summit may be seen, at 1.48 mi. Steep climbing starts at 1.61 mi., the grade moderating at 1.70 mi., followed by a steep pitch up rocks at 1.81 mi. A short level stretch and a trail junction are reached at 1.89 mi. Here the original trail, now abandoned, continues straight ahead and climbs up a very steep couloir with vertical rock face on L. The preferred route turns L over a small hump, descends slightly, turns R at 1.91 mi. and makes a steep climb to top of couloir at 1.95 mi., rejoining the old route. From here it is a short scramble following painted arrows over the bare rocks to the summit at 2.06 mi. where there are unobstructed views in all directions. Both Rainbow Falls and Beaver Meadow Falls may be seen when the leaves are off the trees. From the summit a trail descends SE 1.03 mi. and meets the Dix Trail at its junction with the trail from Round Pond. It is then another 2.21 mi. back to the start at the Ausable Club Road.

Distances: Ausable Club Road to turn off from Dix Trail, 0.56 mi.; to first lookout at bare spot, 1.16 mi.; to summit of Noonmark, 2.06 mi.; Ascent from road 2175 ft. Elevation, 3556 ft.

Noonmark via Round Pond and Felix Adler Trail

This route provides an alternative approach to Round Mt., Noonmark and Dix and although being longer it has the advantage of saving 200 or more ft. in elevation. It is 1.30 mi. longer to Noonmark than the Stimson Trail (200 ft. less climbing) but only 0.12 mi. longer to Dix than the blue trail from St. Huberts (310 ft. less climbing). The start is marked with a DEC sign and a parking area on Route 73, 1.10 mi. SE of parking space at Chapel Pond. The section of trail from the road to the Dix Trail from St. Huberts is maintained by the Adirondacks 46ers.

Leaving the SW side of the road (0 mi.) and following blue DEC markers, the trail climbs up the steep roadside on a traverse, heading S and SE through a hardwood forest. It swings SW at 0.29 mi. and climbs at easy to moderate grades to a height of land in a small col at 0.53 mi. Descending at an easy grade a junction is reached at 0.55 mi. (Trail L leads 55 yds. past a campsite to shore of Round Pond.) Turning R the trail follows around the N shore of Round Pond and passes PBM 1733 ft. at 0.89 mi. near end of pond. Now heading W the trail crosses a wet, marshy spot around an inlet to the pond, and starts climbing moderately at 0.97 mi. After crossing a brook from R at 1.16 mi., the grade gets steeper as the trail climbs steadily up the ravine into a notch. The grade rounds off at 1.60 mi. and becomes fairly level through the pass S of Round Mt. The trail descends slightly at 1.78 mi., crosses a brook from R at 1.82 mi., and continues with easy going to a brook flowing S, which it crosses, and joins the ATIS maintained Dix Trail from St. Huberts at 2.33 mi. (Trail R with ATIS markers leads to St. Huberts, 2.21 mi.; L, marked with blue markers, leads to Bouquet River lean-to, 1.89 mi. and Dix Peak, 4.49 mi.)

The trail to Noonmark crosses the Dix Trail from St. Huberts and is now marked with ATIS markers and axe blazes. It heads W and climbs at an easy grade coming to a steep pitch at 2.59 mi. and another at 2.80 mi. Then leaving the dense forest growth, the trail climbs steadily at moderate grades up the SE shoulder of Noonmark, over bare spots and through scrub birch, poplar and spruce. Some natural steps in the rocks are reached at 3.09 mi. Continuing through many ferns, a bare spot below the summit is reached at 3.27 mi. as the trail levels off. Climbing a steep pitch at 3.33 mi. the trail reaches the summit at 3.36 mi. and joins the Stimson Trail coming up the NW shoulder.

Distances: Chapel Pond Road to Round Pond, 0.55 mi.; to Dix Trail, 2.33 mi.; to summit of Noonmark, 3.36 mi. Ascent from Chapel Pond Road, 1975 ft. Elevation 3556 ft.

Round Mt. via S. Burns Weston Trail

Round Mt. stands between Noonmark and Giant, and its cliffs rising above Chapel Pond are popular with rock climbers. The trail, named for S. Burns Weston, starts at the foot of the hill on the southern approach to the Ausable Club, 0.16 mi. from the Route 73 parking lot found 3 mi. S of Keene Valley and opposite the start of the Roaring Brook Trail to Giant. It is marked with a sign.

Leaving the road (0 mi.), the trail climbs toward the SE. The grade is easy at first but soon gets steeper and then levels off at

0.14 mi. high above the Chapel Pond Road. The trail is now mostly level or climbing at easy grades, soon passing through a blowdown area in a hemlock forest and reaching a height of land at 0.63 mi. Then descending slightly a gully is crossed at 0.78 mi., and the trail starts climbing at easy to moderate grades through a hardwood forest, again descending a slight grade at 0.90 mi. and leveling off from 0.98 mi. to 1.02 mi. Again climbing at easy to moderate grades, a brook from R is crossed at 1.24 mi. which is followed up a short way.

The climbing now becomes more difficult as the trail heads more to the S and climbs a series of slides, reaching the first at 1.40 mi. A second slide is reached at 1.52 mi., on which are passed two lone, white pines on R, and a third slide at 1.58 mi. The grade becomes easy at 1.88 mi. as the trail zigzags over bare spots and reaches a steep pitch at 1.99 mi., with a rock face on R at top of pitch. The trail emerges from the woods at 2.08 mi. and swings toward the SE, following cairns at an easy grade over the bare rocks, the result of a forest fire. The continuation of the Weston Trail up the W side of the mountain from the Dix Trail enters on the R at 2.24 mi., and the summit is reached at 2.27 mi. from which are obtained fine views of Giant and other high peaks.

Distances: Ausable Club Road to summit of Round Mt., 2.27 mi. Ascent, 1820 ft. Elevation, 3100 ft.

Round Mt. from Dix Trail

The Weston Trail (see above) continues down the W side of Round Mt. and joins the trail to Dix. To climb Round Mt. via this route, take the Dix Trail S 1.61 mi. from the Ausable Club Road to the height of land between Noonmark and Round Mt. (0.60 mi. N of trail from Round Pond. See above.)

Leaving the Dix Trail (0 mi.), the Weston Trail climbs steadily to a bare spot at 0.10 mi., swings S and then E as it crosses a shoulder and descends to a small brook at 0.16 mi. The trail follows up the brook a short way and then climbs through a fern-covered area to a bare spot at 0.30 mi. The top of a slide is reached at 0.35 mi. Continuing at a not too difficult grade, the trail climbs through a burned over area among scrub birch and wanders over bare spots. A small brook is crossed at 0.50 mi. and soon recrossed twice, after which the trail gets steeper for a short distance. The trail up the N side of the mountain enters on the L at 0.74 mi. and the bare summit is reached at 0.77 mi.

Distances: Ausable Club Road via Dix Trail to Weston Trail, 1.61 mi.; to summit of Round Mt., 2.38 mi. Ascent, 1720 ft. Elevation, 3100 ft. Chapel Pond Road via Round Pond to Dix Trail, 2.33 mi.; to Weston Trail, 2.93 mi.; to summit of Round Mt., 3.70 mi. Ascent, 1520 ft.

Giant via Roaring Brook Trail

The full name for Giant Mt., Giant of the Valley, comes from the beautiful valley stretching S from Elizabethtown known as "Pleasant Valley." The natives corrupted the name and it became known simply as "The Valley." Hence the mountain, which from the E appears to be a veritable giant, was named "Giant of the Valley."

The trail begins on the Chapel Pond Road (Route 73) opposite the southern approach to the Ausable Club (0.55 mi. S of the main road to the Club and 3 mi. S of the High Peaks sign in Keene Valley Village). Park beside the road. Leaving the road (0 mi.), the trail heads E along the R bank of the brook and enters the woods at 0.10 mi. where the trail soon divides. (The R bank leads to the foot of Roaring Brook Falls.) Keeping L for Giant, the trail starts a steady climb, and at 0.33 mi. a side trail on R leads to a lookout on Roaring Brook. Just before this junction, the grade moderates and then continues at an easy grade to another side trail on the R at 0.57 mi. (This leads 60 yds. to the big slide and the top of Roaring Brook Falls where there is an excellent view of the valley.)

Keeping L the trail climbs slightly and reaches a long level stretch through a hemlock grove at 0.70 mi. Continuing with the slide visible on the R the trail reaches a junction on the R side of the slide at 1.06 mi. (Above this point to the L, the old trail was carried away by the slide.) Turning R the trail crosses the slide following rock cairns to a trail junction on the far side of the slide at 1.12 mi. (Trail R leads to the Nubble, 0.81 mi., and Giant's Washbowl, 1.01 mi. (See below.)

The Giant Trail turns L and climbs through the woods along

the L side of the slide. Two brooks are crossed from their L banks at 1.23 mi. and 1.34 mi. (last water) before rejoining the old trail at 1.41 mi. at an outlook over the slide. The trail now swings away from the slide and Roaring Brook but follows up the general course of the ravine as it climbs up the ridge above the slide. Climbing is now steady on a moderate to fair grade, becoming steeper at 1.77 mi. as the trail becomes badly eroded. A bare rock lookout on R is reached at 2.35 mi. offering a view of the Range and the peaks to the S and SW. In the valley below may be seen the Ausable Club and Bradley's. The trail continues at a steep grade, zigzagging through thick conifers, the general direction swinging to the NE. The grade moderates about 80 yds. before reaching a junction at 2.88 mi. where the Giant Ridge Trail enters on the R. (This trail, cut in 1954 to replace the abandoned Dudley Trail, descends to the Nubble Trail, the Washbowl and Chapel Pond with excellent views from the open ridge. See below. Distance to Route 73, Chapel Pond Road, 2.22 mi.)

Above the junction, the climbing is easier as the trail to Giant climbs to the top of the ridge at 3.04 mi. where the summit is in full view. Descending slightly, the trail becomes fairly level and passes a bare rock lookout toward Rocky Peak on the R at 3.11 mi. The final steep climb starts at 3.23 mi. A junction is reached at 3.47 mi. where the East Trail from Rocky Peak Ridge enters on the R. (See Section B8 for East Trail description.) The PBM on the bare summit is reached at 3.60 mi. where excellent views are obtained. One looks directly down to the Ausable Club golf course to the W and Round Pond to the S while major peaks are seen from the S to the W and NW. To the E lie Lake Champlain and the Green Mts. of Vermont.

The trail beyond the summit, after passing a lookout at the N summit, leads down the steep N shoulder of Giant to the col between Giant and Green. A trail junction in the col leads L to Hopkins (see below), and R around the N and E shoulders of Green to Route 9N. (See Sect. B7.)

Distances: Route 73 to side trail leading to top of Roaring Brook Falls, 0.57 mi.; to trail to Giant's Washbowl and Nubble, 1.12 mi.; to bare rock lookout, 2.35 mi.; to Giant Ridge Trail, 2.88 mi.; to East Trail, 3.47 mi.; to summit of Giant, 3.60 mi. Ascent, 3375 ft. Elevation, 4627 ft. Order of height, 12.

Giant's Washbowl and Nubble

From the Roaring Brook Trail at 1.12 mi. (see above) a trail to the Giant's Washbowl and the Nubble turns R. Leaving this junction (0 mi.), the trail climbs easily at first and then steeply to a junction at 0.16 mi. Taking the R fork, the trail continues to climb at a moderate to fair grade, becoming easy at 0.45 mi. and reaching the height of land in the pass below the Nubble at 0.54 mi. Descending at an easy grade through hardwoods and ferns, a second junction is reached at 0.84 mi. (Trail L leads around N side of Washbowl, close to water's edge, past campsite at 0.15 mi., and after a short climb joins Giant Ridge Trail at 0.24 mi. Distances from junction.) Going R, the main trail continues on the level through conifers along the S side of the pond, passes a fireplace at 0.91 mi. and joins the Giant Ridge Trail at 1.01 mi. at a point 0.23 mi. below the junction of the Giant Ridge Trail with the L fork.

Taking the L fork above at 0.16 mi., the trail to the Nubble continues to climb steadily, the grade moderating occasionally, passing a spring at 0.58 mi. and leveling off at 0.63 mi. where it dips into a sag at a small spring and starts climbing again. A steep pitch is reached at 0.72 mi. after which the trail levels off and comes to a junction at 0.79 mi. (Trail R along bare rocks with good views leads to the SE summit of the Nubble at 0.03 mi., and continuing along the bare rocks, the NW summit is reached at 0.10 mi. Distances from junction.) Continuing straight ahead, the main trail descends slightly over rocks, enters woods at 0.81 mi. and doubles back toward the N at 0.83 mi. It soon swings E again and descends a steep pitch. After crossing a bare spot at 0.95 mi., the trail descends through hurricane damage, swinging around considerably. Care is needed here to follow it. After passing through a sag, the trail descends gradually along the ridge, passing a lookout over the Washbowl at 1.11 mi., and joins the Giant Ridge Trail at a brook crossing at 1.23 mi. This junction is 0.30 mi. above the Washbowl.

Distances: Roaring Brook Trail direct to Giant Ridge Trail at Washbowl, 1.12 mi.; via Nubble Trail to Giant Ridge Trail above Washbowl, 1.23 mi. (1.43 mi. if side trail to summit of Nubble is included.)

Giant from Chapel Pond via Giant Ridge Trail

This trail, completed in 1954, leads up the rocky ridge above the Giant's Washbowl to a point on the Roaring Brook Trail 0.72 mi. below the summit of Giant. There is ample room for cars in the Chapel Pond parking area on Route 73, 1.30 mi. SE of the Roaring Brook Trail. The trail to Giant is 0.20 mi. further SE.

Leaving the road (0 mi.), the trail crosses a bridge at 0.02 mi. over a small brook from its L bank, then crosses and recrosses a brook bed (old outlet from the Washbowl, present outlet now underground) as it climbs at a moderate grade. At 0.25 mi. the trail bears R, and at 0.29 mi. swings sharply L, the first of five such switchbacks as the trail climbs through white birch and beech trees. The grade steepens between the third and fourth switchbacks but moderates at 0.46 mi., just beyond a large boulder off the trail on the L. Becoming steep again, the trail momentarily dips into a sag to cross the bed of the old outlet again and then pitches up, rounding off at about 0.56 mi. and coming to a lookout on a bare rock ledge at 0.65 mi. Here one can look directly down to the Chapel Pond Road. Sawteeth, Gothics, Armstrong and the two Wolf Jaws are in full view. There is an interesting rock profile at 290°. The trail now makes a slight descent to a junction at the S end of the Giant's Washbowl at 0.70 mi. (Trail L skirts the SW side of the pond and leads 1.01 mi. through the pass below the Nubble to the Roaring Brook Trail. See above.)

Swinging R the trail to Giant leads into the woods E of the pond near the underground outlet, and on easy grades swings around the pond at some distance to the E. After a pitch up at 0.81 mi., a trail junction is reached at 0.93 mi. (Trail L descends 0.09 mi. to the Dudley campsite on N side of Washbowl and joins above-mentioned trail at far end of pond, 0.15 mi. beyond campsite. See above.) Straight ahead another junction is reached at 1.00 mi. (Here the trail over the Nubble from Roaring Brook Trail enters on the L. See above.)

Bearing R the Giant Ridge Trail climbs steadily up through the conifers. At 1.10 mi. there is a sharp line of demarcation between the conifers and the white birch, marking the extent of the 1913 forest fire. Here the climbing becomes quite steep. An open spot on the bare rocks offering views is reached at 1.24 mi. Above here the climbing is easier and mostly in the open with a few steep pitches as the trail wanders up over bare granite, marked with cairns, and through patches of scrub. The trail makes a steep pitch from 1.43 mi. to 1.50 mi. and reaches a long, steady climb up a bare face at 1.62 mi., entering the scrub conifers on the level at 1.75 mi. The trail soon descends and detours around a steep pitch at 1.78 mi., reaching the bottom of the col at 1.81 mi. where there is a short, level stretch. Starting up again the trail comes out in the open at 1.89 mi. and levels off as it enters large conifers at 2.01 mi. Soon starting up again the going is mostly easy through the conifers to the junction with the Roaring Brook Trail at 2.22 mi., 0.72 mi. below the summit of Giant. From here the route to the top is described above under the Roaring Brook Trail.

Distances: Chapel Pond Road to Washbowl, 0.70 mi.; to side trail to Dudley campsite, 0.93 mi.; to trail over Nubble, 1.00 mi.; to Roaring Brook Trail, 2.22 mi.; to East Trail, 2.81 mi.; to summit of Giant, 2.94 mi. Ascent, 3050 ft. Elevation, 4627 ft. Order of height, 12.

Mossy Cascade Trail to Hopkins

For naming of this summit see "Spread Eagle and Hopkins" in the Keene Valley Region, Sect. B1. The start of the trail is S of the Route 73 bridge across the East Branch of the Ausable River 2 mi. S of Keene Valley. Proceed along the E bank of the river past a house to a junction at 0.37 mi. with a tote road.

The trail now swings R on the tote road but turns L away from tote road at 0.50 mi. and soon reaches the L bank of the brook again which it follows up in a general SE direction, then swings to the E and NE. A steep pitch is reached at 0.73 mi., after which the trail is high above the brook climbing steadily through a stand of hemlocks. Mossy Cascade is passed in the ravine below at 0.79 mi. after which the trail is close to the brook. The trail crosses and leaves the brook at 0.91 mi., the grade soon leveling off and becoming easy. Steep pitches are reached at 0.99 mi. and 1.05 mi. Continuing on a level stretch through a second growth of hardwoods, a yellow property line is crossed at 1.18 mi.

The grade becomes moderate at about 1.27 mi., followed by a steep climb at 1.37 mi. leading up to a lookout at 1.45 mi. The going now becomes easy with a gradual descent at 1.53 mi. reaching bottom of col at 1.65 mi. Then traversing to the SE, the trail soon swings N climbing steeply and reaches an open ledge with a view to the S at 1.73 mi. Still climbing steadily, a small ledge offers another lookout at 1.82 mi. The trail climbs up an interesting monolithic ridge of granite at 1.88 mi. after which the going is easy, up and down along a ridge. Moderate climbing starts at 2.22 mi., and the junction with the Ranney Trail is reached at 2.30 mi. (See below.)

As the grade eases, the trail heads NE and N through a wet area, then follows up a small brook at 2.51 mi. and soon crosses it. The climbing becomes steeper again at 2.79 mi. as the trail ascends the ravine between Hopkins and Green, crossing and recrossing the brook as it makes its way among the rocks and ferns. After passing a rock face on the L at 2.90 mi., the grade is easy to a trail junction in the col at 2.97 mi. (Trail R leads 3.02 mi. via a shoulder of Green Mt. to Giant. See below.) Turning L the trail heads W and climbs steeply, the grade becoming easy at 3.04 mi. as the trail makes its way over bare granite to the summit of Hopkins at 3.17 mi. where there are many blueberry bushes. The view is unobstructed in all directions except to the NE, 22 major peaks being discernible. (Trail W with ADK markers leads to Keene Valley. See Keene Valley Region, Section B1.)

Distances: Trail sign to junction with tote road, 0.37 mi.; to Mossy Cascade, 0.79 mi.; to first lookout, 1.45 mi.; to Ranney Trail, 2.30 mi.; to trail via Green to Giant, 2.97 mi.; to summit of Hopkins, 3.17 mi. Ascent from Route 73, 2120 ft. Elevation, 3183 ft.

Ranney Trail to Hopkins

This trail to Hopkins starts from the iron bridge 0.50 mi. S of Keene Valley Center, follows up the course of the brook S of Spread Eagle and joins the Mossy Cascade Trail at a point 0.67 mi. below the trail junction in the Hopkins–Green Mt. col and 0.87 mi. below the summit of Hopkins.

Because the start of the trail is reached by a private road which may have a locked chain at the entrance bridge over the Ausable River, cars should be parked at the parking area on W side of Route 73, 0.40 mi. S of the High Peaks sign in Keene Valley Village. Turn E across iron bridge on private road 0.10 mi. S of the parking area.

Leaving the highway (0 mi.), follow dirt road R after crossing the river. Continue straight ahead to sign marking start of Ranney Trail on R at far end of clearing at 0.26 mi. The trail enters the woods on a lumber road following along the R bank of the brook on easy to moderate grades through a lumbered area. Crossing the brook at 0.72 mi., the trail climbs a steep pitch along an old lumber road, then turns sharp L at 0.85 mi. It now climbs to the SE along L bank of the brook. A N-S yellow-painted property line is crossed at 0.96 mi. followed by crossing a tributary brook from its L bank. At 1.13 mi. the trail makes a moderate pitch up and is now high above the L bank of the main brook in the ravine below. Climbing continues at moderate grades, wth occasional steeper pitches and easier stretches, to the junction with the Mossy Cascade Trail which comes in on the R at 1.78 mi. Turning L the route from here to the summit of Hopkins is the same as for the Mossy Cascade Trail. (See above.)

Distances: Route 73 to start of trail, 0.26 mi.; to Valley Trail, 0.38 mi.; to Mossy Cascade Trail, 1.78 mi.; to Hopkins–Green col and trail to Giant, 2.45 mi.; to summit of Hopkins, 2.65 mi. Ascent from Route 73, 2140 ft. Elevation, 3183 ft.

Giant from Hopkins via Green Mt.

Due to its length and the fact that there are no open views between the summit of Hopkins and Giant, this trail is not maintained in the manner of the other trails on Giant. However, it does provide an interesting wilderness trip for those who like to get off the beaten path. The climb up the N shoulder of Giant, which is quite steep, joins the trail to Giant from Route 9N via Green (See Sect. B7.)

Leaving the junction with the Mossy Cascade Trail in the Hopkins–Green col (0 mi.), the trail makes a short descent and then climbs steeply to 0.04 mi. The grade is then easy to moderate with a level stretch through a stand of thick spruce from 0.21 mi. to 0.24 mi., followed by moderate to steeper grades after which is covered with heavy timber. Elevation, 3400 ft.

Starting down an easy grade at 0.43 mi. the trail enters a slash area from which Giant and the main peak of Green may be seen. Continuing the easy descent with a few steeper pitches, the bottom of the small col is reached at 0.53 mi., having lost about 100 ft. in altitude. Climbing easily for a short distance the trail becomes fairly level on a very enjoyable section as it slabs along below a ridge of Green and enters a swampy area with lush moss at 0.69 mi.

At 0.97 mi. the trail starts down again on a moderate grade with occasional easy stretches and crosses a large tributary to Beede Brook (Putnam Brook on 1955 Elizabethtown topog) at 1.12 mi. Continuing the easy to moderate descent as the trail slabs a shoulder of Green, the trail crosses the main stream (may be dry) at 1.66 mi. a short distance below the height of land in the pass between Green and Giant. The trail from Route 9N joins from the L in the col. At this point the trail begins its last steep ascent. Switchbacks and easy natural rock steps gain great elevation in a short time. At 2.79 mi., the trail reaches a scrub timber ridge which looks down upon the slides on the west face of Giant. From this overlook the remaining 0.23 mi. to the top is a gentle climb through corridors of scrub evergreens until the summit bench mark is reached at 3.02 mi.

Distances: Hopkins–Green col to W summit of Green, 0.39 mi.; to Beede Brook, 1.66 mi.; to summit of Giant, 3.02 mi. Ascent from Hopkins–Green col, 2450 ft. Elevation, 4627 ft. Order of height, 12.

Snow Mt.

This low promontory E and a little S of Rooster Comb is well suited for a short afternoon climb and offers fine views of the surrounding higher peaks. The climber has a choice of various routes, making several round trips possible by going one way and returning another.

1. Via W. A. White Trail: From St. Huberts take the W. A.

White Trail just N of the gate (see Section B2) and follow it to trail junction at 0.95 mi. where the W. A. Trail turns L. Continuing straight ahead, the trail climbs at an easy grade to another junction at 1.09 mi. (R fork is short cut descending to Deer Brook Trail. See below.) Taking L fork, the trail continues climbing at an easy grade, slabbing end of ridge, crosses Deer Brook at 1.39 mi. and joins the trail up from Deer Brook at 1.74 mi. which enters on the R. Continuing straight ahead on level ground, another junction is reached at 1.89 mi. (Trail L leads 1.00 mi. to Rooster Comb.) Turning R the trail is level for a short distance, soon starts a steady climb and comes out on bare rocks at 1.99 mi. Entering the woods again, it climbs over more bare rocks at 2.09 mi. and reaches the first summit at 2.14 mi. Crossing this summit the trail heads SE toward the Round Mt. Noonmark col for a few yds. over bare rocks and then swings sharp L, descending into a small sag and climbing to the broad, flat summit of Snow Mt. at 2.19 mi. Side trails radiate to ledges where views are obtained. Nearby peaks are Giant, Round, Noonmark, Dix, Dial, Nipple Top, Bear Den, Hurricane (with fire tower), Rooster Comb, Porter and the Brothers.

Distances: Lake Road N of gate to departure from W. A. White Trail, 0.95 mi.; to short cut to Deer Brook, 1.09 mi.; to Deer Brook Trail, 1.74 mi.; to junction with trail to Rooster Comb, 1.89 mi.; to summit of Snow Mt., 2.19 mi. Ascent, 1035 ft. Elevation, 2360 ft.

2. Via Deer Brook: This approach to Snow Mt. starts 0.10 mi. N of bridge over Ausable River on Route 73, 1.95 mi. S of High Peaks sign in Keene Valley. This is also an approach to the W. A. White Trail and the Range. (See above.) Leaving the highway (0 mi.), the trail heads W on the S side of Deer Brook and comes to a junction at 0.10 mi. Trail straight ahead leads 0.50 mi. up the rugged, rocky ravine of Deer Brook. Trail L on tote road is much easier and is recommended if carrying heavy packs. It rejoins trail up ravine in 0.55 mi. (Data for trail up ravine are: Starting (0 mi.) from junction at 0.10 mi., trail follows up R bank of Deer Brook, easy going, and crosses to L bank at 0.10 mi. Here the going becomes very difficult along foot of rock face. Trail recrosses brook at 0.15 mi. and again at 0.20 mi. Now climbing up the rocky L bank, the trail recrosses the brook at 0.35 mi. and returns to L

bank at 0.40 mi. It now climbs up under the steep rock face of the gorge and crosses to the R bank at 0.45 mi., after which it climbs out of the gorge and rejoins the tote road at 0.50 mi.)

Turning L the tote road heads S at an easy grade and reaches a lookout on L at 0.25 mi. It then swings W, the grade becoming steeper at about 0.40 mi., and rejoins the trail up the ravine which enters on the R at a trail crossing at 0.65 mi. (Trail L leads 0.20 mi. to route described above under (1) at 1.09 mi., and connects with W. A. White Trail.) Keeping straight ahead for Snow and Rooster Comb another junction is reached at a brook at 0.80 mi. (Avoid old trail to L. Trail straight ahead leads 0.05 mi. to falls.)

Turning R the trail crosses the brook and turns downstream a few yds. on L bank and then swings NE away from brook on tote road. At 0.90 mi. it swings L and climbs steadily at an easy grade to junction with trail from St. Huberts on L at 1.30 mi. From here the route is the same as described above under (1) at 1.74 mi.

Distances: Route 73 to reentry trail from Deer Brook ravine, 0.65 mi.; to trail from St. Huberts, 1.30 mi.; to junction with trail to Rooster Comb, 1.45 mi.; to summit of Snow Mt., 1.75 mi. Ascent, 1360 ft.

3. Via Rooster Comb Trail: From Route 73 to ADK Rooster Comb Trail via Sachs Road (see Keene Valley Region, Sect. B1) to junction with ATIS trail on L at 1.20 mi. Turning L the trail descends and crosses a small brook and heads SE mostly on the level through white birch and other hardwoods. Another brook is crossed at 1.45 mi. after which the side trail to Snow Mt. enters on the L at 1.55 mi. From here the route to the summit is the same as described above under (1) at 1.89 mi. (Trail R connects with trails to Deer Brook and St. Huberts.)

Distances: Route 73 to ATIS Trail to Snow Mt., Deer Brook and St. Huberts, 1.20 mi.; to turn off to Snow Mt., 1.55 mi.; to summit of Snow Mt., 1.85 mi. Ascent, 1360 ft.

SECTION B3

UPPER AUSABLE LAKE REGION

Following the sale of higher level land by the Adirondack Mountain Reserve to the State of New York in 1978, all trails around and approaching the shores of the Upper Ausable Lake have been closed to the public. However, the trunk line trail from Marcy over Bartlett Ridge to the nothern end of the Lake at the Warden's Camp is still open to the public as are the trails joining it from the Range Trail from between Haystack and Basin, and from Sawteeth. The Warden's Camp also may be reached by the trail descending from between Colvin and Blake Mountains to the southern end of the Lower Ausable Lake and over the carry between the two lakes.

This Warden's Camp near the boat house at the northern end of the Upper Ausable Lake has radio communication with the Ausable Club office during the summer months.

It should be especially noted, however, that the Upper Ausable Lake Region cannot be reached by way of the Lower Ausable Lake. There is no trail along its shores, no bushwhacking is allowed, there are no boats for rent, and use of portable boats brought in by the public is prohibited.

In addition, no camping is allowed on the privately owned land near the lakes—roughly, the land below the 2500-foot level.

However, there are still many interesting trips available to the public in this region provided one is willing to do a lot of climbing and descending. Camping is allowed on State land, generally above the 2500-foot level. If fires are built, all soil of vegetable origin must be removed from the burning area and stones placed around it. No fires should be built where there is not plenty of water available with which to extinguish the fire. (See Section A, subsection on Campfires.) In the area recently purchased by the State, no established campsites have yet been developed.

Trails Described	Year Measured	Total Miles
Round Trip over Sawteeth, Colvin and Indian Head	1953	10.90
Warden's Camp to Sawteeth Summit	1953	2.80
Warden's Camp to Colvin Summit	1953	2.90
Warden's Camp to Summit of Marcy via Bartlett Ridge	1953	5.26
Warden's Camp to Summit of Haystack via Bartlett Ridge	1953	3.45
Warden's Camp to Summit of Haystack via Haystack Brook	1953	4.35
Summit of Colvin to Elk Lake–Marcy Trail	1953*	5.35
Tammy Stowe Trail–Loop from Sawteeth Trail	1978	1.00

* Section between Pinnacle and Elk Lake–Marcy Trail was measured in 1978.

All trails described in Section B3 are maintained by the Adirondack Trail Improvement Society (ATIS).

One popular trip for seasoned and ambitious climbers is a trip over Sawteeth and Colvin including Fish Hawk Cliffs and Indian Head (for the reverse), from the boat house area at the northern end of the Lower Ausable Lake. During July and August, climbers may ride the bus which leaves hourly 9:00 A.M. through 5:00 P.M. for the Lower Lake from the Ausable Club. Also, those reaching the Warden's Camp at the northern end of the Upper Ausable Lake after traversing Sawteeth and Colvin may climb Marcy, Haystack or other mountains of the Great Range with exit routes to Keene Valley (See Section B1), Sanford Lake (See Section B5), or Heart Lake (See Section B6). A third route through this region leads from the summit of Colvin along the crest of the Colvin–Blake–Pinnacle Ridge to the Elk Lake–Marcy Trail by means of which one may head for the Marcy region or to the Elk Lake Region (See Section B4).

Round Trip over Sawteeth and Colvin

From the Lower Ausable Lake climb Sawteeth via the easier Pyramid–Gothics Trail approach (See Section B2, Sawteeth via the

Pyramid–Gothics Trail) or by way of the so-called "Scenic Trail" (See Section B2, Sawteeth from Lower Ausable Lake).

From the summit of Sawteeth, descend 0.10 mi. to the junction of the Scenic Trail and the trail from the Upper Ausable Lake Warden's Camp. Following the latter trail R, descend through conifers and ferns somewhat steeply down a ridge at the end of which a switch-back leads steeply down to a brook at 1.10 mi. from Sawteeth's summit. This is a possible campsite. From here, the trail climbs slightly, then works along the mountain side to the upper junction with the Tammy Stowe Trail coming in from the R at 1.30 mi. (See below). Continuing downward through a mixed forest, the lower start of the Tammy Stowe Trail is reached at 2.00 mi. From here, the descent is moderate with steep pitches to Shanty Brook which is crossed at 2.60 mi. Beyond the brook at 2.64 mi. the route joins the trail from the Warden's Camp to Marcy, Haystack and the Great Range. (See below). Shortly below this junction, the route reaches flat land which it crosses to the Warden's Camp at 2.80 mi.

Turning L (N) at the Warden's Camp, one follows the Carry Trail between the Upper and Lower Ausable Lakes. Crossing flat land and a number of short bridges over gullies, the Carry Trail reaches Shanty Brook at 3.05 mi. (0.25 mi. from the Warden's Camp) and soon gets close to the Ausable River. At 3.40 mi., there is a rustic bench beside some attractive rapids with a spring nearby. Continuing along the river for some distance, the trail then bears away from it, crosses a brook and joins a tractor road at 3.70 mi. At 3.75 mi., within sight of the Lower Ausable Lake, the trail for Colvin turns R and at 3.80 mi. crosses the Ausable River on a bridge.

Following up the R (N) side of the brook flowing from the Colvin–Blake col, the trail recrosses to the L bank at 4.05 mi. and climbs steeply to 4.10 mi. Climbing is now very steady above the brook, reaching brook level at 4.25 mi. where the brook forks. The trail follows up the L bank of the L fork a few yards, then crosses it. This area offers possible camping sites. Beyond the crossing, the trail continues between the two forks, both of which are heard but not seen. Small brooks are crossed at 4.35 mi. and at 4.40 mi. after which a very steep pitch is encountered at 4.50 mi. Climbing continues steadily up a hogback, the grade moderating at 4.80 mi. and reaching a trail junction in the col at 4.90 mi. (Trail R leads to Blake Peak, 0.55 mi.; the Pinnacle, 3.15 mi., and the Elk Lake–Marcy Trail at 4.55 mi.) (See below.)

Turning L, the Colvin Trail climbs steeply, the grade moderating at 5.10 mi., after which the trail crosses a ridge and dips into a slight sag at 5.20 mi. The going is now relatively easy up the S ridge of the mountain. A lookout is reached at 5.65 mi. offering a view over the Upper Ausable Lake to North River Mountain, Cheney Cobble and Allen. It is then only a few yards to the summit at 5.70 mi. where another lookout presents splendid views of the Range and Sawteeth directly across the Lower Ausable Lake which is seen directly below.

From the summit of Colvin, descend via routes described in Section B2, Mt. Colvin from Lake Road. The trail via Fish Hawk Cliffs and Indian Head leads directly to the Lower Ausable Lake boat house. (In summer, the last bus leaves the lake at 5:00 P.M.) Other choices of descent lead to the Lake Road 2.75 mi. from the Ausable Club or via the more picturesque route along Gill Brook which intersects the Lake Road 2.00 mi. from the Club house. At a point 1.05 mi. below Colvin's summit, one may turn R to climb Nipple Top and return to St. Huberts over Dial and Bear Den Mountains. (See Section B2, Henry Goddard Leach Trail to Nipple Top via Bear Den and Dial.)

Round Trip Distances: Lower Ausable Lake dam to summit of Sawteeth via Pyramid–Gothics Trial, 2.18 mi.; to Warden's Camp, 4.98 mi.; to Lower Lake end of Carry, 5.98 mi.; to summit of Colvin, 7.88 mi.; to Lower Lake boat house via Fish Hawk Cliffs and Indian Head 10.90 mi.

Total ascent and descent, 4500 feet.

Marcy, Haystack and the Great Range from the Warden's Camp

Climbers reaching the Warden's Camp at the northern end of the Upper Ausable Lake via Sawteeth or Colvin (See above) may ascend Marcy, Haystack and other peaks of the Range by the trail leading NW toward Haystack. 1.50 mi. up this trail a R fork gives access to the Range Trail between Haystack and Basin following the valley of Haystack Brook. At 2.70 mi., a very steep trail leads to the summit of Haystack. Beyond this junction, the trail to Marcy descends 600 feet into Panther Gorge to join the Elk Lake–Marcy Trail (See Section B4). The distance from the Warden's Camp to Marcy's summit by this route is 5.26 mi.; ascent 4000 feet (counting loss by descent to Panther Gorge). Exit routes to Keene Valley, Lake Sanford, and Heart Lake are described in Sections B1, B5, and B6. Details follow:

Starting at the Warden's Camp (0 mi.), the trail heads NW across a flat, grassy area with little undergrowth. At 0.05 mi., a private trail now closed to the public branches L. Going straight ahead of Marcy and Haystack, the grade is easy as the trail reaches the Sawteeth trail junction at 0.16 mi., the latter trail turning R.

Going straight ahead to Marcy and Haystack, the gentle grade continues as the trail remains S of a tributary to Shanty Brook. The climbing becomes steeper at 0.45 mi. and moderates at 0.55 mi. Four small brooks are crossed at 0.60 mi. and 0.75 mi. At 0.90 mi., the Sage's Folly trail, now closed to the public, turns off to the L, and then at 1.50 mi. the trail forks again with the R fork leading via the valley of Haystack Brook to the Range trail between Haystack and Basin.

The L fork, leading to Marcy and to Haystack by the shortest route, crosses a ridge with little descent and in 0.20 mi. reaches Crystal Brook where a trail closed to the public leads L to the SW end of the Upper Ausable Lake. Crossing Crystal Brook at 1.70 mi., the trail for Marcy and Haystack starts a slow, steady climb up the side of Bartlett Ridge heading WNW. Between 2.10 mi. and the top of the ridge at 2.40 mi. there is still evidence of damage by the hurricane of 1950. At the ridge top, the trail levels off through a conifer forest. A brook is crossed at 2.50 mi. and another brook at 2.55 mi. At 2.70 mi., a junction is reached. The R fork leads steeply to the summit of Haystack in 0.60 mi., ascending 1180 feet.

Taking the L fork for Marcy, one proceeds on the level for 0.15 mi. before descending the W side of Bartlett Ridge through a conifer forest. Views of Marcy and Skylight may be had through the trees. The grade moderates a bit at 3.10 mi., then becomes steeper, finally slackening at 3.35 mi. and joining the Elk Lake–Marcy Trail at 3.45 mi. just before it crosses Marcy Brook. (Not to be confused with the Marcy Brook in the Heart Lake region.) Turn L for Elk lake, 9.00 mi. The trail for Marcy continues across the brook, 1.18 mi. to the col between Skylight and Marcy and 1.96 mi. to the summit of Marcy. (See Section B4.) Panther Gorge lean-to is 25 yards downstream on the L bank of the brook.

Distances: Warden's Camp to fork leading up Haystack Brook to the Range trail, 1.50 mi.; to fork leading to Haystack by shortest route, 2.70 mi.; to junction with the Elk Lake–Marcy Trail 3.45 mi.; to Skylight–Marcy col, 4.63 mi.; to summit of Marcy, 5.26 mi. Ascent from the Warden's Camp counting 600 feet of descent down Bartlett Ridge, 4000 feet.

It is interesting to note that the first trail to Marcy, cut by Old Mountain Phelps and other guides about 1861, followed the above described route to the junction of Bartlett Ridge with the upper slopes of Haystack where the trail to Haystack forks at 2.70 mi. From here, it descended into Panther Gorge NE of the present trail, reaching Marcy's summit via the slides E of the brook descending from the Skylight–Marcy col. It was over this trail in 1861 that Old Mountain Phelps and other guides including Henry Holt led the first women to ascend Marcy. These women were Miss Mary Cook and Miss Fanny Newton. The trail was abandoned after 1873 when men working for Verplanck Colvin's survey cut a new trail up the Marcy Brook valley and into the Skylight–Marcy col via the route of the present Elk Lake–Marcy Trail. The present trail from the Warden's Camp over Bartlett Ridge was cut about the turn of the present century.

Prior to 1950, a herd path (never a formal trail) led from the crossing of Marcy Brook through Panther Gorge to join the Phelps Trail from Keene Valley in the Marcy–Haystack col. Since the 1950 hurricane, blowdown has made travel through Panther Gorge very difficult, even by rock-hopping Marcy Brook; but views, especially of the wet weather waterfall from Marcy, are rewarding.

Haystack via Bartlett Ridge from Warden's Camp

This is the shortest and most used route from the Warden's Camp to the summit of Haystack.

Follow the trail described above to Marcy, Haystack and the

Great Range from the Warden's Camp to the spot on Bartlett Ridge at 2.70 mi. where the Marcy trail turns L to descend towards Panther Gorge. Turning R the trail heads NNE and at 2.75 mi. starts one of the steepest climbs in the mountains, ascending through a spruce and balsam forest. Timberline is reached at 3.15 mi. after which the trail is marked with cairns and paint blazes on the rocks. Care is needed in following these. Summit of Haystack is reached at 3.45 mi. (In descending by this route, the trail heads W towards Skylight and then SW towards Allen.) The view from the summit is considered to be one of the finest in the Adirondacks with about 27 major peaks discernible. (Trail straight ahead leads 0.55 mi. over Little Haystack to Range Trail. (See Section B1.)

Distances: Warden's Camp to Haystack Brook Trail to Range, 1.50 mi.; to fork leading to Marcy via Panther Gorge, 2.70 mi.; to summit of Haystack 3.45 mi. Ascent from Warden's Camp, 3100 feet.

Haystack and the Great Range via Haystack Brook Valley

Follow the trail for Marcy and Haystack from the Warden's Camp to a R fork at 1.50 mi. Turning R at this junction, the trail is fairly level with slight ups and downs through many ferns until a sharp descent is reached and a brook crossed at 2.10 mi. The trail now climbs the opposite bank through second growth grown up following a landslide. Entering first growth timber again, the trail continues to slab Haystack at an easy grade. Small brooks are crossed at 2.50 mi. and 2.55 mi. after which the trail comes near the R (W) bank of Haystack Brook at 2.65 mi. and turns upstream. After crossing a fair-sized tributary where it joins Haystack Brook at 2.70 mi., the trail starts climbing, getting progressively steeper as it ascends through a spruce and balsam forest on a beautiful duff trail. Haystack Brook is heard but not seen. A ladder is reached at 2.90 mi. followed by a short breather, then a second ladder at 2.95 mi. The trail levels off above the second ladder, crosses a brook at 3.00 mi. and soon starts climbing again. Two small ladders assist the climber at 3.20 mi. after which the trail levels off at 3.25 mi., crosses a wet spot and a brook and joins the Range Trail at the site of the former Sno-Bird lean-to at 3.35

mi. (To the R this trail leads to JBL via the Shorey Short Cut and Slant Rock Camp, 4.67 mi.; JBL via Basin and Saddleback, 5.07 mi. and much more difficult. See Keene Valley Region, Section B1.)

Going L on the Range Trail, with blue DEC markers, the trail recrosses the above brook at 3.40 mi. and starts a steep rocky climb to a trail junction at 3.80 mi. (To the R the Range Trail leads over a low summit to the Phelps Trail from JBL, 0.53 mi.; the Van Hoevenberg Trail from Adirondak Loj, 1.22 mi.; and Mt. Marcy, 1.81 mi. See Keene Valley and Heart Lake Regions.)

The trail to Haystack turns L from the Range Trail and is marked with cairns and paint blazes. It climbs steeply up the bare rock cone of Little Haystack and reaches its summit at 3.95 mi. Elevation, 4700 feet. This little peak offers a magnificent close-up view of Marcy. Between Marcy and Little Marcy on the R a glimpse of Wright Peak may be had. The trail descends steeply about 100 ft. into the spruce-filled col at 4.00 mi. and then climbs at an easier grade up the bare N ridge of Haystack, reaching the summit at 4.35 mi. (Trail S from summit is the shortest trail to the Warden's Camp; also, via a R fork 0.60 mi. down the mountain, it leads to the Elk Lake–Marcy Trail. (See above and Section B4.)

Distances: Warden's Camp to Sawteeth Trail, 0.16 mi.; to fork L leading to Marcy and shorter Haystack Trail, 1.50 mi.; to Haystack Brook, 2.65 mi.; to Range Trail, 3.35 mi.; to turnoff from Range Trail, 3.80 mi.; to Little Haystack, 3.95 mi.; to summit of Haystack, 4.35 mi. Ascent from Upper Lake, 3070 ft. Elevation 4960 ft. Order of height, 3.

The Colvin–Blake–Pinnacle Ridge to the Elk Lake–Marcy Trail

The Colvin–Blake–Pinnacle Ridge, though offering no summits with 360 degrees views, is a beautiful series of peaks covered, where winds haven't interfered, with virgin forests of spruce and balsam underlain with moss-covered rocks. The best views are from Colvin, from a lookout south of Blake and from the Pinnacle; but there are frequent narrower vistas as well—of the Ausable Lake and the Elk Lake valleys, and the higher mountains beyond.

Since the 1978 sale of land of the Adirondack Mountain Reserve to the State of New York, all land along the trail traversing this ridge south of its junction with the trail leading to Indian Head (See Section B2, Indian Head) is now public land. Though the Pinnacle Trail from Inlet Camp on the Upper Ausable Lake is now closed in its lower reaches to the public, a trail constructed in 1978 from the base of Pinnacle Mountain gives access to or from Elk Lake–Marcy Trail.

Access to the summit of Colvin is described in Section B2 as well as here in Section B3. From the summit of Colvin (0 mi.), the trail leads S practically on the level, passes a lookout on the R at 0.05 mi. and continues downward at an easy grade. It dips into a slight sag at 0.50 mi., crosses a small ridge and starts a steep descent at 0.60 mi., reaching the Colvin–Blake col and junction with trail R to Lower Lake at 0.80 mi. (Junction to Carry, 1.10 mi.)

Straight ahead the trail climbs steadily, becoming easy at 0.90 mi. and crossing a low shoulder. Very steep climbing starts at 1.00 mi., the height of a small ridge being reached at 1.25 mi., the summit of Blake Peak at 1.35 mi. Elevation 3960 ft. Order of height among the original 46 peaks, 43. The summit is wooded but views of Elk Lake may be had through the trees on the L.

Blake Peak was named for Mills Blake, Colvin's assistant and closest personal friend. The two worked and lived together for 48 years until Colvin died in 1920. Neither married and they were both free to devote their lives to the work of the Adirondack Survey. Blake's title was that of Chief Clerk and Assistant of the Adirondack survey. It is therefore very fitting that the peak next to Colvin bears his name. The old USGS topog map shows the elevation to be 4000 ft. It was therefore included in the original 46 major peaks, but more accurate survey methods have indicated it to be slightly under 4000 ft.

A minor summit of Blake is crossed at 1.40 mi. after which the trail drops into a col at 1.55 mi. The climbing is then easy over several knolls reaching Lookout Rock on the R at 1.75 mi. affording a good view of the Upper Lake with the boathouse directly below. The first summit S of Blake is reached at 1.80 mi. and in another 40 yards the trail passes through the "lemon squeezer" (two large boulders on either side of the trail). The trail now descends gradually, reaching a lookout through the trees on the L, slightly off the trail, toward Elk Lake at 2.10 mi. The descent becomes steep at 2.20 mi., reaching a col with many ferns and a slight level stretch at 2.40 mi. The trail climbs steeply from the col but soon starts to descend, becoming quite steep at 2.60 mi. and reaches the next col at 2.85 mi. A steep pitch leads over a shoulder of the third summit at 2.90 mi. followed by a descent to the next col, which is reached at 3.20 mi. The trail reaches another summit at 3.50 mi. and gradually descends to another col at 3.70 mi. At 3.75 mi. a junction is reached with the spur trail leading L which climbs steeply at first, then more gently to reach the summit of the Pinnacle at 3.95 mi.

From the trail junction below the Pinnacle summit at 3.75 mi. from the summit of Colvin, the trail descends moderately, then steeply to a point at 4.31 mi. where a trail closed to the public leads off R to the Upper Ausable Lake. Turning L at this point, the trail descends with steep pitches to a flat area beyond which a steep descent leads to a beautiful brook below a waterfall reached at 4.70 mi. This is a possible campsite. From the brook crossing, the trail climbs gently, slabbing the L hillside to an area of rough hiking among boulders. It rounds a rocky prominence at 4.96 mi. and soon reaches easier and more or less level walking to a brook crossing at 5.24 mi. Another larger brook is crossed at 5.29 mi. beyond which lies the junction with the Elk Lake–Marcy Trail at 5.35 mi. from the summit of Colvin.

This junction is 8.87 mi. from the road to the Lower Ausable Lake (See Section B2, Mt. Colvin from Lake Road) and 11.62 mi. from the Ausable Club.

The junction is also 5.99 mi. from the summit of Marcy and 4.97 mi. from Elk Lake, both via the Elk Lake–Marcy Trail (See Section B4).

Distances: Lake Road to summit of Colvin, 3.52 mi.; Summit of Colvin to Colvin–Blake col and junction with trail R to Lower Lake, 0.80 mi.; to summit of Blake, 1.35 mi.; to Lookout Rock, 1.75 mi.; to summit of Pinnacle, 3.95 mi.; to junction with the Elk Lake–Marcy Trail, 5.35 mi. Ascent from the Lake Road, about 3850 ft.; from the Ausable Club, 4500 ft.

The Tammy Stowe Memorial Trail

This trail was constructed in 1976 in memory of Mrs. Putman Stowe who was a summer resident for many years on the Upper Ausable Lake.

Turning R from the Sawteeth trail from the Upper Ausable Lake (See above), at 0.80 mi. from Shanty Brook and 0.96 mi. from the Warden's Camp, this trail heads E pretty much on the level through a notch. After about 0.25 mi., it turns L as it approaches the steep bluff to the N from its E side. Climbing is gradual at first but soon becomes steep. A fork in the trail offers alternate routes, the R fork presenting spectacular climbing on log ramps, the L fork by-passing this rather difficult passage. The trail reaches the ridge top at about 0.75 mi. from the Sawteeth Trail and descends a short distance W to an opening which offers a spectacular view of the Upper Ausable Lake. A short distance down the ridge, a side trail to the L leads to a fine view of Basin and Haystack. Slabbing northerly down the ridge, the Stowe Trail joins the Sawteeth Trail in a surprisingly short distance. This is at a point about 1.50 mi. from the Warden's Camp, 2.00 mi. via the Stowe Trail.

Distances: From point of departure from the Sawteeth Trail to regaining it, 1.00 mi. Round trip from the Warden's Camp, about 3.50 mi.

APPENDIX TO SECTION B3

The following is a reprint of an article entitled "The Sale of ADK Reserve Lands to N.Y.S." by Jim Goodwin, appearing in 1978 in the *Adirondac*, which summarizes the history of this area, events leading up to the recent sale of the property, and the present status of recreational activities thereon.

On June 10th, 1978, on the summit of Noonmark and in the presence of some 80 people, Peter A. Berle, Commissioner of the

Department of Environmental Conservation, and Morgan K. Smith, Chairman of the Board of the Adirondack Mountain Reserve (AMR) exchanged documents to complete the sale of approximately 9000 acres of higher level land by the AMR to the State of New York.

Behind this event lay many years of significant conservation history. In 1887, five years before the New York State Legislature created the Adirondack Park and nine years prior to creation of the State's "Forever Wild" policy, a group of summer residents in the Keene Valley–St. Huberts area learned that the land around Ausable Lakes was about to be lumbered. Wishing to preserve these beautiful lakes from the scourge of the lumberman's axe, they proceeded to buy not only the lakes and their surrounding land, but also additional land stretching from Dix to Indian Falls, including the summit of Marcy and the upper Johns Brook Valley. Their purchase became known as the Adirondack Mountain Reserve. In 1920, thanks to a large bond issue voted by the New York State Legislature, the State bought much of the land thus preserved, leaving the Adirondack Mountain Reserve bounded by the summits of the Great Range and the Colvin–Nipple Top ranges as far as the top of Noonmark. The sale on June 10th reduced the AMR to 7000 acres of low land, which still includes both Ausable Lakes and land between them, and the Ausable Club Clubhouse.

The June 10th purchase gave the State ownership of most of 14 mountains, 12 of which were over 4000 feet in altitude. These latter peaks were Haystack, Basin, Saddleback, Gothics, Armstrong, Upper Wolf Jaws, Lower Wolf Jaws, Sawteeth, Blake, Colvin, Nipple Top and Dial. The two lower peaks are Bear Den and Noonmark. The boundary line between AMR and State land is now, in general, at the 2500-foot level, in most cases 0.50 to a mile in trail distance above the valley floor.

Along with the sale of land, the AMR gave the State of New York permanent easements to the effect that no further development beyond maintenance of present structures can take place within the present Reserve. This assures that the land will remain "forever wild" open space. The easement also grants to the State permanent rights of way for foot travel by the public over all trails on Reserve land north of the Warden's Camp on the Upper Ausable

Lake. However, all trails around and approaching the Upper Ausable Lake described in the Ninth Edition of the *Guide to Adirondack Trails*, 1977 edition, in Section B3 are now, by agreement, closed to the public. Trails from the Elk Lake–Marcy trail to Panorama Bluff, and to Mud Pond Landing on the inlet, are also closed (described in Section B4 of the *Guide*). This closing has resulted from complaints by owners of camps on the Upper Lake that some hikers have been camping illegally in the area and in some instances breaking into and burglarizing buildings.

It should also be noted that use of the trails inside the Reserve which are open to the public is limited to the extent that fire building, camping, off-trail hiking, rock climbing, boating, hunting, fishing, and bringing along pets are prohibited. There is no trail along the Lower Ausable Lake. Bushwhacking is not allowed and no boats are available for rent. Hence, those reaching the southwestern-upper-end of the Lower Ausable Lake may reach St. Huberts or Keene Valley only by climbing over Colvin, or from the Warden's Camp by way of Sawteeth, the Great Range, or Marcy.

Two trails open to the public do cross the Adirondack Mountain Reserve in the vicinity of the Upper Ausable Lake, connecting the Marcy–Great Range area and the Colvin–Blake–Pinnacle Ridge. One is the trail from Marcy and Haystack to Colvin and Blake via the Warden's Camp and the carry between the two lakes with connections from the Great Range trail between Basin and Haystack, and a trail from Sawteeth (described in Section B3 of this new reprinting of the *Guide*). The other is a trail leading from the Elk Lake–Marcy trail 0.25 miles east of its crossing of the inlet to the Upper Ausable Lake. This mile of newly-constructed trail on State land crosses two brook valleys to join an older trail 0.85 miles from the top of the Pinnacle. From here, the Blake Peak and the Colvin–Pinnacle Ridge Trail leads to St. Huberts either directly by way of the Gill Brook–Indian Head trail complex, or by way of Nipple Top, Dial, and Bear Den mountains.

The trail between the Pinnacle and Colvin, though offering few wide angle views south of Colvin, is a fascinating ridge route amid lush vegetation with many narrow-angle vistas. There is no dependable water between the brook crossing at the base of Pinnacle Mountain and Gill Brook.

As formerly, hikers using the approaches to and through the Adirondack Mountain Reserve are required to park their cars in a parking lot on AMR land a short distance up the road across Route 73 from the start of the Roaring Brook–Giant Trail. This is about half a mile from the Ausable Club Clubhouse. Though most of Noonmark is now State-owned, its approach trail, along with the trail to Dix, crosses private land for about half a mile.

The road from the Clubhouse to the Lower Ausable Lake is closed to private vehicles, including bicycles, but is open to foot travel. During July and August, the Ausable Club operates a bus over this road hourly between 9:00 A.M. and 5:00 P.M. The public is welcome to ride this bus for the fare of $1.00 each way. Tickets may be purchased in the lobby of the Clubhouse.

In short, as in the past, the public may continue to use most Adirondack Mountain Reserve trails with certain restrictions on trail use. Now, with the new purchase of land by the State, they may camp on State land above the AMR boundary line which is located in general at the 2500 foot level. Camping here is limited only by DEC restrictions. The dividing line lies one half to one mile above the valley floor and is well-marked. Access to the Upper Ausable Lake, however, is now closed to the public.

SECTION B4

ELK LAKE REGION

To reach the Elk Lake Trail System, leave the Adirondack Northway (Interstate 87) at exit 29 (0.2 mi. beyond milepost 94), and travel W on the Blue Ridge Road 4 mi. Turn N on a dirt road marked by a sign and proceed 5.2 mi. to a parking lot near the lake where cars may be parked. Much of this area in the vicinity of Elk Lake and surrounding the parking lot is private, and hikers are allowed to use the trails to Marcy, Dix and Boreas mountains, but the building of fires, camping, hunting, fishing and off-trail hiking are not permitted except to Elk Lake Lodge patrons. These restrictions do not apply to trailless ascents of Macomb, South Dix, East Dix and Hough because they are on State Land. The map that accompanies this *Guide* shows the point at which the trails from the parking lot reach the Public State Land. During the hunting season, all trails in the vicinity of Elk Lake are closed to the public.

Hikers in the vicinity should sign the DEC register at the parking lot and note their objective. They should also sign out when they return. This is a precaution for their own safety in case of an accident in the woods. The Marcy, Dix and Boreas Trails are maintained by the DEC, a total of about 24 mi.

Trails Described	Year Measured	Total Miles
Elk Lake–Marcy Trail	1965*	10.96
Dix via Hunters Pass from Elk Lake Road	1955**	7.31
Dix via Yellow Trail from Lumber Clearing	1955	2.26
Boreas Mt. from Clear Pond	1955	3.21

* Four Corners to Marcy measured in 1954.
** Elk Lake Road to Slide Brook clearing remeasured 1961.

Elk Lake–Marcy Trail

Leaving the DEC sign posts across the road from the parking lot (0 mi.), the trail, marked with blue disks, climbs through second growth conifer trees over a hill and descends to a suspension bridge across the Branch (the outlet to Elk Lake) at 0.38 mi. At 0.51 mi., it strikes a gravel lumber road, turns L to cross Nellie Brook, and then leaves the road, turning R at 0.52 mi. The trail climbs steeply, then levels off and turns sharp L on an old lumber road at 0.71 mi., finally turning R at 0.75 mi. on a gravel lumber road which it now follows for 1.61 mi. through a recently lumbered area. Taking a R fork at 1.05 mi., the trail crosses Nellie Brook at 1.08 mi. and climbs over a ridge, descending to cross Guideboard Brook at 1.74 mi. At 1.96 mi., a private trail from the R comes in from Elk Lake Lodge. Taking a R fork of the lumber road at 2.21 mi., the trail reaches a point at 2.36 mi. where it leaves the gravel lumber road, turning L.

The trail climbs over a hill and descends to Guideboard Brook, striking it just below a beaver dam at 2.65 mi. Passing the beaver pond on its E side, the trail crosses the main branch of Guideboard Brook at the head of the pond at 2.77 mi. It then crosses and recrosses a tributary following up the valley of the latter stream on its NE side. Intersecting an old wood road at 2.83 mi., it turns sharp L from the wood road at 2.84 mi. in a raspberry patch. The trail then climbs with steep pitches to where it intersects the main valley of Guideboard Brook shortly below the top of the pass through the Boreas–Colvin Range, reached at 3.34 mi. (Elevation, 2650 ft.) Now descending moderately through a lumbered area a small brook may be found at 3.45 mi. as the trail makes its way up and down along the mountainside in a NW direction. An overgrown lumber road is crossed near a corduroy bridge at 3.98 mi., followed by easy ups and downs and then a moderate climb to another height of land at 4.26 mi. (Elevation, 2590 ft.) Descending steadily at a fair grade, a view of Marcy may be had at 4.55 mi. as the trail continues descending, crosses a wide lumber "thruway" and reaches the edge of an old lumber camp clearing that is now almost unrecognizable at 4.73 mi.

Turning sharp L past the ruins of the lumber camp, the trail turns R again around the end of a long tumbled-down building at 4.76 mi. and joins a wide lumber road at 4.86 mi. Turning L and then R at 4.88 mi., the trail leaves the lumber road and crosses the property line of the Adirondack Mountain Reserve at 4.91 mi. Now descending moderately, the trail crosses another trail at 5.14 mi. near the inlet to the Upper Ausable Lake. The latter is a private trail of the AMR.

Crossing the inlet at 5.19 mi. (elevation, 1994 ft.) on a large log, the trail continues NW across a swamp with many corduroys, making travel difficult. The footing improves at 5.58 mi., and the trail finally slopes up out of the swamp at 5.65 mi., levels off and then climbs at an easy grade. At about 6.10 mi. the grade steepens, climbing becomes steady and a trail junction is reached at 6.48 mi. (Trail R is the private ATIS trail leading 1.25 mi. to Marcy Landing on the Upper Ausable Lake.)

Continuing straight ahead through a hardwood forest over fairly level ground, the trail enters the State Forest Preserve and reaches a fair pitch up at 6.61 mi. A second pitch is reached at 6.93 mi., the trail then leveling off through a conifer forest. A large boulder resembling a whale is passed on the L at 7.34 mi., and a small brook from the R is crossed at 7.37 mi. After passing a painted BM on the L at 7.50 mi., the trail crosses a fair-sized brook on logs at 7.56 mi. A small bog is traversed shortly before Marcy Brook (not to be confused with the brook of the same name at Marcy Dam) comes into view at 7.79 mi. Following up the L bank of Marcy Brook on a tote road, the trail turns sharp R away from the brook at 7.83 mi. and swings L along the course of the brook. The trail looks down on Marcy Brook and comes to the confluence of two tributaries at 8.27 mi. Crossing both brooks (PBM 3012 ft. on large rock between brooks), the trail again looks down on Marcy Brook and crosses another tributary. Entering a thick conifer forest at 8.66 mi., the trail comes in behind Panther Gorge lean-to on Marcy Brook at 9.00 mi. There is a large pool located here which may be used for a dip. Shortly past the lean-to, the ATIS trail from Bartlett Ridge and Haystack enters on the R at 9.02 mi. (This leads 1.35 mi. to the summit of Haystack. See Upper Ausable Lake Region, Section B3.)

The blue trail turns left across Marcy Brook and climbs 1100 ft. within the next mile. The grade varies, sometimes moderate to easy, sometimes steep. After crossing a tributary from L at 9.11 mi., the trail ascends a steep pitch and soon enters a blowdown area. After another steep stretch, the grade becomes moderate to easy at 9.38 mi. and reaches another pitch at 9.71 mi. where the trail is quite rocky. There is a good view of Haystack and Marcy through the trees at the top of the pitch. The trail continues climbing steadily, eroded here and there in the brook bed and levels off at 10.03 mi. The going is now easy as the trail crosses a brook just before reaching the former Four Corners lean-to and a trail junction at 10.18 mi. (PBM 4348 ft.) End of blue markers. (The trail L with red markers leads 0.52 mi. to summit of Skylight. The yellow trail straight ahead is the Sanford Lake–Marcy Trail and connects with trails to Lake Colden. See Sanford Lake Region, Section B5.)

Turning R with yellow markers towards the N, the trail to Marcy climbs steadily up a rocky and eroded stream bed which is frequently quite wet. At 10.37 mi. there is a big boulder on the L which has split away from the mountain forming a crevice. A few yds. through this crevice there is a lookout toward Gray Peak. The grade moderates at 10.41 mi. but soon steepens again, the footing in many places being over bare granite. A good lookout on the R is reached at 10.61 mi. with views over Panther Gorge toward Haystack. The timberline is reached at 10.65 mi. A prominence known as Schofield Cobble is crossed at 10.72 mi. where the trail dips slightly. Water can sometimes be found in the sag to the L of the trail. Here the final steep climb begins up the bare rock cone to the summit of Marcy at 10.96 mi. Above the timberline the trail is marked with small rock cairns, and in fog or rain great care is needed in following this part of the trail.

Distances: Elk Lake to Nellie Brook Trail, 0.64 mi.; to height of land in pass between Pinnacle and Boreas, 3.34 mi.; to second height of land, 4.26 mi.; to old lumber camp, 4.73 mi.; to ATIS Panorama Bluff–Mud Pond Landing Trail, 5.14 mi.; to Upper Ausable Lake Inlet, 5.19 mi.; to Panther Gorge lean-to, 9.00 mi.; to ATIS Haystack Trail, 9.02 mi.; to trail junction at the site of the former Four Corners lean-to, 10.18 mi.; to the summit of Marcy,

10.96 mi. Ascent, 3350 ft. from Ausable Inlet, 4200 ft. from Elk
Lake. Elevation, 5344 ft. Order of height, 1.

Dix via Hunters Pass

There are two DEC trails to the summit of Dix from Elk Lake,
both coinciding for the first 4.33 mi. on the E side of the East
Inlet. The route marked with red DEC discs leaves the parking
lot (0 mi.) and joins a tote road that comes in from the R at 0.51
mi. It crosses Little Sally Brook at 0.59 mi. and, continuing to the
NE at an almost level grade, reaches a height of land at about
1.00 mi.

From here the grade is slightly down or almost level, the trail
swinging R at 1.53 mi. where there is a good view of the slides
on Macomb through the opening in the trees. Big Sally Brook is
crossed at 1.61 mi., and the dirt lumber road ends at another brook
crossing at 1.69 mi. From here the lumber road becomes a wet,
soggy, grassy tote road at a section where there was a stretch of
corduroy footbridge before lumbering spoiled the old trail. The
wet section ends as the trail branches R from the grassy tote road
at 1.84 mi. and follows the old route, crossing a yellow property
line into the State Forest Preserve at 1.88 mi.

PBM 2290 ft. in the middle of the trail is passed at 1.94 mi.
and a fair-sized brook is crossed at 1.98 mi., soon followed by a
mudhole section. The foot of the big slide on the R is reached as
the trail crosses the first of three orange-colored brooks (results
of the slide) at 2.16 mi. This slide, which came down from Macomb
in 1947, has several branches, all of which offer a route up the
mountain. The third brook is crossed at 2.22 mi. at the foot of
another branch of the slide. (The lower regions of the slide are
overgrown and the general course of the various branches of the
slide are no longer easily discernible.) A good-sized brook which
is crossed at 2.25 mi. provides a ready access to the route of the
slide. (See Trailless Peaks, Sect. C, for ascent of Macomb.)

The marked trail reaches a small clearing on the L, and a
brook is crossed at 2.32 mi. Slide Brook lean-to is found on the
far side of the brook on the L at the edge of Slide Brook Clearing.

There has been some question as to which brook, the one at 2.25 mi. or the one at 2.32 mi., is Slide Brook. In reality both are Slide Brook since by unusual circumstance Slide Brook divides in its downward course about 0.2 mi. E of the trail and forms these two branches, both of which ultimately flow into the East Inlet of Elk Lake.

Another brook is crossed at the far edge of Slide Brook Clearing at 2.40 mi. after which the trail continues descending at a moderate grade to 2.48 mi. From here the trail climbs gradually, crossing a brook from the R at 2.66 mi. and passing a painted BM (2387.8 ft.) on the R at 2.84 mi. A rock cairn on the R at 3.10 mi. marks the beginning of a route up Hough Peak via the old tote road. The trail continues ascending gradually and reaches the height of land at 3.19 mi., after which it descends at an easy to moderate grade. A small brook is crossed at 3.38 mi. soon after which the downgrade becomes steeper, reaching another small brook at 3.53 mi. where the grade levels off. Continuing an easy descent, a lean-to (1959) on the L is reached just before crossing Lillian Brook at 3.66 mi., where there is a nice pool for a dip.

Climbing steadily from the brook, the grade rounds off at 3.76 mi., soon starts down at a moderate grade and passes PBM 2320 ft. on the L at 3.83 mi. A steep down pitch is reached at 3.87 mi., followed by rough going up and down along Dix Pond but at some distance above the pond. The trail descends close to the shore near the end of the Pond at 4.10 mi. and enters the first of two lumber clearings side by side at 4.27 mi. Passing into the second and larger clearing, a trail junction at the side of the clearing is reached at 4.33 mi. (Yellow trail R is an alternative route up Dix, climbing 2600 ft. in 2.26 mi. See below.)

Continuing straight ahead with the red markers, the longer trail (2.98 mi.) heads N toward Hunters Pass, leaves the clearing in a few yds., and crosses to the R bank (Nipple Top side) of the East Inlet at 4.43 mi. A fireplace is located here. Following the brook, the trail starts climbing steadily at about 4.60 mi. and reaches a painted BM (2465.4 ft.) at 4.79 mi. The going becomes easy again as the trail passes through many small clearings quite a way above the main stream. An excellent tributary (may be the last water) is crossed at 5.49 mi. just before entering the last clearing. There is a fireplace here. Leaving the clearing at 5.52 mi., the trail comes close to the main brook bed at 5.63 mi. and passes a vertical rock face on the L at 5.80 mi. where there is a steep ascent to 5.87 mi. Continuing at a moderate grade, a spring is passed at 6.00 mi. and PBM 3234 ft. is reached at 6.12 mi. near the height of land in the rock-strewn pass.

Crossing to the other side of the pass the trail commences the very steep ascent of Dix, climbing 1623 ft. in the next 1.19 mi. Two interesting overhanging rocks and an inviting chimney are passed shortly after leaving the PBM. Swinging to the L the climbing is exceedingly steep along the foot of a cliff. As altitude is gained, the trail swings around to the R and levels off at 6.28 mi. The respite is short lived as the struggle with the mountain starts in again, and the trail climbs very steeply along the foot of another cliff. A short, level stretch heading S leads to a breathtaking view over a ledge toward Nipple Top at 6.48 mi. "Balanced Rock" lookout is reached at 6.54 mi. Still climbing steadily, another very steep pitch is soon reached followed by a breather and then fairly steep climbing to a painted BM (4371.4 ft.) a few yds. before the junction with the blue trail from St. Huberts at 6.89 mi. (Trail L leads 6.28 mi. to Ausable Club Road. See St. Huberts Region, Sect. B2.)

Turning R with blue markers, the climbing continues steadily up the ridge through the scrub spruce, getting steeper at 6.97 mi. and rounding off at 7.14 mi. as the long bare crest of the summit is approached. A Coast and Geodetic Survey Triangulation Station is passed on the L at 7.26 mi. and the Colvin bolt on the summit, placed here in 1873 by Verplanck Colvin, is reached at 7.31 mi. The views are unobstructed in all directions. Elk Lake with its many islands lies to the SW, Lake Champlain and the Green Mts. to the E, and to the NW one looks over Nipple Top to the high peaks of the Great Range. (The trail straight ahead leads over the Beck-horn (pointed peak at end of ridge) and descends very steeply 2.26 mi. to the big lumber clearing mentioned above.)

Distances: Elk Lake Road to Slide Brook Clearing, 2.33 mi.; to tote road turnoff for Hough Peak, 3.10 mi.; to height of land, 3.19 mi.; to lean-to at Lillian Brook, 3.66 mi.; to Dix Pond, 4.10 mi.; to yellow trail in lumber clearing, 4.33 mi.; to East Inlet crossing, 4.43 mi.; to Hunters Pass PBM, 6.12 mi.; to St. Huberts Trail, 6.89 mi.; to summit of Dix, 7.31 mi. Ascent: 3000 ft. from Elk Lake Road; 2600 ft. from lumber clearing; 1623 ft. from Hunters Pass. Elevation, 4875 ft. Order of height, 6.

Dix via Yellow Trail from Lumber Clearing

Take the red-marked Dix Trail from Elk Lake to the trail junction in the large lumber clearing at 4.33 mi. (See above.) Leaving the junction (0 mi.), the trail heads NE climbing the ridge on a traverse through a hardwood forest at a moderate to fairly steep grade, reaching a short easy stretch at 0.29 mi. At 0.51 mi. the trail reaches a brook and climbs in and out of the brook bed to 0.60 mi. where the grade eases momentarily only to be followed by a fairly steep pitch. The grade moderates at about 0.66 mi. Steep climbing starts again through birch and balsam at 0.88 mi., followed by a short respite before a very steep pitch at 1.01 mi., which leads up to a lookout back toward Elk Lake and Clear Pond. Still climbing steeply, the trail offers a couple of breathers before rounding off at 1.29 mi. and dropping into a slight sag at 1.50 mi.

Looking up to Hough indicates there is still climbing to be done. After two steep pitches, the trail rounds off at 1.67 mi. and drops into a slight sag at 1.74 mi. Stiff climbing continues with some moderations and several steep pitches before coming out on the rocks at 2.04 mi. Following paint blazes, the trail climbs up the rocks and reaches the Beck-horn at 2.09 mi., a name given by Old Mountain Phelps because of its resemblance to the beckiron on a blacksmith's anvil. Continuing S of the rocks, the trail drops into a sag, climbs through blueberry bushes and reaches the Colvin bolt on the summit of 2.26 mi.

Distance: Lumber clearing to summit of Dix, 2.26 mi. (6.59 from Elk Lake Road). Ascent from clearing, 2600 ft. Elevation, 4875 ft. Order of height, 6.

Boreas Mt. from Clear Pond

The fire tower on this mountain has been abandoned and is unsafe to climb. It was to have been removed in 1976. However, by walking around the summit splendid views both to west and to the east may be obtained. The trail starts from the Elk Lake

Road, 3.30 mi. N of the Blue Ridge Road (2.1 mi. S of Elk Lake Lodge). It is marked by a DEC sign in a grassy field just after crossing Clear Pond outlet. Cars may be parked here. Recent lumbering operations have forced considerable relocation of the central section of this trail.

Leaving the road the trail, marked with red DEC markers, heads westerly across the field and enters the woods, a mixture of hardwoods and conifers. At 0.12 mi. it begins a gradual descent, losing about 100 ft. before it reaches an old gravel lumber road at 0.34 mi., turns left and crosses the Branch (Elk Lake outlet) on an old log bridge. Continuing on the lumber road, it crosses a small stream on logs at 0.84 mi., passes a clearing at 0.90 mi. and at 1.10 mi. joins a road from the R in a clearing. (This is the Boreas Trail leading back to Elk Lake Lodge 2.20 mi. The condition of this trail is not reported.) Continuing straight ahead, the trail becomes grassy, draws near a stream at 1.24 mi. and at 1.27 mi. turns abruptly L up a short pitch of trail to join a recent gravel lumber road on which it turns R. It follows this unattractive road for the next mile ascending at a steady but moderate grade. At 1.51 mi. there is a road branching L, the trail continuing straight ahead. A stream is crossed at 1.53 mi., and views of the fire tower on the summit are seen at 1.67 mi. and 1.74 mi. Another road enters from the R at 1.78 mi., and a stream from the R is crossed at 1.94 mi. Just beyond this, the tower is seen straight ahead. Another road diverges L at 2.18 mi., and the observer's cabin in a grassy clearing is reached at 2.33 mi. The trail goes around the cabin to the L, crosses a stream of good water and at 2.35 mi. begins to ascend. At first the grade is moderate, but after crossing a stream from the R at 2.63 mi., it becomes moderately steep. A brook from the L is crossed at 2.66 mi., and the grade eases briefly at 2.71 mi. but soon becomes steeper. Still climbing steadily, a spring is passed on the L at 2.90 mi. At 3.09 mi. the climb becomes quite steep, easing off at 3.12 mi., and at 3.16 mi. the crest of the ridge is reached. The trail swings L and S along the ridge through the conifer woods, coming to the summit at 3.24 mi.

Distances: Elk Lake Road to the Branch, 0.35 mi.; to the big gravel lumber road, 1.28 mi.; to the observer's cabin, 2.33 mi.; to the summit of Boreas, 3.24 mi. Ascent from the road, 1925 ft. Elevation, 3776 ft.

Wallface from Scott Clearing
Photo by Tom Dunn

SECTION B5

SANFORD LAKE REGION

Sanford Lake and the mining area of Tahawus can be reached by turning NE from Route 28N on a road at the National Lead Company sign, 7.30 mi. N of Aiden Lair. Another approach is from Schroon River on Rt. 9 and exit 29 (at 94.2 mi.) of the Northway via Blue Ridge Road which joins the above road about 1.6 mi. NE of Route 28N at the site of the Old Tahawus Post Office where David Henderson built the lower works of the old MacIntyre Works. (**Note:** Beyond here there seems to be no place for camping along the road or at the points where the trails begin. Refer to the map which accompanies this *Guide* to see where the trails reach State land where camping is allowed.) Continuing N from the junction, the road crosses the railroad tracks and the Hudson River at 6 mi. and comes to a fork at the W end of the bridge across Sanford Lake. Across the Bridge is the mining area of the MacIntyre development of the Titanium Division of the National Lead Company. The village of Tahawus was moved to Newcomb in 1965 after rich deposits were discovered under the site. The whole area around Sanford Lake is a desert of mine tailings.

Take the L fork at the Sanford Lake bridge (0 mi.) for the road to the parking lot beyond the old Tahawus Club at the Upper Works (3.5 mi.). A parking lot on the L for the trail to Duck Hole via Bradley Pond is reached at 2.0 mi. The parking lot on the R at 3.0 mi. is for the Opalescent River–Twin Brook Trail to Marcy.

2.80 mi. N from the bridge one of the old 1854 MacIntyre Iron Works' furnaces still stands with trees growing from it. The former Tahawus Club trails have been opened to the public through the courtesy of the National Lead Company, but the building of fires, camping, hunting, fishing and off-trail hiking are not permitted on their property or on the adjacent land belonging to the Finch, Pruyn and Company, Inc.

Trails Described	Year Measured	Total Miles
Mt. Marcy via Opalescent River and Twin Brook	1956	11.37
Skylight from former Four Corners lean-to-site	1955	0.52
Mt. Marcy via Hanging Spear Falls and Flowed Lands	1956	13.74
Mt. Marcy via Calamity Brook from Upper Works	1956	10.11
Indian Pass from Upper Works	1955	4.42
Indian Pass–Calamity Brook Crossover	1955	2.14
Duck Hole via Bradley Pond	1958	8.52
Duck Hole via Henderson Lake from Upper Works	1958	6.93
Duck Hole and Cold River from Coreys and Axton	1958	10.31
Shattuck Clearing from Coreys and Axton via Calkins Creek Truck Trail	1970	10.69
Shattuck Clearing from Coreys via the Stony Creek Horseback Assembly Area	1976	11.23
Horse Trail along SE side of Cold River Valley	1976	9.50
Santanoni Preserve Trails	1976	
Moose Pond Horse Trail		11.5 (est.)
Newcomb Lake to Cold River Horse Trail		11 (est.)

Mt. Marcy via Opalescent River and Twin Brook
(Sanford Lake–Marcy Trail)

Because of mining operations, this trail now starts from a parking lot on the old Tahawus Club Road on the W side of Sanford Lake, 2.80 mi. N of the junction at the Sanford Lake bridge and 0.20 mi. beyond the old MacIntyre Iron Works' furnace. There are DEC signs and a register. This Marcy Trail has yellow DEC markers.

Leaving the parking lot, the trail goes southeasterly on a dirt road. At 0.10 mi. where the road reaches the Hudson River it turns R and at 0.12 mi. crosses the river on a suspension bridge. Trending S by E, the trail joins roads entering from the L at 0.40 and 0.50 mi. At 0.58 mi. it crosses the N end of Lake Jimmy on a log and plank bridge. At 0.75 mi. the abandoned Mt. Adams Trail continues straight ahead and the Marcy Trail goes R trending southerly. A brook from the R is crossed on a log bridge at 0.98 mi. and at 1.07 mi. a swampy area is crossed on corduroy. At 1.22 mi. the trail joins a gravel lumber road from the L and at 1.40 mi. it turns sharp L on another gravel road, turning sharp R from this road at 1.45 mi. The trail now follows the NE shore of Lake Sally with occasional glimpses of the lake through the trees. At 1.88 mi. there is a last view of the lake, and the trail goes SE. At 2.62 mi. it reaches the Opalescent with a view of the stream. The trail now follows an old tote road, crossing a marshy area on bridges at 2.77 mi. and coming to the edge of the river at 2.82 mi. Continuing easterly, now near the river and a distance from it, the trail joins a gravel lumber road at 3.66 mi. Continuing on the gravel road, the trail branches R at 3.75 mi. and crosses the Opalescent on a suspension bridge at 3.82 mi., joining the old Buckley tote road at 3.87 mi. Going L on the tote road with a slight upgrade, a corduroy bridge is crossed at 4.17 mi. and lookouts L toward Mt. Adams are reached at 4.77 mi. and 4.80 mi. Still following the tote road, Lower Twin Brook is crossed on a corduroy bridge at 4.90 mi. A trail junction at Twin Brook lean-to is reached at 5.14 mi., having gained only about 200 ft. in elevation from the parking lot. (Trail L with red markers in front of the lean-to is an alternative route to Marcy via Hanging Spear Falls, Flowed Lands and Lake Colden, rejoining the yellow trail near Buckley's Clearing. It is 2.63 mi. longer but more interesting. Follow this trail 0.04 mi. for water. See below.)

Taking the R fork with yellow markers, the trail follows up the course of Upper Twin Brook still on the level. A small tributary is crossed at 5.39 mi. and a N-S gravel lumber road is crossed at 5.43 mi. The trail starts up an easy grade at about 5.65 mi., crosses a small brook from R at 5.72 mi. as the grade becomes moderate and joins a tote road at 5.86 mi. Turning R with tote road the trail branches R from tote road at 5.92 mi. and recrosses it at 5.95 mi. From here the climbing becomes fairly steady up a fair grade with occasional moderate and easy stretches as the hardwoods give way to the conifers, but the footing is quite treacherous, especially in wet weather due to slanting, slippery corduroys. A tributary is crossed at 6.25 mi. as Upper Twin Brook is heard below on the L. The trail crosses to the R bank of Upper Twin Brook at 6.69 mi., crosses back to the L bank at 6.95 mi. and recrosses to the R bank at 7.28 mi. A tributary is crossed at 7.34 mi. as the grade becomes easy to moderate with occasional steeper sections. Another small brook crossing is reached at 7.69 mi. and then the climbing becomes steady up a rocky, eroded trail. A short breather is reached at 7.83 mi. as the footing becomes better, and the trail levels off through the col between Cliff Mt. rising sheer on the L and a spur of Mt. Redfield on the R at 8.06 mi. Starting down, the trail descends easy to moderate grades over more corduroys, passes through what is known as Buckley's Clearing, though now much overgrown, at about 8.33 mi. and comes to a trail junction at 8.45 mi. where the red trail mentioned above enters on the L from Lake Colden. (BM 3266.7 ft. painted on rock.) Continuing R on the level with yellow markers, Uphill lean-to is reached at 8.52 mi. and Uphill Brook. As the trail follows up the course of the Opalescent River, a marshy section with logs is passed at 8.67 mi. and a trail junction is reached at 9.01 mi. where Feldspar Brook joins the Opalescent from the R. (Blue trail L leads across Feldspar Brook with side trail across Opalescent to nearby Feldspar lean-to and 6.85 mi. to Adirondak Loj. See Heart Lake Region, Section B6.)

Continuing with yellow markers, fairly steep climbing starts at 9.10 mi. as the trail follows up the course of Feldspar Brook through a dark forest of spruce, balsam and white cedar. Some of the latter are quite large. A tributary from the R is crossed at 9.11 mi. The trail is very rocky and eroded with many exposed roots as the grade alternately moderates and steepens. A BM (3686 ft.) painted on a tree is passed at 9.36 mi., and the grade moderates as the footing becomes better at 9.42 mi. The going gets rough again at 9.51 mi. as the trail is high above the L bank of Feldspar Brook. The grade becomes easier at 9.81 mi. shortly before passing a spring and levels off at 10.00 mi., brook level being reached at the foot of Lake Tear of the Clouds, highest lake source of the Hudson River, at 10.25 mi., elevation 4346 ft. Across this little body of water, fringed with spruce and balsam, the rocky dome of Tahawus (Mt. Marcy) rises in clear view. The trail forks at a large boulder at 10.27 mi., the L branch continuing along the S shore of the lake. The R branch ascends the bank and passes in front of the former Lake Tear lean-to site at 10.30 mi. Descending to the lakeshore route at 10.32 mi., the trail continues mostly on the level until it reaches the trail junction at the former Four Corners lean-to site at 10.59 mi. This marks the divide between the St. Lawrence and Hudson watersheds. (Blue trail straight ahead leads 10.18 mi. to Elk Lake and connects with trails to Upper Ausable Lake. See Elk Lake Region, Section B4. Red trail R towards the S leads 0.52 mi. to summit of Skylight. See below.)

Turning L with yellow markers towards the N the trail to Marcy climbs steadily up a rocky and eroded stream bed which is frequently quite wet. At 10.78 mi. there is a big boulder on the L which has split away from the mountain forming a crevice. A few yards through this crevice there is a lookout toward Gray Peak. The grade moderates at 10.82 mi. but soon steepens again, the footing in many places being over bare granite. A good lookout on R is reached at 11.02 mi. with views over Panther Gorge towards Haystack, and timberline is reached at 11.06 mi. A prominence known as Schofield Cobble is crossed at 11.13 mi. where the trail dips slightly. Water can sometimes be found in the sag to the L of the trail. Here the final steep climb begins up the bare rock cone to the summit of Marcy at 11.37 mi. Above timberline the trail is marked with small rock cairns and by trail markers nailed to sticks that are propped up in crevices. In fog or rain great care is needed in following this part of the trail.

Distances: To the Opalescent River, 2.62 mi.; to gravel lumber road at river, 3.66 mi.; to trail junction at Twin Brook lean-to, 5.14 mi.; to trail junction near Uphill lean-to, 8.45 mi.; to trail junction near Feldspar lean-to, 9.01 mi.; to the former Lake Tear lean-to site, 10.30 mi.; to trail junction at the former Four Corners lean-to site, 10.59 mi.; to summit of Marcy, 11.37 mi. Ascent from Sanford Lake, 3800 ft. Elevation, 5344 ft. Order of height, 1.

(Editor's note: Since both the East River and the Buckley Tote Road trails terminate within one mile and a half of each other, the DEC decided in 1980 to abandon the Buckley Tote Road and to no longer maintain the trail from Twin Brook lean-to to Uphill lean-to.)

Skylight

From the former Four Corners lean-to site on the SW side of Marcy (see Sanford Lake–Marcy Trail or Elk Lake–Marcy Trail) a trail, marked with red disks, branches S and ascends Skylight. Leaving the former lean-to (0 mi.), the trail makes a steady, wet and rocky climb up through the thick conifers. An open shot at 0.37 mi. offers a fine view toward Marcy and Haystack. After timberline is reached at 0.40 mi., the climbing is easy to the bare summit at 0.52 mi. where excellent views of the surrounding mountains are to be had, 30 major peaks being discernible. From timberline to the summit, the trail is marked with rock cairns. Legend states that if a climber fails to carry a rock from timberline to place on one of the two huge cairns on the summit it will surely rain.

Distance: Site of the former Four Corners lean-to to summit of Skylight, 0.52 mi. Ascent from former lean-to, 578 ft. Elevation, 4926 ft. Order of height, 4.

Mt. Marcy via Hanging Spear Falls and Flowed Lands

Take the yellow-marked Sanford Lake–Marcy Trail to trail junction at Twin Brook lean-to at 5.14 mi. (See above.) Leaving the junction (0 mi.) and taking the L fork with red DEC markers in front of the lean-to, the trail crosses Upper Twin Brook at 0.04 mi., passes a clearing on L and heads N, following up the course of the Opalescent River at some distance from the L (or E) bank on the level or easy grades. A lumber loading station is reached at 0.28 mi. where the gravel lumber road in back of Twin Brook lean-to joins the red trail on the R. Straight ahead on a tote road the trail ascends an easy grade to 0.43 mi. and descends gradually, branching R from the tote road at 0.53 mi., soon levels off and enters the State Forest Preserve at 0.63 mi. Continuing on the level, a side trail on the L at 1.02 mi. leads to Gorge lean-to.

Continuing with red markers, the trail crosses a branch at

1.10 mi. and reaches the rocky bank of the Opalescent at 1.12 mi. Following up the L bank, the trail veers R away from the river at a pile of rocks at 1.18 mi. and climbs with easy to moderate grades as it swings to the NE. A brook from R is crossed at 2.21 mi., and the climb up beside the gorge of the Opalescent begins to steepen. A side trail on L at 2.24 mi. leads 45 yds. to the brink of the ravine and a spectacular view of Hanging Spear Falls. With a certain volume of water, the falls are divided by a rock which has the appearance of a spearhead. A second side trail at 2.28 mi. leads back 70 yds. to this same lookout point. Still climbing, another lookout is reached at 2.35 mi. where one can look down on the river far below in the gorge. The grade eases off at 2.43 mi. as the trail nears the head of the ravine heading N, ascends a steep pitch at 2.53 mi. and follows along the L bank of the Opalescent at an easy grade to the dam at the outlet of Flowed Lands, which is reached at 2.74 mi., having climbed about 750 ft. from Gorge lean-to. (Livingston Point lean-to on the E shore of the lake may be reached by the unmarked trail on the R.)

Crossing the dam, with a view of the MacIntyre Range, a lean-to (1959) is reached at 2.80 mi. Now climbing up and down along the W shore and crossing two small brooks, the trail comes to a side trail on the R at 3.03 mi. leading a few yards to Flowed Lands lean-to. (A trail S along the lakeshore from the lean-to leads about 100 yds. to a nice, cold spring just above the level of the lake.) The trail continues over a slight knoll and descends to a trail junction at 3.21 mi. at the level of the lake where the two Calamity lean-tos are located. (Blue trail L is the Calamity Brook Trail leading to Indian Pass and Tahawus Upper Works. See below.)

Continuing with red markers for Lake Colden and Marcy, the trail crosses the bridge over the Calamity Brook outlet of Flowed Lands (PBM 2760 ft.) and follows around the NW shore of the lake back some distance from the shore line. At 3.57 mi. it climbs at an easy grade in back of a rocky promontory, levels off at 3.70 mi. and descends to the level of the lake where it crosses Herbert Brook on a bridge at 3.95 mi. not far from where the Opalescent flows into the lake. This brook, flowing from the col SW of Algonquin Pass, offers a route up trailless Marshall (also known as Clinton or Herbert). At 4.04 mi. McMartin lean-to is visible on the opposite bank of the Opalescent and may be reached by crossing the stream on the stones. (If the water is high, continue on red trail 0.28 mi. to bridge just past Colden Dam.) Climbing slightly over a low ridge, descending to cross a small swamp on a bridge at 4.13 mi. and climbing over another low ridge, the ladder and trail junction at Colden Dam at the outlet of Lake Colden are reached at 4.27 mi. Here the outlet joins the Opalescent River. (Blue trail straight ahead leads 0.46 mi. to the ranger's camp on the NW shore of Lake Colden and connects with trail up Algonquin from Lake Colden and the trail through Avalanche Pass. See Heart Lake Region, Section B6.)

Turning R and descending the ladder, the red Marcy Trail crosses the outlet, passes a PBM (2767 ft.) and at 4.32 mi. reaches the log crib bridge over the Opalescent where there is another trail junction. (Yellow trail straight ahead leads to the three Colden lean-tos and around the SE shore at Lake Colden. See Heart Lake Region, Section B6.) Leaving the junction (0 mi.), crossing the bridge and bearing R, a trail leads 0.07 mi. to Opalescent lean-to on the L bank of the Opalescent River. At 0.18 mi. a side trail on the R leads 0.04 mi. to McMartin lean-to. Continuing straight ahead, Flowed Lands Landing is reached at 0.23 mi. (A double-size lean-to was build in 1958 between the Opalescent and McMartin lean-tos. Another lean-to has since been built on L bank of the Opalescent about 50 yds. above the bridge.)

Crossing the bridge and turning L, the Marcy Trail follows up the L bank of the Opalescent at easy to moderate grades and crosses a brook from R on a bridge at 4.61 mi. A view of falls in the Opalescent is reached at 4.65 mi., and a ladder is ascended at 4.95 mi. Lookouts over the river in the narrow, rock-walled flume below are reached at 5.06 mi. and 5.11 mi. The trail has been rerouted up and over near a painted BM (3076.8 ft.) to avoid a washout at 5.25 mi., and at 5.30 mi. it crosses a tributary at its point of confluence with the Opalescent. Soon veering away from sight of the river, another brook is crossed at 5.43 mi. and the grade gets a bit steeper at 5.50 mi. as the trail climbs through many rocks and over exposed roots. Moderating at 5.65 mi., a height of land is reached at 5.83 mi., after which the trail descends and crosses a small tributary just before reaching the junction near

Buckley's Clearing with the yellow Sanford Lake–Marcy Trail via Twin Brook, which enters on the R at 5.94 mi. End of red markers. Turning L follow yellow trail to summit of Marcy. (See above.)

Distances: Twin Brook lean-to to Gorge lean-to, 1.02 mi.; to Hanging Spear Falls, 2.24 mi.; to dam at Flowed Lands outlet, 2.74 mi.; to Flowed Lands lean-to, 3.03 mi.; to blue trail junction at Calamity lean-tos, 3.21 mi.; to trail junction at Colden Dam, 4.27 mi.; to yellow trail at bridge near Colden lean-tos, 4.32 mi.; to junction with yellow Sanford Lake–Marcy Trail near Uphill lean-to, 5.94 mi.; to blue trail junction near Feldspar lean-to, 6.50 mi.; to former Lake Tear lean-to site, 7.79 mi.; to blue trail junction at former Four Corners lean-to, 8.08 mi.; to summit of Marcy, 8.86 mi. (13.74 mi. from Sanford Lake). Ascent from Sanford Lake, 3600 ft. Elevation, 5344 ft. Order of height, 1.

Mt. Marcy via Calamity Brook from Upper Works

This is the shortest trail to Marcy from the SW. It starts at the parking lot just beyond the buildings at the Upper Works (old Tahawus Club locations), 3.70 mi. N of the junction at the Sanford Lake bridge. At the start it is marked with red DEC markers and follows an old tote road up the course of Calamity Brook to Flowed Lands.

Leaving the parking lot signpost (0 mi.) the trail follows a gravel road N on level ground and comes to a fork at 0.11 mi. (L fork is yellow-marked trail connecting with red trail from Duck Hole to Adirondak Loj via Indian Pass. See below.) Keeping R with red markers, the trail becomes quite rocky and crosses the outlet of Henderson Lake (Hudson River) at 0.22 mi. a short way above its confluence with Calamity Brook. Continuing pretty much on the level, the trail comes close to the R bank of Calamity Brook at 0.36 mi. and crosses a small tributary at 0.77 mi. Following up the course of the brook at easy to moderate grades, sometimes being high above it, the trail crosses Calamity Brook on a suspension bridge at 1.18 mi. This is a good place for a trail lunch on the large flat rocks in the brook.

The trail continues along the tote road and passes remains of an old rock crib dam (relic of original MacIntyre Mines) at 1.24

mi. Continuing along with easy ups and downs, with an occasional steeper pitch, the trail swings away from the brook to avoid swamps, eventually returning to and crossing Calamity Brook on a log bridge immediately before joining the blue trail from Indian Pass which enters on the L at 1.70 mi. (See below.) End of red markers.

Turning R with blue markers the trail follows up the R bank of Calamity Brook, still mostly on the level, and crosses a secondary course of the brook at 1.90 mi. The trail joins an abandoned tote road at 2.01 mi. Climbing at easy to moderate grades the trail veers away from the brook, getting steeper at 2.45 mi., followed by easier grades and leveling off at 2.63 mi. where the brook may be heard on the R. There are several brook crossings in this area where one may get a refreshing drink. Now climbing again at easy to moderate grades the trail descends a steep grade before crossing Calamity Brook on the 2nd suspension bridge at 2.79 mi. The old tote road is rejoined again at 2.91 mi. In times of low water the tote road can be followed across Calamity Brook on stones, thus saving one some extra steps. Now climbing again at easy to moderate grades and crossing several small brooks, the course of the trail takes one through some very muddy sections caused by poor drainage.

The trail pitches up at 3.92 mi., comes to a height of land at 3.98 mi. and then descends slightly to Calamity Pond, now mostly a marsh. The trail now bears R staying on higher ground while making its way around the pond and passing through a beautiful stand of cedar. The other side of Calamity Pond is reached at 4.14 mi. Here (PBM 2681 ft.) is the monument to David Henderson, Manager of the MacIntyre (Adirondack) Iron Works, whose accidental death at this spot on September 3, 1845 has given the name of "Calamity" to the stream, the pond and the mountain to SSW. Proceeding pretty much on the level, the trail passes close to a secondary course in the brook at 4.31 mi. and 4.50 mi. and reaches the two Calamity lean-tos at Flowed Lands where it joins the red trail from Twin Brook lean-to via Hanging Spear Falls at 4.55 mi. End of blue markers. Turn L across Calamity Brook outlet of Flowed Lands for Lake Colden and Marcy, following red markers. (See above.)

Distances: Upper Works to Calamity Brook crossing, 1.18 mi.; to second crossing at blue trail from Indian Pass, 1.70 mi.; to third crossing, 2.79 mi.; to Henderson Monument at Calamity Pond, 4.14 mi.; to red trail junction at Calamity lean-tos, 4.46 mi.; to trail junction at Colden Dam, 5.52 mi.; to yellow trail at bridge near Colden lean-tos, 5.57 mi.; to junction with yellow trail near Uphill lean-to, 7.19 mi.; to blue trail junction near Feldspar lean-to, 7.75 mi.; to former Lake Tear lean-to site, 9.04 mi.; to blue trail junction at the former Four Corners lean-to site, 9.33 mi.; to summit of Marcy, 10.11 mi. Ascent from Upper Works, 3600 ft. Elevation, 5344 ft. Order of height, 1.

Indian Pass from Upper Works

Take the road on the W side of Sanford Lake. This trail starts at the parking lot just beyond the buildings at the Upper Works (old Tahawus Club location), 3.70 mi. N of the junction at the Sanford Lake bridge. It is marked with yellow DEC markers and follows easy grades to Indian Pass Brook at 3.91 mi. and then climbs abruptly to Summit Rock at 4.42 mi.

Leaving the parking lot signpost (0 mi.), the trail follows a gravel road N on the level and comes to a fork at 0.11 mi. (R fork is red-marked trail to Marcy via Calamity Brook and Lake Colden. See above.) Keeping L with yellow markers the trail crosses the outlet of Henderson Lake (Hudson River) on a bridge at 0.24 mi. Continuing on the level along what is now a jeep road, the trail comes to another fork at 0.43 mi. and branches R away from the jeep road. Following an old tote road over easy ups and downs, the trail reaches a more pronounced downgrade at 0.93 mi., crosses a couple of brook beds and levels off at 1.06 mi. Again descending at 1.28 mi., the trail enters a small clearing and rejoins the jeep road at 1.37 mi. Here the trail turns sharp R. Again branching R from the jeep road at 1.53 mi. just before the road crosses Indian Pass Brook, the trail follows up the L bank of the brook and comes to a trail junction at 1.59 mi. End of yellow markers. (PBM painted 1839.7 ft. Trail L across the swinging bridge is the red-marked trail to Duck Hole and the Cold River country. See below.) Continuing straight ahead with red DEC markers up the L bank of the brook, the trail forks at 1.64 mi. where the old route goes L. Going R, the trail enters the State Forest Preserve at 1.71 mi. and reaches Henderson lean-to on the L bank of Indian Pass Brook at 1.75 mi.

Passing behind the lean-to, the trail veers away from the brook and comes to an old lumber clearing at 2.01 mi. A trail junction is reached at 2.06 mi. at the far end of the clearing where the trail is again close to the L bank of Indian Pass Brook. (Trail straight ahead with blue markers is the Indian Pass-Calamity Brook cross-over and leads 2.14 mi. over the foot of the MacIntyre Range to the Marcy Trail via Calamity Brook. See below.) Turning L across the brook on a log bridge, the trail climbs up the opposite bank at an easy grade, passes between two large rocks at 2.16 mi., crosses a small tributary at 2.58 mi. and comes to Wallface lean-to on the R bank of Indian Pass Brook at 2.73 mi. where the morning sun comes pouring in. (PBM 2025 ft. located 15 ft. N of N corner of lean-to.) The brook has been heard all the way from the last crossing at the trail junction but not seen until shortly before reaching the lean-to.

Still pretty much on the level the trail follows up the general course of the brook but soon loses sight of it again. Just before reaching a large rock on the R at 2.91 mi. there is a view ahead of the perpendicular cliffs on Wallface Mt. After crossing three small tributaries, the outlet of Wallface Ponds, flowing from the L, is crossed at 3.24 mi. From here the trail crosses various courses of this brook, caused by spring freshets, and the footing is wet and boggy. The R bank of Indian Pass Brook is again approached at 3.52 mi. and the brook finally crossed at 3.91 mi. where there is a chiseled square BM, painted 2209.3 ft. Here there is a view of Wallface up the brook. The trail now climbs about 450 ft. in the next 0.51 mi. Moderate at first, the grade gets steeper as the trail makes it way up among the rocks and boulders, passing around a tremendous boulder on the R at 4.02 mi. The trail climbs higher above the gorge on the L, ascending two steep pitches, and coming to a slight downgrade at 4.18 mi. followed by a level stretch. Starting up again at 4.31 mi. the trail comes to a steep pitch, ascends a ladder and comes to a turnout on the L at 4.42 mi. Here, just a short way off the trail, is Summit Rock from which the view of

Wallface Mt. across the gorge and of Henderson Mt. and Santanoni
Peak to the SW is unobstructed. This is not the top of the pass,
the height of land being 0.46 mi. further up the trail and about
200 ft. higher, but it offers the best views and is the usual objective
from either end of the pass. From Summit Rock it is 5.80 mi. to
Adirondak Loj. (See Heart Lake Region, Section B6.)

   Distances: Upper Works to junction with red trail from Duck
Hole, 1.59 mi.; to Henderson lean-to, 1.75 mi.; to Indian Pass–
Calamity Brook Crossover, 2.06 mi.; to Wallface lean-to, 2.73 mi.;
to last crossing of Indian Pass Brook, 3.91 mi.; to Summit Rock,
4.42 mi. Ascent from Upper Works, 870 ft. Elevation, 2660 ft.

Indian Pass–Calamity Brook Crossover

   This trail connects the Indian Pass Trail 2.06 mi. N of the
Upper Works with the Calamity Brook Trail 1.70 mi. NE of the
Upper Works. It leads SE over a low shoulder of Marshall in the
MacIntyre Range and provides a route to Marcy from Axton and
Coreys via Duck Hole, but it only saves 0.46 mi. over taking the
yellow trail S to its junction with the Calamity Brook Trail and
requires considerable more climbing than the latter route. It is
marked with blue DEC markers. If coming from Indian Pass, the
blue trail saves 1.40 mi. compared to using the yellow trail.

   Starting (0 mi.) from the junction with the Indian Pass Trail
in the lumber clearing at 2.06 mi. (see above), the trail climbs
easily at first, crosses a small tributary and follows up the L bank
of a larger brook. Crossing to the R bank at 0.20 mi., the trail
continues up the brook and turns L away from it at 0.35 mi.
Climbing for a short distance, the grade becomes easy to moderate
as the trail reaches and crosses the brook again at 0.53 mi. Crossing
the brook twice more, the trail turns away from it at 0.59 mi.
and climbs steadily in and out of a rocky brook bed, a branch of
the former brook. Climbing becomes steeper as the trail makes a
switchback and reaches the top of the ridge at 0.88 mi. in a small
col at about 2430 ft. elevation, having gained about 500 ft. over
the trail junction, most of which is lost in descending the other
side of the ridge.

   Descending at an easy to moderate grade, the trail reaches a grassy meadow and brook at 1.00 mi., skirts the meadow and follows down the brook, crossing and recrossing it several times. Swinging away from the R bank at 1.19 mi., the trail climbs slightly over a low ridge and continues descending at easy to moderate grades, coming near the brook again at 1.46 mi. After leaving the State Forest Preserve and entering private land at 1.55 mi., the descent becomes steeper until a beaver swamp is reached at 1.68 mi. The trail climbs part way around the swamp to the R, then climbs away from it over a ridge and descends to the swamp again near its outlet. Crossing the swamp and outlet on logs from 1.83 mi. to 1.86 mi., the trail follows down a soggy tote road to the L of the outlet pretty much on the level, makes a short climb up to dry ground at 1.97 mi. and is joined by the red trail from the Upper Works on the R bank of Calamity Brook at 2.14 mi. and an elevation of 1970 ft.

Distances: Indian Pass Trail to top of ridge, 0.88 mi.; to Calamity Brook Trail, 2.14 mi.

Duck Hole via Bradley Pond

This trail leads to Duck Hole through the pass between Henderson Mt. on the E and the Santanoni Range on the W. It provides access to the trailless summit of Panther Peak. In the pass near the height of land, and to the W of the trail but not visible from it, is situated Bradley Pond. The trail starts from the old Tahawus Club road on the W side of Sanford Lake 2.00 mi. N of the junction at the Sanford Lake bridge. It is marked with a DEC sign and a large parking lot provides off-road parking. Since the trail as far as Santanoni lean-to (formerly Bradley Pond lean-to) is on private land, no camping is permitted.

Leaving the road (0 mi.), the trail heads W following blue markers and immediately joins a lumber road with a surface of coarse stone. It swings N at 0.58 mi. and the stone surface gives way to gravel at about 1.00 mi. After climbing gradually, the road crosses a bridge over the outlet of Harkness Lake at 1.14 mi., swings R and then L up over a slight rise, levels off shortly and then climbs to the point at 1.74 mi. where the trail turns R leaving the road. The trail follows down a tributary of Santanoni Brook, crosses it, goes through a grassy lumber clearing, crosses Santanoni Brook and climbs a bank to a junction with the formerly used trail at 2.03 mi. Here, the route turns L and follows up the valley of Santanoni Brook, veering away from the brook for a time but later coming close to it, climbing at a steady, moderate grade. At 3.25 mi., an attractive series of cascades is passed and at 3.41 mi. the junction with the abandoned trail to Santanoni is reached. This latter trail is now closed to the public. Continuing on, the Duck Hole Trail reaches a high point at 3.52 mi. followed by a short descent, half way down which the herd path to Panther, now closed to the public, used to lead off to the L. From here, the trail climbs gradually through intermittent swampy areas to the Santanoni lean-to at 4.28 mi. where it crosses onto State land. This is the highest point on the trail, elevation, 2950 ft.

Beyond the lean-to, the trail descends gradually, then steeply over broken-down log bridges, crossing and recrossing a stream. At 4.94 mi. it crosses the L fork of the main brook, turns R on relatively flat ground and heads to the N, down the main valley. It crosses a large tributary from the L at 5.67 mi. and at 5.89 mi. uses a beaver dam to negotiate a beaver swamp. Below this the trail continues for a time on flat ground, then climbs above a swamp, descends, and after more travel on the flat crosses to the E bank of the stream at 6.93 mi. Crossing once more to the W side at 7.63 mi. the trail climbs over a ridge and descends to Duck Hole Pond at 7.79 mi. Following along above the pond, the trail crosses a rock crib dam at 7.87 mi. and a spillway dam at 8.04 mi. beyond which are two lean-tos and the site of a former ranger station.

Beyond the first lean-to at 8.08 mi. the trail joins the Ward Brook trail from Coreys (red markers) and the Northville–Placid Trail (blue markers) which coincide at this point. The blue and red markers may be followed W along the fire truck trail 1.24 mi. to the two Cold River lean-tos.

Distances: Old Tahawus Club Road to point where trail leaves lumber road, 1.74 mi.; to Santanoni lean-to, 4.28 mi.; to trail junction near Duck Hole lean-tos, 8.08 mi. Ascent to height of land at Santanoni lean-to, 1200 ft. Descent to Duck Hole, 800 ft.

Duck Hole via Henderson Lake from Upper Works

This route to Duck Hole involves much less climbing than the route via Bradley Pond. Take the Indian Pass Trail from Upper Works, yellow markers, to junction with red-marked trail at 1.59 mi. (0.16 mi. S of Henderson lean-to. See above.) Here the trail to Duck Hole turns L following red markers. (Trail straight ahead with red markers leads 2.83 mi. to Summit Rock in Indian Pass and 8.63 mi. to Adirondak Loj on Heart Lake.)

Leaving the junction (0 mi.) the trail immediately crosses Indian Pass Brook on a swinging bridge and turns L downstream on a tote road. At 0.08 mi. the trail swings R away from the tote road. Continuing in a southwesterly direction the trail traverses a 6 foot high beaver dam at 0.28 mi. and comes to a trail junction at 0.60 mi. (Unmarked trail L leads 0.06 mi. to private dock near head of Henderson Lake).

Turning sharp R and heading NW, the going is easy as the trail follows up the L bank of an inlet to Lake Henderson. A long corduroy over a wet section is reached at 0.66 mi. after which the trail crosses the brook. Recrossing the brook at 0.77 mi., the trail veers away from the L bank, approaches the R bank of another brook at 0.81 mi., which it follows up and passes some interesting cascades at 0.86 mi. At 0.91 mi., the trail encounters a beaver pond which it passes on the W side. Crossing to the L bank at 1.33 mi., the trail veers away and continues at some distance from the brook. Recrossing the brook at 1.43 mi. and 1.50 mi., the property line of the Sanford Lake Rod and Gun Club, lessee, is reached at 1.52 mi. Moderate grades begin here. After passing between twin rocks at 1.72 mi., the grade levels off at 1.84 mi. and comes to a slight descent at 1.89 mi. at L bank of a small brook, having gained 372 ft. in elevation above Lake Henderson. The going is easy through the pass, the trail passing between large rocks at 2.03 mi. and coming to a junction at 2.26 mi. (Unmarked trail straight ahead on corduroy leads 60 yards to private dock on Upper Preston Pond. The height of land in the pass marks the divide between the St. Lawrence and Hudson watersheds, the Preston Ponds draining into the Cold River, then into the Raquette River and finally into the St. Lawrence at the St. Regis Indian Reservation near Massena.)

Turning sharp R, the red trail heads E and soon starts to climb along bank of a brook (outlet of Hunter Pond). Crossing the brook at 2.36 mi. and following up the R bank, the grade gets steeper at 2.43 mi. Turning away from the brook at 2.55 mi. and swinging L, the trail levels off; heading N, it passes little Hunter Pond on its E side from 2.65 mi. to 2.77 mi. Heading NW and climbing again, a steep pitch is ascended just before leveling off in a pass at 2.81 mi. Starting down an easy grade, the trail meets the L bank of a brook and crosses it at 2.88 mi. Below this, a beaver pond is encountered which in 1976 required bushwhacking along its E bank. Following down the brook, sometimes in and out of it on either bank, the trail descends a steeper section and crosses back to the L bank at 3.06 mi. where it encounters a fairly level and wet stretch before reaching the remains of Piche's lumber camp at 3.20 mi. The area around the remains was once a large clearing, but is now completely grown up.

Leaving the camp area, and crossing the brook again at 3.29 mi., now enlarged by a branch from MacNaughton Mt., the trail follows down the R bank on easy grades. Veering away from the brook at 3.50 mi. and descending over old corduroys, lower Preston Pond becomes visible through the trees on the L at about 3.70 mi. Still descending gradually, a small vlei, about 65 yds. wide, is reached at 3.99 mi. at about pond level. Heading W up easy to moderate grades, the National Lead Company property line is passed at 4.19 mi. as the trail enters the Forest Preserve. Descending moderately and making another easy climb, a height of land is reached at 4.38 mi. after which the trail zigzags down in a northerly direction to the NE bay of Duck Hole Pond at 4.43 mi. Going around the N end of the bay, the trail climbs over a low ridge to a height of land at 4.59 mi., descends slightly and climbs again to 4.67 mi. After a short, level stretch a steep descent brings one to the bottom of the grade at 4.80 mi. A beaver dam on L at 4.82 mi. provides a route around the beaver bog, after which the L bank of Roaring Brook is reached where the trail crosses and joins the blue-marked Northville-Placid Trail on the far bank at

4.86 mi. (Blue trail R leads 11.83 mi. to the junction of the N-P trail with the Averyville road, 1.2 mi. S of the DEC sign at the Old Military Road intersection in Lake Placid. This sign marks the offical northern terminus of the N-P trail.)

Turning L downstream to the SW with red and blue markers, the trail pitches up from 4.98 mi. to 5.01 mi., then descends and crosses a small tributary brook at 5.07 mi. After an easy climb over another rise the trail junction at the site of the former Duck Hole ranger station is reached at 5.34 mi., just before reaching the two Duck Hole lean-tos. This is one of the best campsites in the mountains, with a view of MacNaughton to the E over the pond where the call of the loon is frequently heard at night. Here the blue-marked trail from Sanford Lake via Bradley Pond comes in across the dam. (See above.) Fire truck road W with red markers leads to Axton and Coreys. (See below.)

Distances: Trail junction at swinging bridge S of Henderson lean-to to side trail leading to Henderson Lake, 0.60 mi.; to trail junction near Upper Preston Pond, 2.26 mi.; to Hunter Pond, 2.65 mi.; to Piche's old lumber clearing, 3.20 mi.; to Northville–Placid Trail, 4.86 mi.; to trail junction at site of former Duck Hole ranger station, 5.34 mi. (6.93 mi. from Upper Works.)

Duck Hole and Cold River from Coreys and Axton
(Ward Brook Trail)

This trail is the western approach to the High Peak Region and provides the easiest access to the Seward Range and the Cold River country. It is reached via auto by turning S through Coreys from Route 3 on the Stony Creek Ponds Road near the S end of Upper Saranac Lake, about 12.5 mi. SW from the bridge in Saranac Lake Village and about 9.0 mi. E of Tupper Lake Village. This road is the canoe carry from Upper Saranac Lake to Axton on the Raquette River. At 2.0 mi. from Route 3 the canoe carry branches R on a dirt road leading 0.20 mi. to the parking lot at the launching site. Keeping L on main dirt road, the road swings SE, then E, crosses the outlet of Stony Creek Ponds on an iron bridge at 2.55 mi. and continues E past a horseback assembly area to the DEC parking area with register at 5.85 mi. from Route 3.

This marks the beginning of private property and is as far as cars are allowed to go on the fire truck trail.

Leaving the truck trail (0 mi.), the foot trail following red markers crosses a swamp, then swings SE and climbs to a junction with an old trail from the R at 0.60 mi. The trail is then fairly level or with a gradual upgrade to about 1.00 mi. Continuing mostly on the level with an occasional up and down, the trail crosses a N-S dirt road at 1.23 mi. (To the R this road leads SSW into the valley of Calkins Brook which rises on the W slopes of Seward.)

After crossing a good-sized brook at 1.42 mi., a small clearing is reached at 1.60 mi. Crossing more brooks, the trail passes S of Blueberry Pond, which may be seen through the trees on the L at about 2.27 mi. After passing the pond the trail ascends slightly, crosses several brooks and then dips down to cross a large brook on a bridge at 3.49 mi. Continuing on the level a stretch of corduroy is traversed amid many ferns at 3.59 mi. Crossing another good-sized brook on a bridge at 3.95 mi., the trail continues across two more brooks at 4.31 mi. and 4.52 mi. After passing Blueberry lean-to (1962) the trail emerges from the woods at a clearing where it joins the fire truck road from the L at 4.59 mi.

Continuing SE, the trail follows the truck road from the left at 4.59 mi. all the way to the Duck Hole. At about 4.70 mi. a horse trail comes in from the R and at 4.82 mi. the truck road crosses a large brook on a truss bridge. This is the brook route for climbing Seward, Donaldson and Emmons. (See Section C.) Climbing over a low ridge, the brook from Ouluska Pass, between Seward and Seymour, is crossed on another truss bridge at 5.18 mi. (At top of hill, 200 yds. before this brook, an overgrown tote road leads S into Ouluska Pass.) A third fair-sized brook is crossed at foot of hill just before reaching Ward Brook lean-to at 5.35 mi. The first brook beyond the lean-to at 5.45 mi. is the brook to Seymour.

Still climbing at a moderate grade, an easy stretch is reached at 5.90 mi. followed by more climbing and a dip down over a brook in a clearing at 6.08 mi. where there are two lean-tos. Starting to climb, a gravel bank on L is passed at 6.35 mi. and the trail swings towards the S, dips over a brook (spring on L at 6.42 mi.) and then climbs over 200 ft. to the high point of the truck trail at 7.00 mi. where the trail levels off. (Elevation, 2500 ft.) Starting down at 7.11 mi., the trail descends about 250 ft. and crosses a vlei from 8.04 to 8.08 mi. Climbing slightly to another height of land at a gravel bank at 8.40 mi. (elevation, 2320 ft.) and descending about 100 ft. at a fair grade, the junction with the blue-marked Northville-Placid Trail at the N end of Mountain Pond is reached at 8.67 mi. (Trail R leads 4.13 mi. to lean-to at Ouluska Pass Brook, 6.36 mi. to Seward lean-to, 10.32 mi. to Shattuck Clearing, 24.30 mi. to Long Lake and continues to the West Canada Lakes, Piseco, and Northville. At 3.65 mi. down this trail on Cold River is the old hermitage of Noah John Rondeau.)

Continuing E on the fire truck trail with red and blue markers and a descending grade, the two Cold River lean-tos (No. 3 and No. 4) are reached at 9.07 mi. and Moose Creek, the outlet of Moose Pond, is crossed on a truss bridge at 9.14 mi. at its confluence with Cold River. Climbing the far bank of Moose Creek, the trail follows along Cold River pretty much on the level at a distance from its R (or N) bank, starts to climb over a low ridge at about 10.00 mi., then descends at 10.25 mi. and comes to the site of the former ranger station and trail junction at Duck Hole at 10.31 mi. End of truck trail. The two Duck Hole lean-tos are but a few yards past the trail junction on the R. This is a wild and beautiful spot with its view across the pond. (Blue trail across the dam leads 8.52 mi. via Bradley Pond to Tahawus Club Road 2.00 mi. N of Sanford Lake bridge. Blue trail heading NE past ranger station is Northville–Placid Trail to Lake Placid, 13.81 mi. (see section D) and connects with red trail via Preston Ponds to Indian Pass, 8.17 mi. and Tahawus Upper Works, 6.93 mi. See above.)

Distances: Parking area to Calkins Brook road, 1.23 mi.; to Blueberry Pond, 2.27 mi.; to junction with fire truck trail, 4.59 mi.; to Ward Brook lean-to, 5.35 mi.; to Northville–Placid Trail at Mountain Pond, 8.67 mi.; to Cold River lean-tos, 9.07 mi.; to trail junction at site of former Duck Hole ranger station, 10.31 mi.

Shattuck Clearing from Coreys and Axton via Calkins Creek Truck Trail

This trail, which is the most direct approach to the Cold River at Shattuck Clearing from Coreys and Axton, travels the W side of the Seward Range, much of the time in the watershed of Calkins Creek. Except for the first 1.36 mi., the route is entirely on the Calkins Creek truck trail, a well-graded gravel road maintained by the DEC for fire control. Besides serving as a foot trail, this road is also a leg in the DEC Cold River horse trail system.

At the parking area 5.85 mi. from Rt. 3 on the road from Coreys and Axton, the red-marked Blueberry foot trail to Duck Hole heads E while the Cold River horse trail goes S on an old tote road. From the trail register (0 mi.) follow red markers to junction with the Calkins Creek truck trail at 1.35 mi. (Straight ahead on red trail leads to N-P Trail at Mountain Pond, 7.44 mi., and Duck Hole, 9.11 mi. See above.) Turn R on yellow-marked Calkins Creek truck trail. A horse trail junction is reached at 1.55 mi. (From this point to Shattuck Clearing the truck trail is a part of the Cold River horse trail complex. Horse trail R leads back to parking area; L goes to Ward Brook truck trail.) The road now begins to climb SSW at easy grades punctuated regularly with shallow dips. On R at 2.04 mi. is a gravel bank. After passing a huge boulder crowned with ferns and small birches on L at 2.26 mi., a height of land is soon reached at 2.36 mi. After a slight dip another height of land is reached at 2.55 mi. The gentle descent from the col becomes steeper as the road passes a large boulder on the R at 2.64 mi. After the trail crosses a tributary of Calkins Creek on a culvert at 2.97 mi., the downgrade is interrupted by a slight climb to 3.20 mi. Descending briefly, the road levels off at 3.28 mi. Here on the R an extensive beaver swamp is visible through the trees. Beginning at 3.36 mi. there is a brief descent. Just after passing over a small brook, the road makes an abrupt R turn at an old lumber clearing at 3.41 mi. On a rock on the inside of this turn is BM 1987. The road now goes down the R bank of Calkins Creek which is seen for the first time at 3.56 mi. This stream rises high on the W slope of the Seward Range between Seward and Donaldson. The numerous huge logs strewn over and along the creekbed give some idea of the fierce blowdown area one would encounter upstream. After passing a gravel bank on the R, Calkins Creek is crossed on a bridge at 3.67 mi. The road follows the L bank only to recross the stream on another bridge at 3.87 mi. A dry brook is crossed on a bridge at 4.13 mi. and then a brook is bridged at 4.22 mi. A sharp rise at 4.39 mi. marks the beginning of a series of dips and rises as the road slabs the ridge NW of Calkins Creek. Occasionally a glimpse of Donaldson can be caught through the trees to the L. A large boulder on the R is passed at 4.61 mi., and the junction with the horse trail from Raquette Falls is reached at 4.98 mi. Continuing in a roller coaster fashion, at 5.86 mi. a break in the trees directly ahead reveals Kempshall Mt. Here the trail descends quickly at 6.18 mi. to a clearing which was the site of the Santa Ana Lumber Company Camp 1. On the R upon entering the clearing are two lean-tos, Calkins Creek No. 1 and No. 2. Located 80 ft. from this point is a horse stable. On the L is Calkins Creek.

Leaving the clearing at 6.25 mi. the road makes the last crossing of Calkins Creek on a bridge at 6.25 mi. Swinging L around a gravel bank, the road climbs steeply away from Calkins Creek, the grade moderating at 6.33 mi.

The remainder of the truck trail to Shattuck Clearing is well defined and therefore is not described here. The total distance to the Clearing is 10.69 mi.

Shattuck Clearing from Coreys via Stony Creek Horseback Assembly Area

This approach to the Calkins Creek truck trail and Shattuck Clearing starts at the horseback assembly area just E of the Stony Creek bridge on the road leading from Route 3 through Coreys to the start of the Duck Hole–Cold River trail. It is 0.54 mi. longer by this route to Calkins Creek and Shattuck Clearing than is the approach from the parking lot at the start of the Duck Hole trail (see above). Also, the last two miles prior to joining the Calkins Creek truck trail are excessively muddy in anything but very dry weather. However, the trail saves 2.76 mi. for those walking from Route 3 to Shattuck Clearing and leads through interesting, wild country. It also gives access to Raquette Falls by means of a 2 mi. side trail.

Starting at the horseback assembly area, the trail follows a gravel road avoiding a R turn at 0.06 mi., and continues up the E side of the Raquette River flood plain. At 1.45 mi., where an obscure lumber road turns R towards the river, the road bears

L, climbing away from the river, following a small brook. Crossing the brook at 1.66 mi., it comes to level ground and reaches a junction at 2.07 mi. with a trail leading R to the Hemlock Hill lean-to. Beyond this, the trail dips down to a junction at 2.21 mi. where the trail to Raquette Falls (2.00 mi.) leads to the R across Palmer Brook.

The Calkins Brook trail climbs beside the brook, bears away from it over a hill, and finally crosses Palmer Brook in a swamp at 2.71 mi. The road then climbs over another hill and descends to cross another brook flowing from the L at 3.42 mi. This marks the end of the gravel-based road, and from here on the trail is very muddy in anything but dry weather, partly because of its use as a horse trail. Another brook is crossed at 3.49 mi., beyond which the trail starts its long, gradual ascent towards the pass leading to Calkins Creek. What looks like the pass top appears at 4.08 mi., but the true pass is still nearly a mile to the E. The trail flanks the side of a ridge to the base of the pass at 4.60 mi., then turns R and ascends steeply to the top at 5.06 mi. (elevation, 2200 ft.). After a short level stretch, the trail descends steeply to its junction with the Calkins Creek Truck Trail at 5.52 mi. From here to Shattuck Clearing, it is 5.71 mi.

Distances: To start of branch trail to Raquette Falls, 2.21 mi.; to crossing of Palmer Brook, 2.71 mi.; to end of gravel-based road, 3.42 mi.; to top of pass, 5.06 mi.; to Calkins Creek Truck Trail, 5.52 mi.; to Shattuck Clearing, 11.23 mi.

Horse Trail along SE side of Cold River Valley

From the site of the former Shattuck Clearing ranger station, the Northville–Placid Trail gives access to the NW side of the Cold River valley as well as to the Long Lake region (see Section D). Also a horse trail route continues S along the truck trail for about 1.00 mi., then turns L (east) and at about 1.50 mi. crosses Moose Creek to two lean-tos. The trail continues easterly, crossing the brook from Couchsachraga and Panther at about 5.50 mi. (see Section C) and reaching two lean-tos on the Cold River above Cold River Flow at about 7.00 mi. From here, the horse trail continues on to the Northville–Placid trail which it intersects at 9.50 mi., shortly after fording the Cold River. This junction is 0.32 mi. from the Cold River lean-tos and 0.85 mi. from the Duck Hole lean-tos and the site of the former ranger station located there.

The Santanoni Preserve Trails

Transferred from private ownership to the State of New York in 1972 through the efforts of the Adirondack Conservancy, this fine area of land offers excellent opportunities for hiking, fishing, and horseback riding. As part of the conditions of the transfer, access for overnight users is controlled by a permit system with the following additional rules:

1. The Preserve will be open seven days a week with a caretaker on duty from 8 A.M. until 6 P.M.
2. All overnight camping will be prohibited in the parking area. Overnight camping will be allowed only on sites which have been developed and marked as primitive tent sites.
3. All persons entering the Preserve will be required to register. Hikers and other day users will be required to sign the interior use register located at the main gate. Overnight campers are required to obtain a free camping permit directly from the caretaker in charge.
4. The speed limit from Old Rt. 28 to the Gate House will be 15 M.P.H.
5. All mechanized vehicles such as snowmobiles, motorbikes and all terrain vehicles will be prohibited.
6. No mechanically propelled boats will be allowed on the waters of the Santanoni Preserve at any time. This includes both outboard motors and electric motors. Seaplanes are also prohibited from landing on these waters.
7. Hunting of both small game and big game will be allowed during the open seasons, with users again being subject to all applicable rules and regulations.
8. Fishing will be allowed on the Santanoni Preserve waters from May lst to September 30th under the following regulations only:
   Brook trout—3 per day, minimum size 12 inches
   Lake trout—1 per day, minimum size 20 inches

Artificial lures only. These special fishing regulations apply to all waters on the Santanoni Preserve.

It should also be understood that hikers must walk the fire truck roads from the gate house to Newcomb and Moose ponds. *Distances:* to Newcomb Lake 4.70 miles; to Moose Pond, 6.00 miles.

Since this area has not yet received heavy use, persons can be reasonably sure of getting a permit for camping. Access to the preserve is by gravel roads to Moose Pond and Newcomb Lake. All cars are prohibited on these roads, but bicycles are often used to cover this distance. Boats are available for rent at Newcomb Lake. Possibilities for ski touring and snowshoeing are excellent and extensive. Access to the preserve is from Highway 28N at the west end of the Village of Newcomb and is marked by a sign. Cars should be parked on the right at the top of the hill just past the gate house. Permits for overnight camping are available at the gate house.

Moose Pond Horse Trail
(Distances estimated)

Starting from the gate house, this trail leads past Moose Pond and connects with the Cold River horse trail approximately 5 miles north of Shattuck Clearing. Leaving the gate house (0 mi.), follow the gravel road which climbs gradually to a junction at 2.00 mi. (Road R leads to Newcomb Lake 2.70 mi.) Bearing L, the Moose Pond Trail continues over the rolling terrain and then descends to a small brook at 3.00 mi. Crossing an open area, the trail comes to an unmarked junction at 4.50 mi. Bearing L, the trail continues along a side hill before climbing to a height of land and arriving at Moose Pond at 6.00 mi. A trail L leads in 0.25 mi. to two campsites on Moose Pond. Bearing R, the trail marked with blue horse trail disks heads away from Moose Pond, crossing Ermine Brook at 7.00 mi., Calahan Brook at 10.50 mi. and reaches a junction with the Cold River horse trail at 11.50 mi. from the gate house.

Newcomb Lake to the Cold River Horse Trail

Starting from the junction with the Moose Pond Trail (2.00 mi. from the gate house), this hiking trail, following good gravel road, proceeds gradually upwards before descending to the S shore of Newcomb Lake at 2.70 mi. (4.70 mi. from the gate house).

At this point (0 mi.), a trail marked with red DEC disks proceeds along the S shore of Newcomb Lake, eventually connecting with the Cold River horse trail. At 1.50 mi., a trail leads R to a lean-to on Newcomb Lake. The trail continues on, crossing a brook at 2.00 mi. and covering another mile on relatively level ground before climbing abruptly over a ridge and descending to Shaw Pond at 4.50 mi. The trail climbs over another ridge crossing Ermine Brook at 5.50 mi. and continues NW and then N as it slabs the side of Little Santanoni Mountain. The trail crosses Calahan Brook at 8.00 mi. and climbs to a height of land at 9.00 mi. before descending gradually to a junction with the Cold River horse trail at 11.00 mi. Trail R (N) leads in approximately 5.00 mi. to the Duck Hole. Trail L (S) leads in approximately 5.50 mi. to Shattuck Clearing. Total distance from the gate house 15.70 mi.

Distances: Gate house to junction on Moose Pond Trail, 2.00 mi.; to Newcomb Lake, 4.70 mi.; to junction with the Cold River Horse Trail, 15.70 mi.

SECTION B6

HEART LAKE REGION

This popular hiking center is reached by turning S from Route 73, 4 mi. SE of Lake Placid Village. There is a sign "Adirondak Loj, 5 mi." at the corner. There is also a DEC sign "Trail to the High Peaks." The first mile of road is in the open, affording fine views of Mt. Marcy and Mt. Colden, also Wright and Algonquin Peaks of the MacIntyre Range, and Indian Pass with Wallface Mt. rising abruptly on the R. At 3.80 mi. from the corner there is a dirt road on the L, marked with DEC signs, which leads to South Meadow. DEC signs indicate the start of the Indian Pass Trail on the R at 4.70 mi. and Adirondak Loj is reached at 4.80 mi. (PBM 2178 ft.). To the L, as you approach the end of the public road from Route 73, there is seen a driveway that leads to the Campers and Hikers Building maintained by the Adirondack Mountain Club. You are asked to register at this building if you park here.

Heart Lake and the surrounding property are owned by the Adirondack Mountain Club. Adirondak Loj offers accommodations to guests by the day or week. (For further information see Section E.) From here starts the shortest approach to Mt. Marcy, as well as trails to Wright and Algonquin Peaks, Avalanche Pass, Lake Colden, Mt. Colden, Indian Pass and Mt. Jo. From nearby South Meadow a trail leads to Johns Brook Lodge.

All of the 48 mi. of trails described in this section are maintained by DEC, except the trails on Mt. Jo, the trail over Boundary to Iroquois, the ADK trail from Lake Arnold to Hopkins Trail junction (see Van Hoevenberg Bypass Trail) and the Mr. Van Ski Trail.

Trails Described	Year Measured	Total Miles
Mt. Marcy via Van Hoevenberg Trail	1966	7.46
Mt. Marcy via Van Hoevenberg Bypass	1971	7.62
Phelps	1970	1.17
Indian Falls–Lake Arnold Crossover	1954	0.74
Algonquin Peak from Heart Lake	1954	3.97
Boundary and Iroquois Peaks	1954*	0.65
Wright Peak from Algonquin Trail	1956	0.43
Wright Peak via Slide from Marcy Brook	Bushwhack	
Wright Peak and Whale's Tail Notch Ski Trails	1958*	3.00
Avalanche Pass Trail to Lake Colden Outlet	1954	3.97
Mt. Colden from Lake Colden	1954	1.62
Trail around Northwest Shore of Lake Colden	1956	1.04
Algonquin Peak from Lake Colden	1955	2.09
Trail from Lake Colden to Indian Pass Trail	1966	3.31
Avalanche Camp to Lake Arnold and Feldspar Brook	1954	3.17
Mt. Colden from Lake Arnold Trail via L. Morgan Porter Trail	1968	1.37
Indian Pass from Heart Lake	1965	6.00
Scott and Wallface Ponds from Indian Pass Trail	1963	2.70
Mt. Jo (Long Trail 1.14 mi.; Short Trail 0.86 mi.)	1959	2.00
South Meadow (Auto Road)		
Mt Van Hoevenberg from South Meadow Road to Foot of Bobsled Run	1955	3.61
South Meadow to Marcy Dam (Fire Truck Trail)	1955	2.80
South Meadow to Johns Brook Lodge	1955	5.27
The Mr. Van Ski Trail	1976	5.65

* Partly estimated.

Mt. Marcy via Van Hoevenberg Trail

This is one of the oldest and most popular trails to Marcy and is the shortest route to the summit. It was laid out by Henry Van Hoevenberg, builder of the original Adirondack Lodge which was destroyed in the great forest fire of 1903. Sections of the original trail have been abandoned and rerouted over the years due to severe erosion. The section from March Dam to Indian Falls was recut in 1968. Also a bypass was built from a point 0.55 mi. above the Falls to the junction of the Hopkins and Van Hoevenberg Trails in 1970.

In the Fall of 1973 the beginning of the trail was rerouted to avoid the Loj area and the extended wet section between the Loj and the Algonquin junction. The new location also makes the trail more accessible to the new parking lot and the Campers and Hikers Building. Leaving this building, (0 mi.), proceed straight ahead across the lower parking area. The Van Hoevenberg Trail begins at the end of the parking area where the DEC (Department of Environmental Conservation) has erected signs and a trail register. The trail, following blue markers, also posted with blue half-mile markers* bears E and then S, soon crossing the blue painted Mr. Van Ski trail from Adirondak Loj. The trail continues S and descends a short steep section where the ADK Loj Hicks Trail comes in on the R at 0.25 mi., turns sharp L and follows the Hicks Trail to a point just before the crossing of the outlet brook from Heart Lake. Here the Hicks Trail turns R, while the trail to Marcy crosses the brook and continues on and crosses the MacIntyre Brook at about 0.40 mi. The trail now climbs and continues high on the S (R) bank of the brook before reaching the abandoned Van Hoevenberg Trail from the Adirondak Loj at 0.97 mi. (Here the rerouted trail to Algonquin Peak with yellow markers heads straight ahead with some ups and downs to its junction with the Whale's Tail Notch Ski Trail at 1.42 mi.) The trail to Mt. Marcy following blue markers turns sharp L onto the original Van Hoevenberg Trail to Marcy Dam. The trail passes a bench mark painted on a

---

* Half-mile markers are blue numbers (some black) on a yellow field for contrast with DEC blue trail markers.

rock on the L side of the trail at 1.15 mi. and reaches a bridge with a railing at 1.45 mi. After crossing a mud hole with corduroy and another bridge at 1.71 mi., Marcy Brook may be heard for the first time on the L at a slight downgrade. After two more bridges, separated by a rocky stretch in a "hog wallow," the trail comes suddenly to the brink of Marcy Brook at 1.91 mi. Below is the boulder-filled stream, which may be crossed at this point giving access to the fire truck trail on the far bank. Directly beyond to the E is Phelps with Table Top to the SE. The trail now follows up the L bank of Marcy Brook, passes another lookout at 2.09 mi., and descends to cross the eighth bridge at 2.16 mi. (PBM 2365 ft.)

The trail crosses the dam where a fine view is afforded of Phelps, Table Top, Colden and Avalanche (Caribou) Mts. It then turns R upstream along the shore of the pond on a dirt road. There is an excellent spring (water flowing from an open pipe) just below the dam on the R bank of the brook. The road downstream is the fire truck trail to South Meadow, 2.80 mi. Just beyond the dam is a hikers' register with the ranger's cabin beyond it.

Marcy Dam (the term has acquired geographical significance) is now a popular camping center. It was built on the site of a lumber dam used for driving logs down Marcy Brook. There are several lean-tos in the vicinity, including Hudowalski lean-to, plus numerous camping sites. These lean-tos are scattered around the lake. However, it is advisable to bring some type of shelter and not to expect firewood at this popular scenic spot.

Swinging SE away from the pond, the trail leads to a lean-to at 2.34 mi. Here the trail forks with the Van Hoevenberg Trail keeping L. R fork with yellow markers is the trail to Avalanche Pass and Lake Colden. See below. Continuing straight ahead at the trail junction with the blue markers, the trail to Marcy follows a tote road. At 2.52 mi. the trail turns L from the tote road crossing Phelps Brook on the log bridge and then continues upstream some distance uphill from the R bank. (The tote road straight ahead is the Marcy ski trail.) A side trail R at 3.04 mi. descends about 40 yds. to Phelps lean-to. Another junction is reached at 3.13 mi. Turning L, the trail joins the ski trail and continues upstream with easy to moderate grades. (A R turn at this junction leads to Phelps lean-to, 0.08 mi.) At 3.31 mi. a red-marked trail diverges L. This

leads to the summit of Phelps Mt., 1.0 mi. (See below.) After crossing
Phelps Brook on a plank bridge at 3.56 mi., the trail climbs steeply
to a junction at 3.69 mi. Turning R off the ski trail, a spring is
passed at 3.77 mi. The trail turns uphill at a moderately steep
grade. At 3.91 mi. a log bench invites the hiker to sit and enjoy
a rather nice view of Phelps. The steady climb eases at 4.10 mi.
Beginning at 4.12 mi., the route of the original Van Hoevenberg
Trail is followed briefly. Continuing at a moderate grade, the trail
levels off after passing log steps at 4.18 mi., leaving the original
trail at 4.22 mi. The blue-marked ski trail joins from the L at 4.27
mi. Following a turn at 4.42 mi. a bridge across Marcy Brook is
reached at 4.52 mi. Just beyond, a path L leads to the site of the
former upper Indian Falls lean-to. Turning R leads to the top of
Indian Falls. Here is one of the finest views of the mountains, looking over the Falls and across the valley to the MacIntyre Range.
Continuing straight ahead, the original trail is met at 4.55 mi. (Turning R leads .05 mi. to the foot of Indian Falls and the yellow-marked
Indian Falls–Lake Arnold Crossover. See below.)

Turning L at the junction, the old trail follows up the L bank
of Marcy Brook, turning away from it at 4.59 mi. About 50 yds.
further it turns L and climbs at an easy grade through a wet section
with corduroys. Marcy Brook is heard on the L. The grade becomes
a little steeper but levels off in a blowdown area at 5.00 mi. and
reaches a height of land and the Van Hoevenberg Bypass Trail
at 5.07 mi. (The trail L with red ADK markers leads to the Hopkins
Trail 1.20 mi. and is an alternate route to Mt. Marcy. The red-
marked trail R leads to the Lake Arnold Trail and Adirondak Loj.
It is also part of the alternate route to Mt. Marcy. See below.)
Continuing ahead on the old Van Hoevenberg Trail, there is an
easy downgrade, leveling off at 5.19 mi. Steady climbing starts at
5.31 mi. with some fairly steep sections over rocks and corduroys,
the grade becoming easy again near a vertical rock face on R at
5.58 mi. The climbing becomes moderate at 5.69 mi. and levels
off at 5.78 mi. After a pitch up at 5.88 mi. the trail is fairly level
with grades easy to moderate as it winds through a wet section.
At 6.20 mi. it starts descending gradually, and at 6.26 mi. the Hopkins Trail, with yellow markers, comes in on the L from Keene
Valley via JBL and Bushnell Falls. The former Hopkins lean-to
site (1962) is about 200 yds. beyond the trail junction on the blue

trail. (See Keene Valley Region, Section B1.) The red-marked Van Hoevenberg Bypass also joins at this point.

Bearing R with the blue markers, the trail continues to descend slightly through a very muddy section. A gradual climb starts at 6.38 mi. up a brook to the site of the former Plateau lean-to. Here the dome of Marcy is in full view. The trail then dips a little to cross a tiny stream which may be the last sure water. It then ascends through thick, stunted spruce, and at 6.88 mi. the Phelps Trail, with red markers, comes in on the L. This leads to the Range Trail and to Keene Valley via Slant Rock and JBL. (See Keene Valley Region, Section B1.)

Swinging R the trail makes a short climb, coming out on bare rocks, then crosses a wet sag at 7.02 mi. and climbs again to come out on the first rocky shoulder of Marcy at 7.12 mi. From this point the trail is level for a short distance and then climbs up the bare rock to the summit at 7.46 mi. Over the bare rocks the trail is marked partly with small rock cairns and with paint blazes. In fog or rain great care is needed in following this part of the trail. Down the W side of Marcy, toward Gray Peak, water can sometimes be found. It takes about 25 minutes to make the round trip to the spring. Descending toward Lake Tear on the yellow trail, water can also be found to the R of the trail in the sag at Schofield Cobble, 0.22 mi. below the summit of Marcy. (See Elk Lake–Marcy Trail or Sanford Lake–Marcy Trail. See Section A, sub-section on Mt. Marcy, for description of view.)

Distances: Adirondak Loj to Algonquin Trail, 0.97 mi.; to Marcy Dam PBM, 2.23 mi.; to ranger station, 2.34 mi.; to junction with side trail to Phelps lean-to, 3.04 mi.; to former Indian Falls lower lean-to, 4.52 mi.; to Indian Falls-Lake Arnold Crossover Trail, 4.60 mi.; to Van Hoevenberg Bypass Trail, 5.07 mi.; to Hopkins Trail, 6.26 mi.; to former Plateau lean-to, 6.64 mi.; to Phelps Trail, 6.88 mi.; to summit of Marcy, 7.46 mi. Ascent, 3166 ft. Elevation, 5344 ft. Order of Height, 1.

Mt. Marcy via Van Hoevenberg Bypass

With the approval of DEC, the Adirondack Mountain Club in 1970 laid out and built 1.92 mi. of trail which connects the

Lake Arnold Trail to the junction of the Hopkins–Van Hoevenberg trails. This new section of trail, which is marked with red ADK markers, in combination with sections of existing older trails, makes possible another route to Mt. Marcy from Adirondak Loj. The by-pass is only 0.16 mi. longer than the Van Hoevenberg Trail and offers some compensating rewards including more interesting views and fewer steep grades. However, excessive use in recent years has made this trail less popular because of excessive mud.

From Adirondak Loj (0 mi.) follow blue DEC markers to Marcy Dam ranger's cabin 2.34 mi. via the Van Hoevenberg Trail (see above). Turn R and follow yellow DEC markers to Avalanche lean-tos 3.42 mi. via Avalanche Pass Trail (see below). Leaving trail junction at Avalanche lean-tos, follow blue DEC markers to the trail junction just after crossing the bridge over Arnold Brook at 4.50 mi. via the Lake Arnold Trail (see below).

Leaving the Lake Arnold Trail, turn L and follow red ADK markers. A medium sized stream, following to the L, is crossed at 4.65 mi. After several short, steep ascents the Van Hoevenberg Trail crossing is reached at 5.24 mi. (Follow blue DEC markers L 0.55 mi. to Indian Falls and blue DEC markers R 1.19 mi. to Hopkins Trail.)

Leaving the Van Hoevenberg Trail crossing, the trail following red ADK markers descends at a gentle grade reaching the first of three bridges at a wet area at 5.40 mi. The third bridge at 5.44 mi. crosses Marcy Brook. At 5.53 mi. the trail steepens, moderating again at 5.58 mi. Oxalis (wood sorrel) occurs in profusion at this point. The trail levels at 5.79 mi. with a view of Mt. Marcy to the R. There is a view of Table Top to the L at a turn in the trail at 5.93 mi. At 6.02 mi., there is an open area with a spring. The trail now enters open woods, and at 6.09 mi. there is fairly open area to the R with views of Wright and a section of the airplane wing. Also the MacIntyre Range and Marshall are visible to the R with Marcy showing up ahead. The trail now enters an open area with small trees and shrubs at 6.24 mi. Looking back-ward, there is a view of Table Top, Whiteface, and Lake Placid Village. At 6.32 mi. there is an open grassy area with ferns and scattered trees. At 6.36 mi. spectacular views of the Range Trail and Giant appear in an area of standing dead trees. Big Slide shows well at 6.37 mi. to the L. Mt. Marcy appears straight ahead at 6.40 mi. and the trail junction with the Hopkins and Van Hoevenberg Trails is reached at 6.44 mi.

Follow the blue DEC markers L via Van Hoevenberg Trail (see above) for a distance of 1.20 mi. to the summit of Mt. Marcy.

Distances: Adirondak Loj to Marcy Dam ranger's station, 2.34 mi.; to Avalanche lean-tos, 3.42 mi.; to Arnold Brook, 4.50 mi.; to crossing of the Van Hoevenberg Trail, 5.24 mi.; to junction with Hopkins–Van Hoevenberg Trails, 6.44 mi.; to summit of Mt. Marcy, 7.62 mi.

Phelps

The red-marked trail turns L from the Van Hoevenberg Trail (0 mi.) at a point 3.31 mi. from the Loj. The trail starts climbing ENE. At 0.08 mi. a log bridge is crossed, and the trail pulls up the ridge away from Phelps Brook. The grade becomes steep at 0.56 mi., leveling off at 0.59 mi. At 0.66 mi. the grade becomes steep again, becoming very steep at 0.74 mi. A lookout is reached at 0.75 mi. with views of Table Top, Marcy, Colden, MacIntyre, MacNaughton, Street and Nye. Climbing less steeply, a blowdown area is traversed at 0.98 mi. which affords views of Basin, Table Top and Marcy. The open rock and stunted growth at 1.05 mi. indicate that the summit is not far away. The trail is now marked with yellow-painted arrows on the rock. At 1.10 mi. there is a lookout with a view of Marcy Dam. The summit, reached at 1.17 mi., affords views of Big Slide, Yard, Giant, the Great Range, the tip of Haystack, Marcy, Gray, Colden and the Santanonis.

Distances: Adirondak Loj to start of red trail, 3.31 mi.; to summit of Phelps, 4.48 mi. Elevation, 4161 ft. Order of height, 32.

Indian Falls–Lake Arnold Crossover

On the Van Hoevenberg Trail to Marcy, opposite Indian Falls, 4.60 mi. from Adirondak Loj (see above), a trail with yellow markers branches and connects with the blue trail to Lake Arnold and Feldspar Brook from the Avalanche lean-tos. (See below.)

Leaving the junction at Indian Falls (0 mi.), the trail makes a short climb and then descends at an easy grade toward the W, staying S of Marcy Brook. The descent becomes moderate at 0.16 mi. and eases off at about 0.38 mi. At 0.50 mi. the trail turns sharp L up a brook at an easy grade. Then swinging R away from the brook at 0.57 mi. the trail soon levels off and reaches the R bank of Arnold Brook at 0.69 mi. Following down the R bank, the trail crosses Arnold Brook at 0.74 mi. and joins the blue trail from Avalanche lean-tos. (PBM 3415 ft.) (Turn R for Avalanche Pass Trail and Avalanche lean-tos, 1.04 mi.; L for Lake Arnold, 0.50 mi.; and yellow trail near Feldspar Brook lean-to, 2.13 mi.)

Distance: Indian Falls to Lake Arnold Trail, 0.74 mi.

The MacIntyre Mountains*

The series of peaks known as the MacIntyre Mts., or the MacIntyre Range, rises loftily against the sky S of Heart Lake, having been named in honor of Archibald McIntyre, the dominating figure in the iron works enterprise that bore his name. Considered by many the noblest group of mountains in the Adirondacks, the range extends for about 8 mi., running NE and SW. Its steep NW slopes form one side of Indian Pass and the SE spur helps to form Avalanche Pass and shadow Avalanche Lake, Lake Colden and Flowed Lands.

The most northerly peak is called Wright Peak, 4580 ft., in honor of Governor Silas Wright. A lesser peak NE of Wright is Whale's Tail. To the SW of Wright is the highest peak of the range and second highest of the Adirondacks, Algonquin, 5114 ft. This peak has also been referred to as Mt. MacIntyre. SW of Algonquin stands Boundary Peak, so named because it is supposed to have marked the ancient boundary between the Algonquin and Iroquois Indians. It is, at present, on the boundary between the towns of Newcomb and North Elba. SW of Boundary is Iroquois Peak 4840 ft. The 1943 survey shows Boundary as also being 4840 ft., but it

---

* The spelling of MacIntyre here conforms to the USGS topog map and is approved by the U.S. Board of Geographic Names. It is used throughout this guidebook to be consistent. However, the man who started the Adirondack Iron works spelled his name McIntyre.

is not rated as an individual mountain among the 46 peaks, being instead a prominence in the range on the way to Iroquois. Still further, SW, and separated from Iroquois by a deep col, is a trailless peak that rises 4360 ft. Colvin called it Clinton for Governor DeWitt Clinton, while making an official survey; ADKers have called it Herbert for Herb Clark, the guide who went with Robert and George Marshall when they became the first people to climb the 46 peaks that were at that time indicated on the maps to be 4000 ft. or higher. The Adirondack Forty-Sixers call it Marshall in honor of Robert Marshall, who died in 1939. The name Marshall is now officially approved by the New York State Board on Geographic Names.

Besides the trail from Heart Lake to Algonquin, and its branches to Wright and Iroquois, this mountain range may also be approached from Lake Colden on the SE.

Algonquin Peak from Heart Lake

From the Adirondak Loj Campers and Hikers Building, take the Van Hoevenberg Trail to the trail junction at 0.97 mi. Here, the trail to Algonquin continues straight ahead (Trail L leads to Mt. Marcy and Avalanche Pass via Marcy Dam). Continuing at an easy grade, and crossing a brook at 1.10 mi., the junction with the Whale's Tail Notch Trail is reached at 1.42 mi. Gradually increasing in grade, the Algonquin Trail continues to a junction with an abandoned trail coming in from the R at 2.33 mi. This is .03 mi. past the unmarked and abandoned Wright Ski Trail leading off to the L (see below). A beautiful cascade on the L is reached at 2.40 mi. In dry seasons this may be the last water. The trail levels off at 2.60 mi., but soon starts climbing again at 2.72 mi. It crosses bare rocks on a rude bridge and climbs steeply to a sharp L turn at 2.90 mi. where there is a rock cobble about 100 ft. off the trail on the R. A short level stretch followed by a steep pitch brings one to the first view of Algonquin straight ahead at 2.95 mi. The grade is now somewhat easier as the trail heads S towards the summit. The spur trail to Wright Peak enters on the L at 3.10 mi. (See below.) In usual seasons a small stream here provides the last water.

The trail now ascends fairly steeply, climbing 912 ft. in the next 0.87 mi. As the spruce becomes dwarfed, one can see over them to the rocky summit and look back towards Lake Placid and Whiteface. The ascent is more gradual at 3.52 mi. and timberline is reached at about 3.57 mi. The last 0.40 mi. of climbing is in the open, and great care should be used in following the rock cairns from here to the summit at 3.98 mi., particularly when the visibility is poor. On top the trail is met by the trail up the SW slope from Lake Colden, marked with paint blazes on the rocks. (See below.)

Splendid views are obtained from the summit. Across Avalanche Pass to the SE, with its many slides and famous dike, is Mt. Colden with Gray Peak directly over its summit. To the L of Gray Peak is Marcy and Skylight to the R. In the distance over the L slope of Marcy may be seen Hough and Dix Peaks. To the NE of Marcy is the Great Range, in the distance to the E is Giant, with Whiteface and Lake Placid to the N. Close at hand to the N is Heart Lake; to the W is Wallface, Indian Pass, Street and Nye, with Flowed Lands and Lake Colden directly below to the S. Several species of alpine flowers may be found near the summit. To find the marked trail on descent keep Whiteface and Heart Lake in line.

Distances: Adirondak Loj via blue trail to yellow trail for Algonquin, 0.97 mi.; to Whale's Tail Notch Ski Trail, 1.42 mi.; to Waterfall, 2.40 mi.; to Blue Trail for Wright Peak, 3.10 mi.; to summit of Algonquin, 3.98 mi. Ascent, 2936 ft. Elevation, 5114 ft. Order of height, 2.

Boundary and Iroquois Peaks

Near the col between Algonquin and Boundary a poorly cut trail turns SW leading over Boundary to Iroquois. This trail was rerouted by the Adirondack 46ers in 1975. It leaves the Algonquin–Lake Colden Trail below the height of land in the col 0.38 mi. below the summit of Algonquin. At this col between Algonquin and Boundary, this "herd path" continues straight ahead from the route down from Algonquin. This is not a maintained trail, and its condition depends upon the amount of usage. Iroquois offers unique views of Wallface and Algonquin. Dix can be seen from Boundary but not from Iroquois. Allow about 20 to 30 minutes from the col to Iroquois.

Distances: Trail junction to Boundary, 0.22 mi.; to summit of Iroquois, about 0.65 mi. Elevation, 4840 ft. Order of height, 7.

Wright Peak

At 0.87 mi. below the summit of Algonquin 3.10 mi. from Adirondak Loj via blue and yellow trails, a trail branches to the E marked with blue DEC markers and leads to the summit of Wright Peak. Leaving the trail junction (0 mi.), the trail climbs steadily, soon heading NE, then SE and E again, and enters an open blowdown area at 0.11 mi. Timberline is reached at 0.21 mi., after which the route is marked with cairns up the bare rock ridge. The grade rounds off at 0.31 mi., and the open and rocky summit is reached at 0.43 mi., where splendid views are obtained.

A bronze plaque on a large vertical rock face just N of the summit commemorates the four airmen who lost their lives in a crash of a B47 at that spot in 1962. Parts of the aircraft are still visible and are scattered around a considerable area very close to the top of the mountain.

Distances: Adirondak Loj to blue trail for Wright Peak, 3.10 mi.; to summit of Wright Peak, 3.53 mi. Ascent from trail junction, 385 ft. Elevation, 4580 ft. Order of height, 16.

Wright Peak via Slide from Marcy Brook

For those who like to bushwhack, Wright Peak may also be climbed by the slide on the SE. Take Avalanche Pass Trail from Marcy Dam to log flume in Marcy Brook. (See below.) This is 0.25 mi. up the brook from the point where the yellow trail suddenly comes out on the brink of Marcy Brook. Cross the brook at the log flume and continue up brook a few yards to first tributary coming in on the R. Bushwhack up tributary to slide. Climb slide to summit.

Wright Peak and Whale's Tail Notch Ski Trails

At a point on the Algonquin Trail 2.30 mi. from the Adirondak Loj Campers and Hikers Building and 1.33 mi. from the junction with the Van Hoevenberg Trail (0.10 mi. below the waterfall), an abandoned ski trail, Wright Peak Ski Trail, turns L, ascends to the ridge running NE from Wright Peak and climbs to the summit of Wright. Thick second growth makes the trail impossible to ski, but a herd path following the ski trail offers an alternate way up Wright for those used to following obscure trails. The distance from the Algonquin Trail is about 1.50 mi.

The Whale's Tail Notch Ski Trail offers an alternate but longer route to Marcy Dam from Adirondak Loj. It is not maintained for summer use. Turning L at a sign post on the Algonquin Trail 1.42 mi. from the Campers and Hikers Building at Adirondak Loj and 0.45 mi. from the Van Hoevenberg Trail, this ski trail climbs steadily up the NW side of Whale's Tail Notch in and out of a small brook with a maximum slope of 15 deg. It levels off in the pass at 0.50 mi. (elevation, 2750 ft.), having gained over 300 ft. The descent on the SE starts at 0.64 mi. and follows down a good sized brook, crossing and recrossing the brook, with a maximum slope of 20 deg. It levels off at 1.03 mi. and follows down the brook's R bank. The side trail leading to Marcy Dam lean-tos from the Van Hoevenberg Trail is reached at 1.22 mi. Turning L a lean-to is passed at 1.25 mi. and the blue Van Hoevenberg Trail is reached at 1.28 mi. just before PBM 2365 at Marcy Dam.

Distance: Adirondak Loj to Marcy Dam PBM, 2.70 mi. (This is via Whale's Tail Notch Ski Trail.)

Avalanche Pass to Lake Colden Outlet

At Marcy Dam the Avalanche Pass Trail, with yellow markers, forks R from the Van Hoevenberg Trail at the lean-to where the hiker's register stands (0 mi.). It crosses a bridge at 0.07 mi. and turns L along a wooded bank avoiding wet ground. (Straight ahead a trail leads 0.09 mi. across a small brook to two lean-tos.) The trail reaches the brink of Marcy Brook at 0.36 mi. where it joins

an old tote road. The trail turns L and continues at an easy grade
along the R bank of the brook, where there is a lean-to at approximately 0.6 mi. It finally crosses the brook on a log bridge at 1.03
mi. and leads up to the two Avalanche lean-tos just beyond the
bridge at 1.08 mi.

At the second lean-to there is a trail junction. (Blue trail L
leads up Marcy Brook to Lake Arnold and Feldspar lean-to, also
to Mt. Colden, to Indian Falls on the Van Hoevenberg Trail, and
to Mt. Marcy via the Van Hoevenberg Bypass Trail.) Continuing
R with yellow markers the trail passes to the L of a wet area and
bears R, leaving the telephone line on the L at 1.11 mi. Continuing
up the R bank of a tributary to Marcy Brook, the trail soon turns
up the slope away from the tributary. (Unmarked trail upstream
leads to wild Caribou Pass.) At 1.21 mi. the trail turns L on a tote
road and reaches a switchback at 1.39 mi. The Avalanche Pass
Trail turns R, climbs steeply and then levels off at 1.64 mi. as it
enters the NE end of the pass. Here at the height of land, during
wet seasons a small waterfall descends from the cliff on the L and
divides into two streams, one flowing NE to the St. Lawrence and
the other flowing SW to the Hudson. This and Wallface Ponds
mark the northernmost sources of the Hudson. The trail now starts
to descend slowly, following closely under the high rock wall on
the R side of the pass. As the NE end of Avalanche Lake (elevation,
2863 ft.) is approached, a rock shelter on the L is passed at 2.10
mi., and the upper end of the lake is reached at 2.15 mi. Geologists
tell us that Avalanche Lake and Lake Colden (elevation, 2764 ft.)
were once one but were separated by a prehistoric slide or slides
which not only divided them in two but lifted one about a hundred
feet higher than the other. The great slides now visible on the
NW side of Mt. Colden occurred in 1869 and 1942.

At Avalanche Lake the precipitous side of Mt. Colden rises
directly from the water and the even more precipitous side of
Caribou (Avalanche) Mt. leaves only room for a trail on the R.
The next 0.50 mi. is quite rugged, especially with packs, but it is
interesting—over ledges, under and around huge boulders, across
crevices, climbing hand and foot, up and down, aided by plank
walks and sturdy ladders. In two places where the precipices come
down to the water, they are skirted by means of plank bridges

bolted into the solid bedrock. The first one of these, which is also the longer, is reached at 2.42 mi. and is known as the "Hitch-Up-Matilda." From this bridge one can look up practically to the rocky summit of Mt. Colden. The trail crosses the second bridge at 2.52 mi. from which one can look across the lake directly into the well-known Avalanche (Colden) Dike. This steep-walled gorge, which was produced by the differential erosion of gabbro and anorthosite, offers an interesting but strenuous route to the summit of Mt. Colden, including a short, vertical rock climb, for those who prefer to get off the beaten path.

The foot of the lake is reached at 2.68 mi. where the trail crosses the outlet and turns R. The site of the original Caribou lean-to was destroyed by the great slide in the fall of 1942. The trail now follows the L bank of the outlet and comes to a fork at 2.99 mi. (The R branch, marked with blue disks, leads to the trail up the MacIntyre Range to Algonquin, and also around the NW shore of Lake Colden via the ranger headquarters to the outlet at Colden Dam. The present Caribou lean-to is located a few yards down this trail on the other side of the brook. See below.) The L branch, with yellow markers, continues through the woods on the SE side of Lake Colden. After crossing several log bridges, a red trail to the L is reached at 3.48 mi. This leads away from the lake to the summit of Mt. Colden, 1.62 mi. (See below.) Continuing straight ahead along the shore, the yellow trail is close to the lake on logs at 3.72 mi. and brings one to the middle of the three Colden lean-tos on the R bank of the Opalescent River at 3.87 mi. The newest lean-to (1955) is situated upstream about 45 yds. Turning R, downstream, the third lean-to is passed at 3.89 mi. The red trail to Marcy (4.45 mi.) enters on the L at 3.92 mi., crossing the Opalescent on a log crib bridge, and the ladder at Colden Dam at the outlet of Lake Colden is reached at 3.97 mi. (Blue trail R at top of ladder leads around NW shore of Lake Colden. See below. Red trail L leads 1.06 mi. to the two Calamity lean-tos at Calamity Brook outlet of Flowed Lands, thence by alternative trails to the Upper Works, 5.52 mi., or via Hanging Spear Falls to Tahawus and Sanford Lake, 9.15 mi. See Sanford Lake Region, Section B5.) There is a total of sixteen lean-tos in the vicinity of Lake Colden and Flowed Lands.

Leaving the junction with the red trail (0 mi.), crossing the bridge and bearing R, a trail leads 0.07 mi. to Opalescent lean-to on the L bank of the Opalescent River. At 0.18 mi. a side trail on the R leads 0.04 mi. to McMartin lean-to. Another lean-to was added to this group in 1963 by the Intercollegiate Outing Club Association. Continuing straight ahead, Flowed Lands Landing is reached at 0.23 mi. A double size lean-to was built in 1958 between the Opalescent and McMartin lean-tos. Another lean-to has since been built on L bank of the Opalescent about 50 yds. above the bridge.

Distances: Marcy Dam ranger station to Avalanche lean-tos, 1.08 mi.; to NE end of Avalanche Lake, 2.15 mi.; to trail around NW shore of Lake Colden, 2.99 mi.; to Mt. Colden Trail, 3.48 mi.; to red trail at bridge near Colden lean-tos, 3.92 mi.; to Colden Dam, 3.97 mi. (6.31 mi. from Adirondak Loj).

Mt. Colden from Lake Colden

Mt. Colden forms the SE rampart of Avalanche Pass and was named by Professor Redfield for David C. Colden, one of the proprietors of the MacIntyre Iron Works. Professor Emmons later renamed it Mt. McMartin in honor of Judge Duncan McMartin, who was one of the leaders in the inception and development of the iron works, but the former name has endured.

The trail starts on the SE side of Lake Colden, 0.44 mi. NE on the yellow trail from the log crib bridge near the Colden lean-tos at the outlet of the lake and 5.82 mi. from Adirondak Loj. It was cut by Arthur S. Hopkins, former Director of Lands and Forests, and Forest Ranger Clinton West. It turns SE away from the lake and is marked with red disks. Leaving the lake (0 mi.), the ascent is gradual at first with the trail passing through a former blowdown area, now mostly grown over. At 0.18 mi. a stream can be heard on the L shortly before passing a beautiful stand of spruce. At about 0.60 mi. the grade becomes quite steep, and the trail swings to the N to avoid the shoulder. Soon it veers to the R, still climbing steeply. A short breather is reached at 0.67 mi. and again at 0.81 mi. A low rock ledge is passed on the L at 1.13 mi. where views of Redfield, Cliff and Marshall can be had. The trail turns L around the upper end of the ledge with the grade becoming quite steep. At 1.18 mi. another steep stretch is reached with many downed trees. Two huge boulders are passed under, with an interesting cave, shortly before coming to an old wooden ladder at 1.32 mi. From here the climbing is less difficult as the trail heads NE along the rocks with the main peak in sight. (When descending via this route care should be taken in following the paint blazes on the open rocks.) At 1.52 mi. a rock wall is reached which one must ascend to reach the summit at 1.62 mi. The actual top is off the trail to the R. This summit rises between Marcy on the SE and Algonquin on the NW. Avalanche Lake and the "Hitch-Up-Matilda" can be seen directly below. The trail continues over the summit and leads 1.47 mi. to the Lake Arnold Trail. (See below.)

Distance: Lake Colden to summit of Mt. Colden 1.62 mi. (7.44 mi. from Adirondak Loj). Ascent from lake, 1950 ft. Elevation, 4714 ft. Order of height, 11.

Trail around Northwest Shore of Lake Colden

Starting (0 mi.) at the trail junction 0.31 mi. from foot of Avalanche Lake and 2.99 mi. from Marcy Dam ranger station (see above), take R fork and cross stream at 0.01 mi., following blue markers. At 0.02 mi. trail L leads 30 yds. to Caribou lean-to. The trail has no steep grades and skirts the swampy upper end of Lake Colden, passing through what used to be a fine forest before the 1950 hurricane created havoc in this section. On the L bank of the first tributary, 0.40 mi. from trail junction, a trail to the R with blue markers leads 2.09 mi. to Algonquin Peak in the MacIntyre Range. (See below.) Turning L across the brook on a foot bridge, also with blue markers, the trail follows down the R bank a short distance, then veers away crossing Cold Brook on a bridge at 0.56 mi. and brings one to the ranger's camp at 0.58 mi. Cold Brook lean-to, with a stove and bunk, is located 0.11 mi. up Cold Brook behind the ranger's camp.

The trail continues in front of the ranger's cabin and after crossing a little bog follows the lakeshore, giving splendid views of Mt. Colden across the lake. At the SW end of the lake a low promontory, known as Beaver Point, is crossed. Here at 0.89 mi.

is located Beaver Point lean-to just off the trail to the L. At 0.92
mi. a side trail L leads about 25 yds. to West lean-to, named for
Clinton West, a Colden Ranger for many years. The trail soon
reaches the ladder above Colden Dam at the outlet of the lake
where the blue markers end. This is 1.04 mi. from the junction
with the yellow trail near Caribou lean-to via NW shore of Lake
Colden, and 0.98 mi. via the SE shore. (Red trail straight ahead
is the Marcy Trail from Sanford Lake via Calamity Brook or Hanging Spear Falls. Turning L and descending the ladder, this trail
crosses the outlet on its way to Marcy, and in 0.05 mi. connects
at the log crib bridge over the Opalescent with the yellow trail
leading past the Colden lean-tos and around the SE shore of Lake
Colden. See Sanford Lake Region, Section B5 and above.)

Distances: Trail junction near Caribou lean-to to Algonquin
Trail, 0.40 mi.; to ranger camp, 0.58 mi.; to Beaver Point lean-to,
0.89 mi.; to West lean-to, 0.92 mi.; to Colden Dam, 1.04 mi. (6.37
mi. from Adirondak Loj.)

Algonquin Peak from Lake Colden

From the trail on the NW shore of Lake Colden (see above),
0.18 mi. NE of the ranger's camp and 0.40 mi. from the trail junction near Caribou lean-to, a trail with blue markers starts up Algonquin Peak in the MacIntyre Range, the trail junction being at a
bridge over a tributary to Lake Colden.

Leaving the junction (0 mi.), the trail follows up the L bank
of the brook at an easy to moderate grade, getting steeper at 0.13
mi. as it climbs through conifers. The top of a cataract is reached
at 0.19 mi. The grade levels off, and a heavy blowdown area is
reached at 0.23 mi. At 0.27 mi. the trail crosses to the R bank at
a pile of logs and continues at an easy grade up the brook, reaching
the end of the heavy blowdown damage at about 0.32 mi. The
trail crosses to the L bank at 0.34 mi. and recrosses again at 0.45
mi. and 0.48 mi. shortly after which the grade becomes steeper.
The foot of a waterfall is reached at 0.60 mi. and the foot of a
slide in the brook at 0.64 mi. The trail climbs the sloping granite
ledges that form the brook bed, from which fine views of the slides
on Colden are obtained.

The trail leaves the slide on the L bank of the brook at 0.70 mi., soon after which a steep pitch marks the beginning of steady, steep climbing with occasional breathers. The grade slackens a bit about 0.88 mi. Crossing the brook at 0.90 mi., the trail follows up pretty much in the brook but mostly on the R bank. Crossing to the L bank at 0.96 mi., a big pool is reached at 0.99 mi. Keeping R, the trail climbs steeply out of the brook and continues very rocky and rough at a steady, steep grade. The dwarfing of the spruce gives promise of a top as the trail approaches the col between Boundary and Algonquin. At 1.71 mi., shortly before reaching the height of land in the col, a trail that is not maintained turns L for Boundary and Iroquois peaks. (See above.)

The Algonquin Trail continues past this junction and emerges from the scrub at the height of land in the col at 1.78 mi. Here the trail turns sharp R and follows paint blazes up the bare rock cone to the summit at 2.08 mi. where it is met by the yellow trail on the N slope from Heart Lake, marked with rock cairns above timberline. (See above.)

Distances: Trail junction at bridge near Lake Colden to rock slide in brook, 0.64 mi.; to trail for Boundary and Iroquois, 1.71 mi.; to summit of Algonquin, 2.09 mi. Ascent from Lake Colden, 2350 ft. Elevation, 5114 ft. Order of height, 2.

Trail from Lake Colden to Indian Pass Trail

From the trail on the NW shore of Lake Colden near the ranger's camp (see below), a trail was cut in 1965 through the col between Iroquois and Marshall, Algonquin Pass, to a point on the Indian Pass Trail 0.90 mi. SE of Scott Clearing via the High Water Route (4.90 mi. from Adirondak Loj.) It is a very steep and rough trail on the Lake Colden side of the pass. It starts just a few yards NE from the bridge over Cold Brook.

Leaving the trail junction (0 mi.) and following yellow markers, the trail starts at an easy grade and follows the L bank of Cold Brook through thick spruce growing up through the hurricane damage of the 1950s. There is a slight pitch up at 0.14 mi., followed by a pitch down where the trail crosses a small tributary. Another tributary is crossed at 0.22 mi. after which there is a pitch up followed by an easy stretch. Cold Brook is crossed at 0.28 mi. The trail then soon reaches the R (S) fork of Cold Brook (not shown on topog). Here it enters the brook for easier going and leaves right away on the same side, again doing this in another 40 yds.

The grade begins to get a little steeper at 0.37 mi., and the R fork is crossed at 0.46 mi. The trail enters the brook at 0.53 mi. and leaves on the same side (R bank) in about 20 yds. The real climbing soon begins. A very steep pitch is ascended at 0.56 mi., followed by a short breather and then up again. A small brook is crossed at 0.62 mi., and at 0.65 mi. the trail crosses the R fork on a slant to the L bank. In about 30 yds. there is another very steep pitch followed by fair to steep climbing. The grade moderates at 0.77 mi., but from 0.85 mi. to 1.03 mi., there are four very steep pitch ups as the trail climbs away from the brook up a shoulder of Iroquois. Slabbing along the shoulder, the grades are moderate, but the footing is rough as the trail approaches the col. A small height of land is reached at 1.43 mi. after which the trail descends a little and then climbs gradually. The top of the pass is reached at about 1.50 mi. The trail continues fairly level for some distance through the grassy col with many ferns and little balsams.

Now descending at easy to moderate grades, the trail crosses a brook and follows down at some distance from its L bank through an open forest. At 2.16 mi. the trail descends steeply and crosses two branches of a large brook from the R bank at 2.19 mi. Veering away from the brook on moderate grades and crossing over a shoulder into another valley, the trail descends through a small couloir at 2.45 mi. and reaches the R bank of another large brook at 2.47 mi. where it turns R and joins an old tote road. The trail veers away from the brook but returns and crosses it at 2.72 mi. After following down the L bank past some very steep falls in the brook, the trail returns to the R bank at 2.84 mi. Continuing down the R bank on the tote road over old corduroys, some interesting bare rock ledges are seen on the L bank and a large chockstone in the brook. The trail recrosses to the L bank at 2.98 mi., veers away from the brook and ascends a steep pitch at 3.21 mi. to get over a low shoulder. After pitching down at 3.24 mi., the trail continues on the level and joins the red-marked Indian Pass Trail at 3.31 mi. Turn L for Summit Rock, 1.10 mi.; R via High Water

Route for Scott Clearing lean-to, 1.12 mi.; turnoff to Rocky Falls lean-to, 2.58 mi.

Distances: Start of trail near ranger's station to height of land in Algonquin Pass, 1.50 mi.; to Indian Pass Trail, 3.31 mi.

Avalanche Camp to Lake Arnold and Feldspar Brook

At the second Avalanche lean-to (0 mi.) on the Avalanche Pass Trail (see above) a trail branches to the L, marked with blue disks. It crosses a fair-sized brook at 0.16 mi. and begins to climb on an old tote road high above the L (SW) bank of Marcy Brook. The grade is steady and the trail full of corduroys, but the climbing becomes easier at about 0.60 mi. and again at about 0.85 mi. At 1.04 mi. the trail divides (PBM 3415 ft.). (Trail to the L with yellow markers leads 0.74 mi. to Indian Falls on the Van Hoevenberg Trail. See above.) Turning R (S) with blue markers the trail crosses Arnold Brook at 1.08 mi. (Trail L is Van Hoevenberg Bypass Trail to Mt. Marcy 3.12 mi.) The trail continues to climb along the R bank of the brook. At 1.44 mi. the trail forks, the trail straight ahead bypassing the former Lake Arnold lean-to and being about 50 yds. shorter. Turning R and climbing, the former lean-to site is reached at 1.54 mi. The yellow-marked trail on R is the L. Morgan Porter Trail to Mt. Colden, 1.37 mi. Crossing the outlet of Lake Arnold, the trail rejoins the direct route at 1.57 mi.

Turning R the height of land (elevation about 3800 ft.) between Colden and a spur of Marcy is reached at 1.79 mi., after which a steady descent begins following the course of a tributary to the Opalescent River. The grade eases off at about 2.05 mi.

Continuing straight ahead with blue markers, the trail continues descending at a fair grade through the conifer forest, crosses a brook at 2.27 mi., comes to a level stretch and passes a spring at 2.40 mi. Descending moderately, the trail comes close to the R bank of a washed-out brook bed at 2.65 mi., this being about the bottom of the grade. Continuing toward the S, a marshy tributary is crossed at 2.71 mi., after which the trail reaches the R bank of the Opalescent River and crosses it on the stones at 2.76 mi. Following down the L bank through marshy grassland, the bridge across the Opalescent to Feldspar lean-to is reached at 3.13 mi.

Turning sharp L, the trail crosses Feldspar Brook at 3.16 mi., not far from the brook's confluence with the Opalescent and joins the yellow Marcy Trail from Sanford Lake at 3.17 mi. (Turn L for Marcy, 2.36 mi.; R for Lake Colden Dam, 2.23 mi. and Sanford Lake via Twin Brook, 8.75. See Sanford Lake Region, Section B5.)

Distances: Avalanche Camp to Indian Falls Crossover Trail, 1.04 mi.; to Van Hoevenberg Bypass Trail, 1.08 mi.; to former Lake Arnold lean-to and L. Morgan Porter Trail, 1.54 mi.; to crossing of Opalescent River, 2.76 mi.; to Feldspar lean-to, 3.13 mi.; to yellow trail at Feldspar Brook, 3.17 mi. (6.59 mi. from Adirondak Loj.)

Mt. Colden from Lake Arnold via L. Morgan Porter Trail

This approach to Mt. Colden from Lake Arnold replaces the now abandoned trail which turned off 0.67 mi. S of Lake Arnold on the trail to Feldspar Brook. The present trail was laid out in 1966 by Rudy Strobel and built by ADK with the approval of DEC, which now maintains it. It has officially been named the L. Morgan Porter Trail in memory of the man who produced the sixth and seventh editions of this guidebook.

The trail starts at the S end of the site of the former Lake Arnold lean-to where the blue-marked trail leads L back to the main trail. The Colden Trail, with yellow DEC markers, turns R and proceeds in a westerly direction, soon swinging SW as it ascends the NE shoulder of the mountain. The climb is not steep and is interspersed with relatively level areas and occasional sharp pitch ups over ledges. An open blowdown area is reached at 0.21 mi., and a view of part of the shoulder is seen at 0.49 mi. There are frequent views to the E and NE along this section. After surmounting a bulge on the shoulder at 0.55 mi., the trail drops until 0.65 mi. when the ascent of the N summit is resumed. At 0.97 mi. the trail comes out on the S end of the N summit, turns L on bare rock and almost immediately turns L into the scrub, dropping into a sag at 1.02 mi. After a short ascent, it descends into the col between the N and S summits at 1.11 mi., where the abandoned trail enters on the L. From here to the main summit, it is 0.26 mi. straight ahead with an ascent of 250 ft.

Distances: Lake Arnold to the summit of Colden, 1.37 mi. (6.23 mi. from Adirondak Loj.) Ascent, 942 ft. Elevation, 4714 ft. Order of height, 11.

Indian Pass from Heart Lake

Indian Pass, or Adirondack Pass as it was formerly sometimes called, is a stupendous gorge between Wallface Mt. and the MacIntyre Range, lying 3 mi. NE of Henderson Lake and about 5 mi. SW of Heart Lake. It is over a mile in length, and its sheer NW wall rises 1000 ft. on Wallface Mt. It was once much deeper, but repeated rock slides have raised its present base and made it very rough and tortuous. At many places among these rocks the ice never melts and the sun never shines. The trail passes above this rock jumble on the SE side of the pass, with Marshall (Herbert), the southernmost peak of the MacIntyre Range, forming the SE side of the pass. Donaldson tells us that the Indian name for the pass was He-no-do-aw-da, The Path of the Thunderer.

The trail begins at a point on the Heart Lake road 0.10 mi. N of Adirondak Loj. From the trail sign on the road follow red DEC markers W 0.11 mi. on a grassy tote road, passing Mt. Jo ski trail on R and bearing L to junction with spur trail from the Loj. The trail is also posted with red half-mile markers.* From the Loj (0 mi.) head N across the lawn toward Mt. Jo, swinging L on tote road and joining the state-marked red trail at 0.10 mi. At 0.13 mi. there is a trail to the R and a sign marked "Mt. Jo." The trail continues W on the tote road along the N shore of Heart Lake, passing several private lean-tos. (See Adirondak Loj, Section E.) The end of the lake is reached at 0.44 mi. where the old Mt. Nye ski trail continues W. This ski trail was constructed for the 1932 Olympics but is no longer maintained. However, it provides a relatively easy approach to trailless Nye and Street. (See Section C.) It is kept cleared for 0.14 mi. to the W property line of the ADK.

Swinging SW the Indian Pass Trail soon climbs gradually to

---

* Half-mile markers are red numbers on a yellow field for contrast with DEC red trail markers.

the top of a short rise where it enters the State Forest Preserve, having been on the private property of the Adirondack Mountain Club up to this point. The trail continues on the tote road through magnificent forest at easy grades, following the general direction of Indian Pass Brook, considered by some to be the W branch of the Ausable River to avoid confusion with the Indian Pass Brook flowing SW out of the pass into Henderson Lake. Shortly past a raspberry patch, a fair-sized brook is crossed at 2.09 mi. Just beyond the brook, a branch trail on the R leads 0.25 mi. to Rocky Falls lean-to on the opposite side of the river. This is the better route to the lean-to with heavy packs. The main trail now climbs abruptly and reaches the second turnoff to Rocky Falls at 2.32 mi. (PBM 2160 ft.) Here a steep trail to the R descends to the river and across to the lean-to (0.10 mi.).

Continuing straight ahead, the Indian Pass Trail crosses several various-sized brooks and reaches Scott Clearing lean-to at 3.78 mi. Crossing the brook in front of the lean-to, a junction and the old lean-to site in Scott Clearing are reached at 3.99 mi., the old fireplace still being visible in the grass on the R. (Trail L is a shortcut leading 44 yds. to the High Water Route described below.) As one enters the clearing, Iroquois is visible dead ahead. This clearing is the site of an old lumber camp, the high dam once making a large pond here. Going R at 3.99 mi. another junction is reached at the stone dam at 4.01 mi. (The blue trail turning R leads to Scott Pond, 1.55 mi. and Wallface Ponds, 2.70 mi. See below.)

Turning L, a third junction is reached in a few yards at the end of the dam. (Here the Low Water Route turns R and can be followed up the gravel flats if the water in the brook is not too high, beaver flooding sometimes making it impassable, the trail following the R bank of the brook as soon as it leaves the bed of the old pond. This route avoids some steep grades and is 0.2 mi. shorter than the High Water Route.)

Going straight ahead with red markers at the end of the dam, the High Water Route swings back toward the clearing, the shortcut entering on L at 4.04 mi. After following up the L bank of a large brook a short ways (same brook that flows by the lean-to), it veers off to the R and climbs a moderate grade. After rounding off at 4.17 mi., the height of land is reached at 4.21 mi. Descending gradually, the trail turns sharp R in about 60 yds. and follows down the R bank of a small brook in a ravine at a moderate to fair grade. Crossing the brook and swinging L away from it with the old dam in view through the trees, the trail starts a moderate climb at 4.31 mi. and reaches another height of land at 4.35 mi. Descending a steep pitch and crossing a small brook, the trail levels off at 4.38 mi. and follows along above the Low Water Route, gradually descending and rejoining it at 4.48 mi.

Turning L the trail crosses a large tributary from its R bank at its confluence with Indian Pass Brook at 4.50 mi. Another large tributary flows from the L at 4.76 mi. out of Algonquin Pass on the SE between Iroquois and Marshall. The trail enters the main brook for a short distance along its R bank at 4.84 mi. At 4.90 mi. the trail over Algonquin Pass from Lake Colden enters on the L. The trail makes a 30 yd. crossing to the L bank at 5.02 mi. After recrossing the brook at 5.08 mi., the trail starts climbing and enters woods of second growth while the main stream turns westward toward its source at Scott Pond. (The stream can be followed about 0.75 mi. to the pond. Ascent, 500 ft.)

The trail becomes steeper as the pass becomes narrower. It clambers over ledges and around huge blocks of rocks. An icy, little stream trickles down the trail. By exploring among the rock caves, ice may be found even in mid-summer. After climbing about 400 ft. in 0.39 mi., there is a short level stretch at 5.47 mi. (PBM 2834 ft. on L, 656 ft. above PBM at Loj) where one can look through the trees at the 1000 ft. vertical cliff on Wallface Mt. This is approximately the divide, the height of land being at 5.54 mi. where there is a DEC sign. However, one must continue on the trail to get the best view. The trail now dips down, then climbs again and gradually descends the other side of the pass until a turnout on the R is reached at 6.00 mi. Here just a short way off the trail is Summit Rock from which the view of Wallface Mt. across the gorge and of Henderson Mt. and Santanoni Peak to the SE is unobstructed. The descent from the top of the pass to this point is about 200 ft. From Summit Rock it is 4.42 mi. to the Upper Works at the Old Tahawus Club location. (See Sanford Lake Region, Section B5).

Distances: Adirondak Loj to Scott Clearing lean-to, 3.78 mi.;

to Scott Clearing and blue trail to Scott and Wallface Ponds, 4.00
mi.; to junction with trail from Lake Colden, 4.90 mi.; to height
of land in Indian Pass via High Water Route, 5.54 mi.; to Summit
Rock, 6.00 mi.

Scott and Wallface Ponds

This trail was cut by the DEC in 1962–63 and follows the
old tote road W from the dam at Scott Clearing.

Leaving the Indian Pass Trail (see above) at the stone dam
(0 mi.) and following blue markers, the trail heads W and makes
a rather difficult crossing at Indian Pass Brook just below the log
flume in the old spillway at the dam at 0.04 mi. Bearing R on
the far shore and then climbing steeply to the L, the trail rejoins
the old tote road at 0.07 mi. Heading S and then swinging toward
the W, the trail climbs steadily at a moderate to fair grade and
crosses a small brook at 0.18 mi. A large brook is heard in the
ravine on the R at about 0.33 mi., and the grade rounds off at
0.50 mi. becoming easy to level. At 0.58 mi. the trail pitches down
and crosses a brook from the L bank at 0.62 mi. followed by an
easy climb. Crossing another brook at 0.67 mi. and following it
up over corduroys for a short distance, a height of land is reached
at 1.12 mi. Descending at an easy to moderate grade, the trail
levels off at 1.21 mi., passes a vlei on the R and climbs easily to
1.38 mi. Heading W and descending easy to moderate grades, the
trail turns sharply to the L (S) at 1.50 mi. where Scott Pond may
be seen through the trees. It then descends to the old dam at
Scott Pond outlet at 1.55 mi.

Following down the L bank of the outlet amid large boulders,
the stream is crossed via a log jam at 1.53 mi. where the trail
climbs back along the R bank to the S side of the pond. Here
good views may be had. One may find the going easier by crossing
the outlet directly below the dam and rejoining the blue trail on
the other side. A beaver dam is passed just above the old stone
dam. Continuing W, the pond is visible through the trees on the
R at 1.84 mi. after which the trail soon heads SSW, crosses a vlei
from 1.91 to 1.95 mi. and immediately bears L at a beaver dam.
Swinging NW around the upper end of the beaver flow, the trail

then heads W and starts climbing at 2.03 mi. After ascending a steep pitch, the trail levels off through a col at 2.14 mi. and then descends to the E shore of a small pond at 2.26 mi. The trail continues to the NW following the general direction of the pond outlet and reaches a second pond at 2.39 mi. where the brook flows N into the pond. These ponds (here referred to as the Second and First Upper Scott Ponds to distinguish them from the nearby Wallface Ponds which flow into the Hudson) flow into Scott Pond and then out to the St. Lawrence.

Continuing W through a small pass with care being taken to detour around some of the wetter sections without losing sight of the trail, the largest of the three Wallface Ponds is reached at about 2.70 mi. These ponds, together with the divided brook in Avalanche Pass, form the northernmost sources of the Hudson.

Distances: Indian Pass Trail at Scott Clearing Dam to Scott Pond Outlet Dam, 1.55 mi.; to Second Upper Scott Pond, 2.26 mi.; to First Upper Scott pond, 2.39 mi.; to largest Wallface Pond, 2.70 mi.

Mt. Jo

On N shore of Heart Lake is Mt. Jo, a low but steep and rocky peak rising 710 ft. above the lake. It was named in 1877 by Henry Van Hoevenberg in honor of his fiancee, Josephine Scofield. There are two routes to the summit starting together at the Mt. Jo sign on the Indian Pass Trail. (See above.) This is 0.13 mi. from Adirondak Loj and about the same distance from the Heart Lake road. Leaving the Loj (0 mi.) and turning R at the sign, the trail is easy at first, climbing to a junction at 0.27 mi. where the Long Trail goes L and the Short Trail turns R.

The Long Trail is less strenuous than the Short Trail, but it is 0.28 mi. longer. It soon crosses a small brook (may be dry in summer) and proceeds westerly without much change in elevation until a R turn and a steep pitch are reached at 0.57 mi. Making the short climb over the rocks, the trail turns sharp L avoiding the bare slide straight ahead. It now starts swinging around toward the R in a northerly direction and comes to a trail junction at 0.70 mi. just before reaching the end of an interesting cliff on the R. (The trail L with blue paint blazes leads 0.19 mi. with little change in elevation to the W property line of the ADK, which is marked with yellow paint blazes. This line may be followed S 0.24 mi. downgrade to the old Mt. Nye ski trail and thence E 0.14 mi. to the Indian Pass Trail at the head of Heart Lake, thereby providing a circuit back to the Loj. On the yellow property line there is a short blue bypass around the "rock garden." Total round trip from the Loj and return, 1.71 mi.)

The Mt. Jo Trail turns toward the NE, crosses a brook bed and climbs steadily up the mountain. At 0.92 mi. at a short level stretch there is a side trail to a lookout on the R, and the rerouted Short Trail enters on the R at 0.99 mi. Ascending a pitch up the trail levels off, heading N, and at 1.02 mi. turns sharp R at a rock wall. Immediately after making the turn, a trail to the L climbs steeply over the rocks to the bare W summit and continues to the N property line. (Data for this blue-painted trail are: Starting (0 mi.) from Mt. Jo Trail, the trail zigzags up the rocks and crosses the W summit at 0.01 mi. Descending a draw to the L, the trail continues down the ridge to the NW and N. At 0.12 mi. it enters an open spot with views of Whiteface, Pitchoff, Cascade and Porter. Descending over the bare spots, a steep descent is made over the end of the rock ledge. Turning sharp L and swinging back to the N, the N property line is reached at 0.18 mi. While this property line has been cut wide like a ski trail, it is somewhat overgrown in places but may be followed downgrade to the E, crossing the W branch of the Ausable River and coming to the NE corner of the Loj property about 90 yds. W of the Heart Lake road. However, considerable bushwhacking is required to get around a vertical drop when going toward the NW corner of the property.)

The trail to the main summit continues straight ahead to the E on a level stretch. The view from the summit is one of the best in the Adirondacks for the least amount of effort. The Rimrock ski trail descends the E slope.

Turning R from the junction at 0.27 mi., the Short Trail soon climbs steeply to the N among many broken rocks, one of which looks like a long needle, to a level stretch and a second junction at 0.55 mi. (Trail R is the original route which has been abandoned due to steepness and erosion.) Turning L the rerouted Short Trail (originally called Crossover Trail) leads off below the ledges and ascends by easy traverses. It passes an overhanging cliff on R at 0.61 mi. and at 0.66 mi. turns sharp L onto bare rocks, where there is a good view. Following the paint blazes on the rocks the trail swings to the R, becomes wooded again and climbs to its junction with the Long Trail at 0.71 mi.

Distances: Adirondak Loj via Long Trail to side trail leading to W property line, 0.70 mi.; to side trail leading to W summit and N property line, 1.02 mi.; to summit of Jo, 1.14 mi.; Loj to summit via Short Trail, 0.86 mi. Elevation, 2876 ft.

South Meadow

South Meadow is a clearing that can be reached by auto. There is a dirt road 3.80 mi. S of Route 73 on the Heart Lake road, and 1.00 mi. NE of Adirondak Loj that leads E 1.05 mi. to South Meadow Brook. At 0.25 mi. from the corner a blue trail leads N 2.09 mi. to Mt. Van Hoevenberg. At 0.85 mi. the road forks, the R branch being the yellow-marked fire truck trail to Marcy Dam, 2.80 mi. Continuing on the L branch, the road reaches South Meadow Brook at 1.05 mi. where there is a small bridge and an old dam, now broken. This is as far as cars can be driven. The red-marked trail straight ahead across the brook is the Klondike Notch Trail to Johns Brook Lodge, 5.27 mi. The trail crosses the brook on a bridge (1954) a short distance N of the old dam. (See below.)

Mt. Van Hoevenberg from South Meadow Road

Mt. Van Hoevenberg is a low mountain N of South Meadow and was named in honor of Henry Van Hoevenberg. On the N side of the mountain approached from Route 73, is the Olympic Bobsled Run. The trail leaves the South Meadow road 0.25 mi. from the Heart Lake road, as described above, and is marked with blue disks.

Leaving the South Meadow road (0 mi.), the trail heads N on the level through a meadow wooded with red pine. The end of the meadow is reached at 0.66 mi. and a brook bed is crossed at 0.94 mi., still pretty much on the level. Easy to moderate grades start at about 1.03 mi. followed by a level stretch. After crossing a brook at 1.18 mi., the trail starts climbing steadily, gets steeper at 1.28 mi. and swings to the R, passing an interesting rock on the R at 1.32 mi. Still climbing steadily, the trail swings more toward the E, now heading about 60°, and reaches a level stretch at 1.40 mi. affording the first view. Climbing again, the trail enters an eroded brook bed, levels off, starts up again and drops into a small sag at 1.66 mi. Ascending three more pitches through the conifers near the summit, a side trail to the open ledges on the R is reached at 2.04 mi. The partially wooded summit is reached at 2.09 mi. but more ledges to the S give splendid views of the Great Range, Phelps, Marcy, Colden, Avalanche Pass and the MacIntyre Range. Descending slightly, an old lean-to site is reached at 2.14 mi. where more views are obtained.

The trail continues N and starts down a steady grade at 2.19 mi., becoming wide cut like a ski trail at 2.30 mi. and reaching the buildings at the head of the bobsled run at 2.80 mi. From here the trail follows down the bobsled return road, reaching a fork and turning sharp R at 3.26 mi. After passing the grandstand at 3.42 mi., the office at the foot of the bobsled run is reached at 3.61 mi. From here a gravel road leads NE to Route 73 at 4.64 mi. at a point 3.00 mi. from the Heart Lake road.

Distances: South Meadow road to summit of Van Hoevenberg, 2.09 mi.; ascent, 740 ft.; elevation, 2860 ft.; to foot of bobsled run, 3.61 mi.; to Route 73, 4.64 mi.

South Meadow to Marcy Dam

The fire truck trail to Marcy Dam leaves the South Meadow road 0.85 mi. from the Heart Lake road, as described above, and is highly recommended when the blueberries and raspberries are ripe. It is a well-graded, gravel road all the way to Marcy Dam and is marked with yellow DEC markers. Just before it crosses South Meadow Brook, 0.20 mi. from South Meadow road, there is a sign and a padlocked gate indicating that private vehicles are not allowed beyond this point. There is a cleared spot nearby for parking.

Leaving the South Meadow road junction (0 mi.), the fire truck trail heads S, crosses the bridge over South Meadow Brook at 0.20 mi. and continues pretty much on the level, reaching the end of the meadow at 0.53 mi. Here the road swings L and starts upgrade. At 1.02 mi., at a bend in the road on a hill, the telephone line crosses the road and enters the woods on the R. After crossing two brooks from L at large culverts, the telephone line rejoins the road at 1.26 mi.

The first of two large tributaries to Marcy Brook is crossed on a truss bridge at 1.80 mi. At about 2.15 mi. the road descends to the R, making a horseshoe curve, crosses a fair-sized brook at 2.21 mi. where it turns L on the horseshoe and climbs back to grade. The road descends a fair grade at 2.35 mi. and crosses the second large tributary on a truss bridge at 2.42 mi. At 2.51 mi. the road has been rerouted, the older route on the R with the telephone line coming close to the main stream of Marcy Brook at one telephone pole from the fork. Here, except when the water is high, the stream may be crossed on the stones, and at the top of a steep gravel bank on the far side is the blue-marked Van Hoevenberg Trail from Heart Lake.

Going L at the fork, the old route rejoins the regular road at 2.61 mi. and the junction with the Van Hoevenberg Trail at Marcy Dam is reached at 2.80 mi. Here, just below the dam on the R bank of Marcy Brook, there is excellent spring water flowing from an open pipe.

Distances: South Meadow road to South Meadow Brook, 0.20 mi.; to first large tributary, 1.80 mi.; to second large tributary, 2.42 mi.; to Marcy Dam, 2.80 mi.

South Meadow to Johns Brook Lodge (Klondike Notch Trail)

This route leads from South Meadow through Klondike Notch in a SE direction and connects with the Phelps Trail (also called Johns Brook Trail) at JBL. Klondike Notch between Table Top and Big Slide Mts. has, apparently due to a cartographer's error, also been called Railroad Notch. This latter name more rightfully belongs to the notch between Big Slide and Porter Mts. where the grades are less, and which years ago was surveyed for a railroad.

The trail, marked with red markers, starts at the signpost (0 mi.) just before reaching the old broken dam on South Meadow Brook and crosses the brook on a bridge (1954) a short distance upstream. Turning downstream, the trail reaches the old tote road opposite the dam at 0.11 mi. and follows it most of the way to Klondike lean-to. Heading SE, the tote road is intersected at 0.25 mi. by the Mr. Van Trail from Adirondak Loj, coming in from the R. At 0.45 mi. the Mr. Van Trail turns L on its way to the Van Hoevenberg bobsled run and cross-country ski area. There is a rocky stretch from 0.57 mi. to 0.69 mi. followed by moderate grades at 0.83 mi. After easing off, steady climbing and another rocky stretch are encountered. Leveling off and climbing again, a reference BM in the trail is reached at 1.33 mi. PBM 2567 ft. is located just off the trail to the L in a dim tote road.

Here the trail swings way around to the R, heading W, and levels off on a switchback. Swinging S again at 1.38 mi. the trail climbs up an eroded brook bed, the original course of the tote road. Soon branching L from the brook bed, the trail rejoins the tote road at 1.49 mi. and climbs steadily. Rounding off at 1.57 mi., the trail is fairly level with a few moderate pitches up and down as it crosses several small brooks flowing from the R. A fairly large brook flowing over bare rock is crossed at 2.17 mi., being the first real good brook on the trail. Descending at 2.43 mi. Klondike Dam lean-to on the L bank of Klondike Brook is reached at 2.58 mi. (Chiseled square BM, painted 2831.9 ft. near SE corner of lean-to.)

The trail follows around in front of the lean-to and climbs at an easy grade along the L bank of the brook, crossing it at 2.65 mi. where the brook makes a right angle turn. Upstream a few yards is a sign indicating a route to Phelps Mt. Continuing through a conifer forest at easy to moderate grades with a few steeper pitches, the height of land in Klondike Notch is reached at 3.55 mi., having gained 1127 ft. elevation over South Meadow. (PBM 3182 ft. just off trail to R.) Now descending at moderate grades, with occasional steeper pitches, through a tall spruce forest heavily damaged by hurricanes, the trail reaches a wet, level stretch at 3.75 mi., climbs slightly out of the swampy area and continues down to a trail junction at 3.99 mi. (Painted BM, 3031.5 ft. on spruce tree. Trail L is the red-marked ADK trail over Yard Mt. to Big Slide Mt., 2.70 mi. Ascent, 1208 ft. See Keene Valley Region, Section B1.)

Continuing the descent at easy to moderate grades with a steeper pitch here and there, a birch tree, bent over by a large blowdown, forms an arch over the trail at 4.49 mi. Black Brook, which has been heard for some time on the R, comes into view at 4.90 mi. Following down the L bank of this brook, the trail is quite soggy for a stretch before it crosses the brook on the stones at 5.21 mi. and reaches the signpost at JBL at 5.27 mi. (PBM 2316 ft. is a few steps down blue trail towards Johns Brook.)

Distances: South Meadow to Klondike lean-to, 2.58 mi.; to height of land in Klondike Notch, 3.55 mi.; to ADK Big Slide Trail, 3.99 mi.; to JBL, 5.27 mi. Descent from height of land to JBL, 866 ft.

The Mr. Van Ski Trail

The Mr. Van Ski Trail was named after Henry Van Hoevenberg, builder of the original Adirondak Loj. At times, Van Hoevenberg used to ride his horse over much of the present route of the trail to pick up his mail on Cascade Road, the present Route 73.

Primarily used by skiers, this trail provides a useful link between the ski touring trial systems of Adirondak Loj and the Van Hoevenberg Nordic Ski Center near the bobsled run. Leaving the Campers and Hikers Building (0 mi.), follow the road leading R into the campground and turn immediately L entering the woods at 0.06 mi. The trail is marked here with blue paint blazes and an occasional ADK or red DEC marker. The trail meets the main Marcy trail at a right angle at 0.18 mi. and continues straight across generally on the level but gradually descending to Marcy Brook which it reaches at 0.76 mi. As of September, 1976, the bridge here was washed out. This can make crossing difficult. Leaving the brook, the trail proceeds mostly on the level but with a few climbs to its junction with the Marcy Dam truck road at 1.29 mi. Continuing straight across the road and the phone line, the trail (now marked with red DEC markers) meets the Klondike Notch

Trail (see above) at 1.87 mi. Here, the Mr. Van Trail turns R and then branches L from the Klondike Notch Trail at 1.98 mi., descending to Klondike Brook at 2.17 mi. (Cross-country skiers should be careful not to use their poles on this bridge, the widely spaced slats of which tend to catch pole tips and break them shortly below the basket.)

Continuing on, the trail reaches the Mr. Van lean-to at 3.37 mi. where it crosses South Meadow Brook on a broken but usable (as of Sept., 1976) bridge. At 3.65 mi., the trail begins climbing towards Hi-Notch which it reaches at 4.33 mi. At 4.35 mi., the Mr. Van Trail joins the Mt. Van Hoevenberg complex of cross-country ski trails, offering several possible routes to the parking lot. The most direct route to the parking lot is found by turning L at this junction and proceeding down to the next junction at 4.45 mi. where the Home Run Trail (still marked with red DEC markers) is followed to the L. Another junction is reached at 5.39 mi. at the bottom of a hill. There is now a L turn and a sign is seen at 5.60 mi. that points R to the parking lot which is reached at 5.65 mi.

Distances: Campers and Hikers Building to Marcy Brook, 0.76 mi.; to Klondike Notch Trail, 1.87 mi.; to parking lot, 5.65 mi.

SECTION B7

CASCADE–KEENE–HURRICANE REGION

This section, comprising at the present about 25 mi. of trail, is centered around the village of Keene and the Mountain House on East Hill. It includes the trails in the vicinity of the Cascade Lakes, the trails near the Mountain House and the various trails to Hurricane Mt. The village of Keene lies 5 mi. N of the village of Keene Valley on Route 73 and 12 mi. W of Elizabethtown on US Route 9N. See Keene Valley Region for bus connections.

Of the trails described in this section about 8 mi. are maintained by the Hurricane Mountain Chapter of the ADK, the rest being maintained by DEC, with the exception of the unmarked trail to Owls Head and the trail through the notch NW of Pitchoff.

Trails Described	Year Measured	Total Miles
Cascade and Porter Mts. from Cascade Lakes	1976	2.80
Pitchoff Mt.	1966	4.90
Notch Northwest of Pitchoff	1958	4.38
Owls Head	1953	0.85
The Crows	1954	3.50
Lost Pond from Mountain House	1954	3.02
Hurricane Mt. from Mountain House	1954	4.14
Hurricane Mt. from South (Route 9N near Beaver Pond)	1954	2.64
Hurricane Mt. from the East (Route 9N near Elizabethtown)	1955	4.93
Giant from Route 9N	1971	7.52

Cascade and Porter Mts. from Cascade Lakes

Cascade Mt., once known as Long Pond Mt., lies to the SE of the Cascade Lakes. High above the lakes is the cascade from which the mountain takes its name. To the SE of Cascade is Porter Mt., once known as West Mt., named in honor of Dr. Noah Porter, President of Yale University from 1871 to 1886, who made the first recorded ascent of the mountain in 1875 with Ed Phelps from Keene Valley.

The trail was rerouted in 1974 by the Algonquin Chapter of the ADK and provides a somewhat longer, but less steep route to the summit. The trail begins on the S side of Route 73 about 0.25 mi. past the end of Upper Cascade Lake (6.80 mi. from Keene, 4.50 mi. from the Heart Lake Road) and is marked with a DEC sign and red disks. Leaving the road (0 mi.), it descends over a small brook and climbs to a small brook bed at 0.10 mi. where the trail levels off. Climbing easily, fairly sure water is reached at 0.35 mi. at the only good-sized brook on the trail. No sure water after this.

The easy grade continues on the far side of the brook, and passing some very old maples, the climbing becomes steeper at 0.70 mi. The trail levels off at 0.90 mi. and at 1.00 mi. drops slightly to avoid a jumble of boulders. The top of the ridge is reached at 1.17 mi. and the grade moderates. Climbing along the ridge Marcy can be seen to the right at 1.52 mi. and a panoramic view is obtained at 1.82 mi.

The trail continues at a moderate grade, reaching a junction at 2.10 mi. The trail to Cascade bears L (R fork leads 0.70 mi. to Porter Mt.) and climbs 300 ft. mostly in the open to the summit of Cascade at 2.35 mi. By continuing on the bare rocks a short distance past the summit bench mark, one can look directly down to the lower end of Upper Cascade Lake. From the summit 30 major peaks can be seen, and one can look directly into Avalanche Pass over a shoulder of Mt. Phelps.

Distances: Highway to trail junction, 2.10 mi.; to summit of Cascade, 2.35 mi. Ascent, 2000 ft. Elevation, 4098 ft. Order of height, 36.

Starting (0 mi.) from above junction at 2.10 mi., and taking the R fork, the trail continues with red markers and descends into the col between Cascade and Porter at 0.20 mi. It then climbs gradually and goes around a very large boulder at 0.55 mi., reaching the summit of Porter at 0.70 mi., which is not as open as Cascade but the views are similar. (The trail continues E along the ridge with red ADK markers, leading either directly 3.84 mi. to Keene Valley near the Garden or to the Keene Valley Airport, 4.54 mi. See Keene Valley Region, Sect. B1.)

Distances: Highway to trail junction, 2.10 mi.; to summit of Porter, 2.80 mi. Ascent, 2000 ft. Elevation, 4059 ft. Order of height, 38.

Pitchoff Mountain

This bare ridge N of the Cascade Lakes offers exceptional views of the surrounding mountains and is a nice, short day's hike. In season, there are a lot of blueberries. Since the start and finish of the trail are 2.70 mi. apart on Route 73, the two-car system is advised. Both ends of the trail are marked with DEC signs. It is better traveled in the direction described herewith, the ascent being less. Take a canteen; there is no water on the ridge.

The trail starts on the N side of Route 73, 0.10 mi. E of the trailhead for Cascade and Porter. (See above.) It is marked with red DEC disks. Leaving the road (0 mi.), it climbs steadily toward the N, then swings to the NE at 0.20 mi. on a more or less level stretch through a conifer forest with easy ups and downs and makes a steep pitch up to a small lookout among white birch at 0.84 mi. Here there is a view of the cascade on Cascade Mt., with the two lakes directly below. A second pitch leads up to another lookout at 0.90 mi., with a near vertical drop on the R, and views of Marcy, Colden and Algonquin in addition to Cascade. Making a moderate descent to the L under the cliff of Pitchoff, the trail becomes very steep and eroded at 1.00 mi. It levels off for a short stretch, becomes very steep, and again levels off at 1.14 mi. where there is a trail junction. (Leaving the junction (0 mi.) and continuing straight ahead on the old route, a very steep climb up the bare rock face, requiring extra precaution, starts at 0.03 mi. and leads up to a balanced rock at 0.11 mi. where there are splendid views in all directions. Following paint blazes over the bare rocks, this route rejoins the newer route at 0.25 mi.)

Turning L at the junction, the newer route (cut in 1965 to avoid the rock climb) slabs around the shoulder of the ridge, descends a short pitch at 1.18 mi. and continues at an easy grade. Passing beneath a bare rock ledge on the R at 1.25 mi., the trail soon gets much steeper, rounds off at 1.39 mi. and reaches the junction with the old route at 1.41 mi. (To the R, it is 0.14 mi. back to the top of the rock climb at the balanced rock.)

Continuing L at the junction, the trail continues NNE, swinging N and gradually rising but with ups and downs as it passes mostly through a nice conifer forest with open stretches. After two steep upward pitches at 1.82 mi. and 1.90 mi., the first and principal summit of Pitchoff is reached at 1.97 mi. where there are two large rocks. Elevation, 3600 ft.; ascent, 1400 ft. Views include those seen at the balanced rock plus views of the Sentinal Range to the N and lesser summits of Pitchoff which appear to be as high as the main peak.

The trail now leads NE, dropping gradually over open rocks and through woods to the col at 2.10 mi. Then a short climb up rocks leads to the second summit at 2.15 mi. Here the trail proceeds along an open ridge with a sheer drop on the R. Descending moderately through conifers, the next col is reached at 2.40 mi. where the trail levels off. Climbing moderately up open rock, the trail passes just below the third summit at 2.58 mi. Now losing very little altitude, the route leads across open rock and through woods alternately, passing over an intermediate height of land at 2.66 mi. and climbing to the fourth summit at 3.01 mi. A triangulation flag station was located here during the 1953 survey. Elevation, 3477 ft. Giant and Rocky Peak Ridge are now in view over the shoulder of Cascade. Across the valley to the WNW Dinosaur Ledge may be seen.

Continuing along the ridge to the NE over open rocks, the trail descends steeply into a small, wooded col at 3.19 mi., then immediately ascends a steep pitch only to drop down again and ascend to a large, bare rock on the left at 3.29 mi. where the trail swings R. After descending into another col at 3.41 mi. the trail climbs up a bare rock hogback and through interesting rock passageways. The bottom of another steep descent is reached at 3.55 mi. where the trail swings L at the foot of a rock face. Swinging R around the end of the ledge, the trail climbs steeply up the rocks to the fifth summit at 3.64 mi. where the views are unobstructed in all directions. To the right, in line with the Spruce Hill Road, will be seen the "Sleeping Elephant."

Straight ahead the trail starts down gradually over the rocks and descends very steeply into the woods, where it doubles back under the peak at 3.72 mi. Here there is a fairly level, grassy stretch for about 130 yds. The trail then becomes very steep and eroded. The descent becomes a little easier at 3.95 mi. As the footing gets better, a spring is passed on the L at 4.06 mi. Following down near the L bank of a brook, a tributary from the L is crossed at 4.33 mi. as the trail continues down near the L bank of the main brook at easier grades. Turning sharp R, the trail makes a steep descent to cross the brook at 4.57 mi. and crosses right back again in about 33 yds. It again crosses to the R bank at 4.64 mi. and returns to the L bank in about 66 yds. The trail now levels off, descending slightly now and then, and reaches the highway, Route 73, at 4.90 mi. Just across the highway is a small parking area constructed in 1979. It is 4.0 mi. from this point to the bridge in Keene.

Distances: Upper end of trail at Route 73 to junction with alternate trail near foot of rock climb, 1.14 mi.; to second junction with old route, 1.41 mi.; to first (main) summit of Pitchoff, 1.97 mi.; to second summit, 2.15 mi.; to third summit, 2.58 mi.; to fourth summit (flag station), 3.01 mi.; to fifth summit, 3.64 mi.; to lower end of trail at highway, 4.90 mi. (4.10 mi. from center of Keene).

Notch Northwest of Pitchoff Mt.

This trail is really an old tote road veering L from the Cascade Lakes Road, Route 73, where the highway turns S 2.3 mi. E of the Heart Lake Road. It heads SE at first and then swings around to the NE, passing through the notch NW of Pitchoff Mt. and joining the upper end of Alstead Mill Road in the town of Keene. While it is not a state-maintained trail and is not marked, it is kept open as a bridle path by the riders from Camp Tree Tops and the North

Country School, and affords a very enjoyable woodland walk with easy grades. It is advisable to park cars at both ends.

Leaving the highway (0 mi.) on a dirt road, a turnout on R at 0.05 mi. affords a parking place. Climbing at a fair grade, the road levels off at 0.39 mi. where there is a road on L to a private camp. The dirt road becomes poorer at 0.43 mi. where it is possible to park and turn around, but the former parking place is preferred.

Now descending slightly on a jeep road, the trail is soon joined by the bridle path on the R and continues with easy ups and downs through a hardwood forest. The jeep road ends at 0.96 mi., the bridle path continuing on the Old Military Road, now merely a tote road. After crossing a small brook from its R bank at 1.00 mi., a large boulder is passed on the L at 1.14 mi. followed by another boulder on the L in a small clearing at 1.57 mi. Here the trail enters the narrow notch between Pitchoff Mt. and the S end of the Sentinel Range and follows the R bank of a small brook. At 1.60 mi. there is a very large, sloping top boulder on R with the brook and a cave under it. By climbing up on the sloping top, a view may be had through the notch. This is a good picnic spot.

Continuing upgrade, a tributary brook is crossed at 1.64 mi. shortly before reaching a pond on R at 1.71 mi. This pond is presently about 3 ft. higher than normal level (1976) because of an active beaver colony dam at the outlet. The tote road trail is under several ft. of water. Hikers can avoid the water by clambering through brush and rocks on L of pond. The height of land in the notch is reached at about 1.96 mi. at an elevation of 2350 ft., having gained 320 ft. from Route 73. After crossing the headwaters of Nichols Brook at 2.13 mi. the trail follows down the L bank and reaches another pond at 2.21 mi., the grade now becoming somewhat steeper on this side of the notch. After crossing the brook at 2.24 mi., the trail descends a rocky stretch and then recrosses to the L bank at 2.52 mi. While the old tote road bridges over the brook may be crossed on foot, they have been blocked off with brush in order to turn the horses aside to ford the stream instead. The brook is crossed again at 2.63 mi. and later recrossed. A badly eroded section is encountered from 2.90 mi. to 3.00 mi., and a tote road enters on the L at 3.46 mi. This heads N and is the old ski trail descending from South Notch. (See Lake Placid Region, Sect. B9.)

Descending gradually, the trail continues down the L bank of the brook on the bridle path and passes a picnic table by the brook at 3.91 mi. Veering away from the brook, it finally comes to a farmhouse at the W end of Alstead Mill Road, a good dirt road, at 4.38 mi., where cars may be parked, having descended 680 ft. from the height of land in the notch. Continuing E, the dirt road turns S at 6.90 mi. and joins Route 73 at 7.40 mi., at a point about 0.80 mi. from the main highway junction in the center of Keene.

Distances: Route 73 at SW end of trail to picnic boulder, 1.60 mi.; to height of land in notch, 1.96 mi.; to old South Notch ski trail, 3.46 mi.; to Alstead Mill Road, 4.38 mi.; to Route 73, 7.40 mi.

Owls Head

This prominent little peak seen on the R side of Route 73 when driving downhill from the Cascade Lakes toward Keene is well worth the half hour scramble it takes to get to the top. The summit is both open rock and thinly wooded, permitting views in all directions.

The trail, which is not marked, starts on the SE side of the highway, 0.70 mi. below the lower end of the Pitchoff Trail, 3.40 mi. from Keene and directly across from a large farmhouse and barns. There is a turnout on the SE side of the highway about 100 yds. above the trail. Leaving the highway (0 mi.), the trail leads down over an embankment of an old road at a reverse angle through a deserted farmyard and orchard, soon following down the L bank of a brook with Owls Head directly in front. The old road crosses the brook at 0.10 mi. where the wagon tracks are followed across a field. Keeping L at 0.25 mi. shortly before a summer cottage, the trail enters a second growth woods, following an old tote road. At 0.30 mi. the route turns sharp L (marked with cairns) away from the tote road, becomes a footpath and climbs over a small hill following a barbed wire fence. A lookout toward the W is reached at 0.45 mi. Climbing again through pine woods and becoming steeper at 0.55 mi., the second lookout is reached at 0.60 mi. Here the trail continues more or less on the level, leaving the woods at 0.70 mi., and coming to the third lookout toward the W at 0.75 mi. There is moderate climbing with the final assault up an outcropping of rock, circling it to the L to reach the summit at 0.85 mi. The summit is rock-covered with a very sharp drop to the S, permitting excellent views toward Hopkins, Green and Giant, also toward Porter, Cascade and Pitchoff. By peeking through the trees, views may be had toward the N and E.

Distance: Highway to summit, 0.85 mi. Ascent, 585 ft. Elevation, 2165 ft.

The Crows

The trail to these two rocky pinnacles, which dominate the landscape at the top of East Hill, starts 0.23 mi. before reaching the Mountain House at the top of the long hill-climb by auto from Keene. Leaving the road (0 mi.), it is marked with red ADK markers (some yellow) and starts out across a field at an easy grade heading N. At 0.17 mi. it enters the woods and starts climbing steadily. The grade moderates at 0.30 mi. but soon starts up again. A rock face is passed on the L at 0.40 mi. as the grade gets easier. The trail passes by the foot of a ledge and then climbs to its top at 0.45 mi. Here there are good views from Giant around to Pitchoff. Swinging R at top of the ledge, the grade is easy to moderate, becoming very rocky at 0.50 mi. A steep pitch up ledges is reached at 0.56 mi., after which the climbing continues at moderate grades with some level stretches over rock ledges affording views. The trail is marked with cairns and paint blazes. Another steep pitch is encountered at 0.71 mi., then a level stretch crossing a shoulder at 0.80 mi. with bare rocks on the L. The trail passes below the W summit of Little Crow on the L at 0.85 mi. The W summit is a wide, flat spot of bare rocks with some trees around it. Continuing almost level, the trail crosses the E summit at 0.94 mi. Elevation, 2540 ft.

The trail now descends gradually over ledges and enters woods at about 1.06 mi., reaching the col between the two Crows at 1.10

mi. Now climbing at a moderate grade on a traverse, the first rock ledge on Big Crow is reached at 1.15 mi. Swinging R and climbing toward the S at 1.17 mi., the trail levels off for a short stretch at 1.23 mi. The last pitch up the bare granite starts at 1.33 mi., and the summit of Big Crow is reached at 1.35 mi. where there are unobstructed views except to the NE. Ascent from road, 1220 ft. Elevation, 2800 ft. Twenty-eight major peaks may be seen from the summit.

The trail continues level over the bare rocks toward the E, starting a steady descent over ledges at 1.41 mi. Continuing a steady descent, the trail enters the woods at about 1.63 mi., leveling off through an overgrown pasture at 1.80 mi. and reaching the edge of an old farm clearing (Crow Mt. Clearing) at 2.00 mi. Crossing the field through the apple trees, a dirt road is reached at 2.08 mi. where there is a trail sign. Descent from Big Crow, 600 ft. Turning R on the road, the short cut trail to Hurricane and Lost Pond enters on the L at 2.16 mi. where there is another trail sign. Continuing down the road, the Mountain House is reached at 3.27 mi.

Distances: Road to lookout ledge, 0.45 mi.; to E summit of Little Crow, 0.94 mi.; to summit of Big Crow, 1.35 mi.; to dirt road at Crow Mt. Clearing, 2.08 mi.; to Mountain House, 3.27 mi.

Lost Pond from Mountain House

From the Mountain House on East Hill (0 mi.), take the dirt road heading E uphill. Avoid R fork just pass the Mountain House which leads to Route 9N at the top of Spruce Hill. Just before reaching Crow Mt. Clearing, a trail branches R at 1.11 mi. (Trail R is short cut for Lost Pond and Hurricane but only saves 0.05 mi. Leaving the junction (0 mi.), the trail enters the woods and crosses a brook at 0.07 mi. Heading 160° on a tote road, the trail soon swings SE and then E, rejoining the dirt road at 0.41 mi. Marked with ADK markers.) The clearing is reached at 1.19 mi. where cars may be parked. The road levels off past the clearing and while passable, is not recommended for good cars. The short cut trail re-enters on the R at 1.57 mi. near a plank bridge, and the trail to Lost Pond and Hurricane branches L from the road at 1.97 mi. where the dirt road is going downgrade toward a clearing.

The trail, now a tote road marked with red ADK markers, is level and heads in a SE direction. A brook is crossed at 2.25 mi., and the Gulf Brook lean-to is reached at a trail junction at 2.28 mi. (Trail R leads to Hurricane. See below.) Going L, still pretty much on the level and not far from R bank of brook in ravine below, a tributary from L is crossed at 2.42 mi. At 2.52 mi. the trail turns sharp L shortly before reaching an old lumber clearing. The trail now climbs steadily toward the N. The L bank of a brook is reached at 2.62 mi., and the brook is crossed at 2.68 mi. A steep pitch is ascended at 2.72 mi. followed by steady climbing. The trail finally levels off through the white birches at 2.84 mi., and the fireplace at the foot of Lost Pond is reached at 3.02 mi. at an elevation of 2830 ft. An unmarked trail continues around the W side of the pond toward Rocky Spur Peak and leads over the Nunda-ga-o Ridge to Big Crow. The Walter Biesemeyer Memorial lean-to is located on this trail at the far end of the pond, about another 0.35 mi. from foot of pond.

Distances: Mountain House to short cut trail, 1.11 mi.; to Crow Mt. Clearing, 1.19 mi.; to start of marked trail, 1.97 mi.; to Gulf Brook lean-to and trail for Hurricane, 2.28 mi.; to beginning of steep climb, 2.52 mi.; to Lost Pond, 3.02 mi.

Hurricane Mt. from Mountain House

Like Whiteface, this mountain stands by itself and gets the weather from all directions. It was used by Colvin as a triangulation station. The fire tower on top is a good vantage point for spectacular views. To the E lie Lake Champlain and the Green Mts. To the S are Giant and Rocky Peak Ridge. To the SW the Great Range and Marcy dominate the view. Porter, Cascade, Pitchoff and the Sentinel Range loom up in the W, while Lost Pond is nestled in the woods under the mountain's protective eye to the N.

The trail, known as the North Trail and marked with red ADK disks, coincides with the trail to Lost Pond at the start. (See above.) Take latter trail to trail junction 2.28 mi. from the Mountain House where North Trail branches R at the Gulf Brook lean-to. The trail crosses Gulf Brook at 2.30 mi. and heads SW and then S. Another brook from L is crossed at 2.37 mi. Avoiding deer run on R, the trail follows up the L bank of brook at a single grade, recrossing at 2.42 mi. and following up R bank. A tributary from L is crossed at 2.47 mi., and soon thereafter the trail becomes eroded and follows up the brook bed, first on one side and then on the other. It leaves the brook bed at 2.60 mi., following up the R bank at a moderate grade, and crosses to the L bank shortly before reaching an unmarked trail with a sign "Glenmore" on the R at 2.71 mi. The trail finally crosses the brook at 2.76 mi. and soon swings away from it, heading E, then SE and S. Climbing is easy to moderate through birch and ferns. A brook from L is crossed at 3.07 mi., and the grade becomes a little steeper at 3.11 mi. The trail reaches and follows up the R bank of a small brook for a short distance at 3.23 mi. Now climbing steadily the trail ascends a steep pitch at 3.60 mi. A small spring is passed on the L at 3.84 mi. as the trail enters the balsams and ascends another steep pitch, leveling off at 3.90 mi. and coming to a trail junction at 3.99 mi. (Trail on R with red DEC disks is the trail from the S, leaving Route 9N near Beaver Pond. See below.) Continuing straight ahead, the trail climbs up through the scrub spruce and comes out on bare rocks at 4.03 mi. Swinging L the trail follows paint blazes over the rocks and reaches the fire tower on the summit at 4.14 mi.

Distances: Mountain House to short cut trail, 1.11 mi.; to start of marked trail, 1.97 mi.; to Gulf Brook lean-to and trail for Lost Pond, 2.28 mi.; to unmarked trail to Glenmore, 2.71 mi.; to red DEC trail from Route 9N, 3.99 mi.; to fire tower on summit of Hurricane, 4.14 mi. (4.09 mi. via short cut trail.) Ascent from dirt road at start of marked trail, 1600 ft. Elevation, 3694 ft.

Hurricane Mt. from the South

This trail leaves the N side of Route 9N at the height of land 1.60 mi. E of where the road from the Mountain House joins the highway near the top of Spruce Hill. It is marked with red DEC disks. Leaving the highway (0 mi.) the trail follows a tote road and climbs fairly steeply at the start, leveling off and becoming a foot path at 0.30 mi. The going is now very easy for about 0.85

mi. as the trail passes through a conifer forest, heading N and then swinging toward the NW. A small brook from R is crossed on a corduroy bridge at 0.55 mi. After crossing a second brook on a log bridge at 0.64 mi., the trail follows up the brook's R bank, veering away from it at 0.69 mi. A short, marshy stretch is traversed shortly before crossing another brook from R on a log bridge at 0.81 mi. The trail is still fairly level through a thick, conifer forest. It approaches a fourth brook and climbs gradually a short distance up its L bank, crossing on a bridge at 1.10 mi. (Last water.)

This is about the end of the easy part, as the trail heads N up the ridge at 1.15 mi. The grade eases off again from about 1.49 mi. to 1.65 mi. A steep pitch is ascended at 1.70 mi. followed by an easy traverse. The grade becomes moderate at 1.78 mi. leveling off again at 1.87 mi. After crossing a wet section of corduroys, climbing becomes steady at 1.99 mi. The conifers give way to birch trees at 2.09 mi., and the grade becomes much steeper at about 2.28 mi. The junction with the ADK North Trail from the Mountain House is reached at 2.49 mi. where the trail levels off. Turning R, the trail climbs up through the scrub spruce and comes out on bare rocks at 2.53 mi. Swinging L, the trail follows paint blazes over the rocks and reaches the fire tower on the summit at 2.64 mi.

Distances: Route 9N to ADK trail from Mountain House, 2.49 mi.; to fire tower on summit of Hurricane, 2.64 mi. Ascent from highway, 2000 ft. Elevation, 3694 ft.

Hurricane Mt. from the East

This approach to Hurricane is used by DEC in manning the fire tower on the summit. It is the shortest of the three trails but is quite steep and follows the telephone line all the way. The start of the trail is reached by taking Route 9N W from the center of Elizabethtown 2.25 mi. to a point where the highway crosses a stream. Here a dirt road branches R and is marked with a DEC sign indicating Hurricane Mt. The dirt road climbs steadily, reaching a gate 2.75 mi. from the highway. Continuing through the gate and entering private land, the route to Hurricane branches L at 3.15 mi. Here the road becomes poorer but can be traversed by cars in dry weather all the way to the parking area in front of the observer's cabin at 3.95 mi. There are several steep grades on this stretch. Turnouts provide parking spots off the road.

Leaving the signpost at the observer's cabin (0 mi.), the trail, marked with red DEC markers, descends slightly behind the cabin and crosses a brook on a bridge. There is a lean-to here on the far side of the brook. Steep climbing starts immediately but moderates at 0.09 mi. and then levels off. Another brook is crossed at 0.18 mi. (last water) and the climbing becomes very steep up an eroded trail high above the brook. A bench is passed at 0.28 mi., and the grade moderates at 0.38 mi. for a short stretch. Then climbing again a second bench is passed at 0.42 mi. soon after which the trail climbs very steeply over stretches of bare rock. Rounding off at 0.52 mi. where there is a view of the Champlain Valley, there is a short, level stretch, followed by a steep pitch, a short breather, and another very steep pitch. Finally moderating at 0.65 mi., the grade becomes fairly easy at 0.84 mi. as the trail emerges from the trees at 0.91 mi. and climbs over the bare rocks to the fire tower on the summit at 0.98 mi.

Distances: Route 9N to gate and private road, 2.75 mi.; to start of footpath at observer's cabin, 3.95 mi.; to fire tower on summit of Hurricane, 4.93 mi. Ascent from highway, 2800 ft.; from observer's cabin, 1300 ft. Elevation 3694 ft.

Giant from Route 9N

This trail is a long but interesting approach to Giant through remote country for those who dislike trails that are too well used. It also offers a relatively easy approach to a rocky promontory known as Owls Head. (To avoid confusion it should be called Owls Head East.) This has a wide view including the east side of Giant, Lake Champlain and the Green Mountains of Vermont.

The trail, marked with red DEC markers, begins at a parking lot about 4.5 mi. west of Route 9 at Elizabethtown on Route 9N. The trail leaves the parking lot (0 mi.) and follows a gravelly jeep road from which it turns left at .09 mi. and becomes a footpath. At 0.27 mi. it intersects a recent jeep road used for lumbering from which it turns L at 0.34 mi. heading SE and entering State

Land at 0.43 mi. At 1.11 mi. it crosses Slide Brook on a bridge and begins to climb moderately, alternating ascents with nearly level areas. A stream from the R is crossed at 1.18 mi. and the trail ascends a hogback, joining a brook which it crosses and re-crosses several times. A striking rock face is passed on the L at 1.57 mi. The trail crosses the brook for the last time at 1.67 mi. and at 1.80 mi. turns sharply R. A boggy area is passed at 1.86 mi. as the trail turns S and climbs steadily but not steeply until a junction is reached at 2.49 mi. (Trail L leads 0.13 mi. very steeply to the summit of Owls Head with its wide view. Climbers ending their trip here should go 0.10 mi. south on the red trail for a striking view of this crag.)

Leaving the junction the trail passes a boggy area on the L at 2.52 mi. and at 2.57 mi. starts to descend in an open area with views S toward Bald Peak, Rocky Peak Ridge and a part of Giant not hidden by Green. Half way down the slope is the view of Owls Head crag. Reentering the woods at 2.60 mi. the trail continues to descend until 2.70 mi. where it swings SW. At 3.04 mi. it starts another descent heading WSW through open woods and at 3.38 mi. reaches an unusually open forest area consisting of widely spaced hardwoods of moderate size. At 3.42 mi. a rock face is visible on the R. There is another descent from 3.75 mi. to 3.81 mi. and at 4.14 mi. the trail comes out on a remarkable bank of glacial gravel high above Roaring Brook. (The one on the E side of Giant.) This is called High Bank on the DEC signs. There is little vegetation on this gravel except birch trees through which there are views S. About 100 ft. E of the trail there is an unobstructed lookout point.

Leaving the gravel bank at 4.17 mi. the trail trends WNW, high above Roaring Brook which can be heard but not seen. A dry brook bed is crossed at 4.41 mi. and at 4.57 mi. there is an outlook 50 ft. on the L with views of the slides on Giant. The trail now climbs steadily but not steeply into the notch between Green and Giant. A stream bed is crossed on a bridge at 4.80 mi. after which the climb slackens briefly to begin again at 4.84 mi. Another stream bed is crossed at 4.93 mi. and the ascent begins to level off in the notch at 5.37 mi. A brook with good water is reached at 5.70 mi. and there is a junction. The trail L leads about

150 ft. to a lean-to. At 6.00 mi. at the top of the notch another junction is reached where there is the last sure water. The trail straight ahead leads over a boulder of Green to Hopkins. (It is 4.15 mi. to Keene Valley via this route and the Ranney Trail. See Section B2.)

Turning L the red trail begins the steep, steady climb up the N shoulder of Giant, climbing 1400 ft. in a little over a mile. Switchbacks and easy natural rock steps help gain elevation rapidly. At 7.27 mi. the trail reaches a ridge which looks down on the slides of Giant's western face. From this overlook it is 0.23 mi. to the summit, an easy walk through scrub evergreens. The summit bench mark is reached at 7.51 mi.

Distances: Route 9N to trail to Owls Head lookout, 2.49 mi.; to High Bank, 4.14 mi.; to lean-to turn off, 5.70 mi.; to junction with trail from Hopkins, 6.00 mi.; to bench mark on summit of Giant, 7.51 mi. Ascent from highway 3327 ft., plus 150 to 200 ft. lost in descent after Owls Head turn off. Elevation 4627 ft. Order of height, 12.

Keene Valley from Hurricane
Photo by R. Meyer

SECTION B8

BOUQUET VALLEY REGION

From sources high in Hunter's Pass on the slopes of Nipple Top and the Dixes, the Bouquet River drops more than 3200 feet in a dozen miles before it foams over Split Rock Falls and enters the pleasant valley through which it meanders for another 30 mi. to Lake Champlain. W of the Bouquet the high peaks rise like a wall; eastward are lower ranges where iron has been mined and smelted for a century and a half. Through the cleft between the ranges runs a natural pathway from the headwaters of the Schroon River to Champlain and the St. Lawrence. Indians followed it for a thousand years before the first white man came. Tradition says that Rogers and his famous rangers were ambushed here, and history records that Gentleman Johnny Burgoyne held a council of war with his allies at the river's mouth en route to Saratoga and defeat.

1.30 mi. N of Split Rock Falls on Route 9 and S of Elizabethtown, near the point where the brawling mountain river becomes a quiet valley stream, stands the Bouquet River Lodge (BRL). Accommodations are not available to the public.

Sunrise Trail to Mt. Gilligan

This mountain, formerly known as Sunrise Mt., rises due E from BRL and affords good views to the W over Pleasant Valley from open ledges just below the summit. The trail also passes several lookouts during the ascent. For the beginning of the trail, turn E from Route 9 on road 145 yds. S of southern entrance to BRL, 3.2 miles from Underwood intersection of Route 73 and Route 9. There is a clearing here for parking cars used by fishermen. Cross Bouquet River on bridge and follow road to R. The trail starts at a sign 0.20 mi. from Route 9 just before reaching a cottage on the L.

Leaving the road at the sign (0 mi.), the trail starts in a narrow strip of woods between a field and a cottage, following ADK markers and paint blazes along a gully. After pitching up out of the gully at 0.08 mi., the trail turns sharp R and starts a steep climb. The grade moderates shortly before following up beside a rock ridge to a lookout on top of the ridge at 0.25 mi.

Entering the woods again, the trail heads S on level to easy grades, swings SE, dips into a sag and ascends a steep pitch at 0.36 mi., after which the going is easy again. A spot which is being overgrown on R at 0.42 mi. provides a view of E. Dix, Spotted, Hough and Dix. Another lookout on L at 0.49 mi. offers a view of Rocky Peak Ridge and Giant. After a stretch of easy climbing, the trail is fairly level along a ridge to the NE, then makes a short descent and crosses an old tote road in a small col at 0.73 mi. Climbing past an interesting overhung rock on the R at 0.74 mi., the trail ascends to bare rocks at 0.79 mi. where excellent views are obtained of Rocky Peak, Giant and the Dix Range with Nipple Top and Dial in the distance and BRL almost due W in the valley below.

The trail continues up the ridge and joins a tote road at 0.80 mi. At 0.90 mi. the trail branches to L through lumbered area avoiding tote road to R and continues on the level. Climbing again at 0.97 mi., the trail pitches up over bare rocks to final lookout at 1.25 mi., where the trail ends. This is about 100 yds below the wooded summit of Gilligan.

Distances: Route 9 to first lookout, 0.45 mi.; to lookout below summit of Gilligan, 1.25 mi. Ascent, 670 ft. Elevation, 1420 ft.

Loope Trail

This trail, originally blazed by P. Fay Loope, is a short loop of about 0.50 mi. making a complete 360° circuit on the hillside behind BRL. Leaving the washstand behind the lodge and heading N along the pipe line toward Stevens Brook, this trail makes an abrupt L turn along an old tote road shortly before reaching Stevens Brook and runs roughly parallel to it. It traverses the top of a rocky shoulder or cliff where one can obtain good views of Split Rock Mt. and Gilligan across the valley of the Bouquet River and then descends to the lodge just S of the back door.

East Trail to Giant Mountain via Rocky Peak Ridge

The East Trail to Giant Mt. via Rocky Peak Ridge is a challenging foot trail marked by exceptional views of the Adirondacks and the Champlain Valley.

A trail, marked with yellow DEC disks, bears W from its beginning at the parking lot on the W side of Route 9, 4.60 mi. N from the Route 73 traffic circle and 1.30 mi. S from the New Russia Post Office. Crossing an open field, the trail passes a small family cemetery on the L and crosses a footbridge at 0.12 mi. Entering the woods, the trail follows an old tote road with a stream on the L. Bearing R at 0.33 mi., it passes through a stand of hemlocks, crosses a recent logging road at 0.65 mi. and reaches a fair-sized stream on the L at 0.67 mi. Leaving the stream, the trail passes through a white birch grove and rejoins the stream at 0.80 mi. Now following a logging road, it leaves the stream at 0.95 mi., probably the last sure water. The trail climbs moderately, with some steep pitches, partly following logging roads until at 1.79 mi. a DEC view sign points to an outlook 50 yds. to the R. A good view can be had of the town of New Russia and the Bouquet River Valley.

Now the trail passes over Blueberry Cobbles with bare rocks, blueberries and small oak trees predominating. At 1.97 mi. a trail junction is reached with a red shortcut trail bearing R for 0.23 mi. to rejoin the yellow trail. The yellow trail, with scenic views, continues L over Blueberry Cobbles (2000 ft.) following open rock marked with yellow arrows. At 2.32 mi., Mason Notch causes the trail to turn R at a large boulder and descend steeply into the col where the red trail joins it at 2.42 mi. Turning sharply R, the trail climbs over the lightly-wooded summit of Mason Mt. (2330 ft.) and at 2.82 mi. begins the descent into Hedgehog Notch. The trail now climbs steeply up the SE slope of Bald Peak (3060 ft.) at 3.86 mi. Good views of Lake Champlain, the Green Mountains, the Dix Range, Rocky Peak Ridge and Giant Mt. are obtained from the summit. Following the ridge, the trail passes a huge, balanced rock at 4.02 mi. and begins the descent into Dickerson Notch at 4.21 mi. After dropping steeply into the col, the trail begins a steep climb with a possible spring at 4.92 mi. At 5.17 mi., the trail passes between large rocks on either side and then passes over open ledges, following cairns, to the summit of Rocky Peak (4060 ft.) at 5.41 mi. Excellent views in all directions include views of Belfry, Makomis, Poke-o-Moonshine and Hurricane.

The trail now follows slightly downgrade through open, alpine-like meadows and then through scrub balsam and birch reaching a footbridge over the outlet of Marie Louise Pond at 6.04 mi. This water is not recommended for drinking. Skirting the N side of this small pond, the trail climbs steadily over open, rocky terrain, following cairns and yellow paint spots. The burned-over summit of Rocky Peak Ridge is reached at 6.66 mi. where there are excellent views in all directions. Total ascent from parking lot, 4190 ft., elevation, 4420 ft., order of height, 20.

Bearing NW, the trail gradually descends into the saddle between Rocky Peak Ridge and Giant Mt. through thick, scrub balsam and begins to climb at 7.40 mi. in a northerly direction. Climbing steeply through spruce and balsam, the trail passes rock ledges and joins the ATIS trail from Route 73 at 7.91 mi., 0.13 mi. below the summit. The climb is now easy and the summit of Giant Mt. is reached at 8.04 mi.

Distances: Parking lot to Blueberry Cobbles, 1.86 mi.; to Mason Mt., 2.73 mi.; to Bald Peak, 3.86 mi.; to Rocky Peak, 5.41 mi.; to Marie Louise Pond, 6.04 mi.; to Rocky Peak Ridge, 6.66 mi.; to ATIS trail from Chapel Pond, 7.91 mi.; to summit of Giant Mt., 8.04 mi. Ascent from parking lot, 4810 ft.; elevation, 4627 ft.; order of height, 12.

Dixes via North Fork of Bouquet River

The trailless Dixes may be approached via an unmarked hunter's trail which starts on the S side of the bridge over the N fork of the Bouquet River on Route 73. The dirt road on the N side of the bridge is the Old Chapel Pond Road which leads to an old bridge abutment and a good campsite. Excellent spring water may be obtained from two open pipes at the entrance to this dirt road.

Leaving the highway (0 mi.), the trail heads SW, following up the R bank of the river, and crosses to the L bank at 0.40 mi. where it climbs above the stream. Soon heading 300° as the river also bends, the trail is back somewhat from the L bank and crosses the outlet of Twin Pond at 0.65 mi. It then climbs over a low rise and descends to a narrow gorge and large pool in the main stream. This is a good picnic spot and is visible from the main trail.

At 0.91 mi. the trail starts to climb high above the river on an easy grade, then descends and crosses the N branch (here flowing from the NW) at 1.19 mi. Heading SW, the trail crosses a large tributary at 1.42 mi. Lilly Pad Pond is just out of sight of the trail to the SE. Continuing to the SW, the trail makes an easy climb with views of Dix from small clearings and then descending gradually reaches the L bank of the S fork of the Bouquet River at 2.29 mi. From the valley of the S fork there are easy approaches to the Spotted Mt.–East Dix Ridge.

The trail continues up the L bank of the S fork, much of the time high above it, as it starts an easy climb up the ravine. A small tributary is crossed at 2.97 mi., and the "Rock of Gibraltar" is passed on the L at 3.09 mi. At 3.32 mi. the trail meets the L bank of the large tributary coming from the side of Dix, at a point just above its confluence with the S fork. (This tributary offers a good route up Dix.) The trail crosses the tributary at 3.34 mi. (end of measurements), becoming quite indistinct due to blowdowns, and climbs along the R (S) bank to the remains of an old hunter's camp where it turns L, flanking the main valley of the S fork. After contouring to the upper reaches of the S fork, it crosses three tributaries from their L banks. Hough may easily be climbed by bearing SW up the third tributary. A route up the great slide of the N face of East Dix may be reached via a tributary from the L, a short distance further up the S fork.

For those skilled in following obscure trails, this route offers the fastest and most direct approach to the Dix Range from the E. While this trail is neither officially marked nor maintained, occasional small, square, white paint spots may be followed to the S fork.

Whiteface from Route 73
Photo by R. Meyer

SECTION B9

LAKE PLACID REGION

Lake Placid is well known as a popular resort, both summer and winter. Also in the spring it attracts the fisherman and in the fall, perhaps the loveliest of the seasons, lures the hunter as well as the hiker. The Adirondack Camp & Trail Club, initiated by Henry Van Hoevenberg in 1910, began the opening of trails in this region. The Lake Placid Club has also had a large share in opening up the natural beauties of the mountains to those who seek recreation in their midst.

This section comprises the principal trails to Whiteface and other trails maintained by DEC in the vicinity of Lake Placid and Wilmington Notch. In addition to the DEC-maintained trails, there is a trail along the shore of Lake Placid from Whiteface Inn, connecting many private homes, from which other trails lead to McKenzie and Moose Mountains (from a branch 0.50 mi. up the lake), Loch Bonnie, Eagle's Eyrie and other points of interest. These trails are maintained by the Shore Owners Association, and except where they connect with the DEC trails, no attempt has been made to include them in the trail descriptions. They are marked with SOA markers, similar in size to DEC and ADK markers.

Trails Described	Year Measured	Total Miles
Whiteface Mt. via Connery Pond and Whiteface Landing	1958*	6.62
Whiteface Mt. via Wilmington Trail	1958	5.34
Esther Mt. from Wilmington Trail	1958	1.24
Trail to McLenathan Bay and Whiteface Landing	1958	4.49
Sunrise Notch Trail	**	3.25
Owen and Copperas Ponds	1958	2.01

	Year	*Total*
Trails Described	*Measured*	*Miles*
Winch Pond from Owen–Copperas		
Pond Trail, N end	1958	0.73
Winch Pond from Owen–Copperas		
Pond Trail, S end	1958	1.88
North Notch Trail	1958	2.41
South Notch Trail	1958	2.72

* Revised 1959

** Not covered by ADK wheel measurements, distance estimated.

Whiteface Mt.

Whiteface Mt. is the prime interest to the hiker in this section since the completion of a ski center with tows, lifts and summit shelter. There are now two trails and a highway to the top. The shortest route and the stiffest climb is from Whiteface Landing at the N end of Lake Placid. (Inquire at the Boat Livery near Lake Placid Village for boat trip.) The most scenic route is from the E, the old trail from Wilmington.

The Whiteface Memorial Highway begins near Wilmington on Route 86. This is a toll road. The approach is well marked with signs. It ends 273 ft. vertically below the summit at the Castle. There is ample parking space here. The top may be reached by the board walk and steps in the open (0.21 mi.) or by a tunnel and an elevator that takes one directly to the observation house.

The views from the summit of Whiteface are expansive and inspiringly varied. Lake Placid, with its wooded islands, and guarded by mountains, lies directly below. Beyond this to the SW and S a tumult of peaks, with Mt. Marcy and the MacIntyres and the Range in the front ranks, fades on the distant horizon. To the E lies the Champlain Valley, bordered on the far side by a long line of Green Mountains. The waters of Lake Champlain show here and there between nearer hills. To the N green stretches of low forested hills and farmlands, dotted with lakes, are spread out before one. If the atmosphere is exceptionally clear, Mt. Royal near Montreal, Canada can be seen.

Whiteface Mt. via Connery Pond
and Whiteface Landing

This trail starts at the former Connery Pond campsite on the
N side of Route 86, 3 mi. NE of the traffic light at the intersection
of Routes 86 and 73 in Lake Placid Village and 0.25 mi. W of
where the river road from Route 73 and the ski jump joins Route
86. It is marked with a DEC sign and red markers. It follows a
fire truck trail over fairly level ground, skirting the W shore of
Connery Pond, and reaches a side trail to Whiteface Landing at
3.10 mi. Heading NE it soon follows up the course of Whiteface
Brook and becomes a footpath shortly before reaching the Whiteface Brook lean-to at 4.15 mi. Climbing gradually through a beautiful conifer forest, the former site of the lean-to is passed at 5.08
mi. Above this point the trail climbs more steeply, and the last
0.75 mi. is very steep over rocks and ledges to the summit at 6.62
mi.

Leaving the highway (0 mi.), the trail follows a dirt road heading NE and crosses a bridge at 0.09 mi. Soon heading N, a private
road branches R at 0.49 mi. Continuing L, the road crosses the
outlet of Connery Pond and comes to a parking area on R at 0.54
mi. Cars may be driven to this point. (Side trail on R leads to
Connery Pond, 0.08 mi.) Private property begins at 0.60 mi. where
the road forks at locked barways. Here the marked trail follows
the relocated route to the L to pass behind a private house on
the shore of the pond. Rejoining the old route at 0.84 mi., where
an opening in the trees affords access to the pond, the road soon
leaves the shore of the pond and climbs gradually to a road junction
at 1.05 mi.

Bearing L downgrade another locked barway is reached at
1.08 mi. The road beyond this point is a fire truck trail, now mainly
a tote road, which was used to remove down timber after the
1950 hurricane. A side trail on L at 1.11 mi. marked with blue
SOA markers (blue SOA on a white field) leads 1.30 mi. to McLenathan Bay dock and the red SOA trail around Lake Placid. (See
below.) Straight ahead and climbing gradually, the remains of an
old shack on R are passed at 1.44 mi., the road finally leveling

off at 2.02 mi. The road pitches down at 2.80 mi., soon becomes a gradual downgrade, crosses the fire tower telephone line at 2.94 mi. and comes to a junction at 3.10 mi (Road L leads 115 yds. to Whiteface Landing on Lake Placid, the lake being visible from the junction. A boat trip to this point will save many miles of walking.)

Turning sharp R, still on a tote road, the trail bears R at a junction at 3.34 mi. and joins the telephone line on R at 3.41 mi. (The telephone line may be used as a short cut to this point, saving 0.23 mi., but it is quite wet for about 90 yds.) Now following the telephone line a brook is crossed in an area of second growth after the 1950 blowdown, and an old sawmill site in a clearing is passed at 3.70 mi. With Whiteface now in full view straight ahead, the tote road makes a short descent and crosses Whiteface Brook from L bank at 3.74 mi. At 3.81 mi. the Sunrise Notch Trail enters on the R, being marked with a sign on a telephone pole, also with a painted blaze and arrow. (This trail leads about 3.25 mi. to Wilmington High Falls on Route 86 and is marked with paint blazes. See below.)

Continuing straight ahead on a gradual ascent the tote road crosses to the L bank on Whiteface Brook at 3.99 mi. At 4.05 mi. there is a side trail on R leading about 20 yds. to a rock-walled spring. Now starting to climb, the tote road gives way to a footpath as the trail recrosses the brook twice and comes to the Whiteface Brook lean-to (1958) on R in a small clearing at 4.15 mi. After crossing a small tributary at 4.34 mi. the grade soon gets steeper and climbs steadily. Whiteface Brook is heard on the L and comes into view at 4.55 mi. where the brook comes cascading down over the rocks. Now following along above the L bank of the stream on a beautiful duff footpath through a conifer forest, the trail reaches an easy stretch at 4.67 mi. Then resuming the climb, a steep pitch is ascended at 4.98 mi., and after crossing a blowdown area, the site of the old Whiteface Brook lean-to on the R is reached at 5.08 mi. (Lean-to destroyed by fire in winter of 1957–1958.)

Above the lean-to site at 5.12 mi. the trail swings R (E), away from the telephone line, on easy to moderate grades, and reaches a small brook which it follows up at 5.41 mi. Leaving the brook at 5.45 mi., climbing becomes steep on a rocky trail at 5.49 mi. "Moses Rock" on L is reached at 5.69 mi. where a small stream in the spring will be found flowing from a cleft in this large boulder. Climbing is a little easier for a stretch, but at 5.84 mi. the trail turns sharp L up the S face of the mountain and climbs very steeply. A breather, with a view to the S, is reached at 6.19 mi., followed by another short, level stretch through the trees at 6.32 mi. Above the timber line, which is reached at 6.36 mi., the trail is marked with paint blazes and climbs very steeply, with much clambering over rocks and ledges, to the S summit at 6.58 mi. The main summit is reached at 6.62 mi.

Distances: Route 86 to Connery Pond parking area, 0.54 mi.; to SOA trail to McLenathan Bay, 1.11 mi.; to junction near White-face Landing, 3.10 mi.; to Sunrise Notch Trail, 3.81 mi.; to White-face Brook lean-to, 4.15 mi.; to summit of Whiteface, 6.62 mi. Ascent from Route 86, 3232 ft.; from Whiteface Landing, 3009 ft. Elevation, 4867 ft. Order of height, 5.

Whiteface Mt. via Wilmington Trail

This trail branches L from the Whiteface Memorial Highway 0.60 mi. from Route 86, just beyond the Twin Brook Motel, and is marked with a DEC sign. It follows up the general course of White Brook and used to ascend Marble Mt. from the N where the original ski development, now abandoned, is located. It avoids the main ski trails by swinging away from the brook, climbing the mountain from the NE and joining the original trail at 2.41 mi. near the summit of Marble Mt. From here it heads SW up the ridge, in and out of the ski trail leading to Whiteface lean-to at 4.72 mi. and then through scrub and over bare rock to the summit of Whiteface at 5.34 mi.

Many climbers shorten their climb by driving to the Atmo-spheric Sciences Research Center, reached by a road turning L from the Whiteface Mountain Highway 0.80 mi. above the North Pole–Santa's Workshop amusement park. Parking cars at the cen-ter, descend to the building by the brook which once housed a ski lift motor and ascend herb paths through thick growth along the former lift line to the top of the ridge where the official trail is intersected at a point 2.41 mi. from the highway. The distance from the center is about 0.75 mi.

Leaving the Memorial Highway (0 mi.), the trail heads W on a dirt road following red markers. It crosses a small brook at 0.08 mi. and reaches the Wilmington Reservoir and dam at 0.27 mi. There is a parking lot at the dam. Continuing past the dam, the trail crosses White Brook at 0.29 mi. and follows up the R bank of the brook at easy grades through a beautiful hardwood forest. At 0.43 mi. it veers gradually to the L away from the brook (last sure water for 3.63 mi.), crosses a tote road at 0.57 mi. and passes a nice stand of birch at 0.80 mi. After crossing a small brook and ascending a short pitch, a boundary post is reached at 0.94 mi. where the trail enters a wildlife management area. Descending over a small brook another boundary post is passed at 1.04 mi. as the trail follows along a yellow-blazed property line. Real climbing starts at about 1.69 mi. where the trail angles up the NE side of Marble Mt. Passing between two interesting boulders at 1.91 mi., a welcome level stretch is soon reached. Climbing again the trail passes S of the summit, soon levels off and is joined by the above mentioned route up the abandoned ski line.

Continuing L, climbing soon starts again as the trail turns L from the ski trail at 2.44 mi. and heads SW up the ridge leading to Lookout Mt. A rock slide is climbed at 2.64 mi., the trail soon turning L away from it and rejoining the ski trail at 2.70 mi. From here the footpath is periodically in and out of the wider cut ski trail, affording views back to the N and E. After passing a bare spot, the grade becomes easier at 2.85 mi. and levels off in the woods at 3.14 mi. After starting up again at 3.25 mi., a small summit is reached at 3.36 mi. Two pitch ups lead to the lookout on R at 3.47 mi. The trail descends slightly, levels off and comes to a trail junction at 3.65 mi. (Unmarked trail R leads 1.24 mi. to summit of Esther. See below.)

Continuing with red markers the trail follows along the ridge with easy ups and downs. At 3.78 mi. a very steep ski trail climbs R to the above trail leading to Lookout Mt. Keeping straight ahead a good spring is passed at 4.06 mi. Climbing starts again shortly before joining a ski trail at 4.55 mi. where there is a good view.

Climbing the ski trail, the foot trail leaves it just before coming to Whiteface lean-to at 4.72 mi. where a ski trail enters on R.

Above the lean-to the trail climbs steeply up the ski trail toward the stone retaining wall on the Memorial Highway. Turning L near the top of the ski trail, the foot trail follows along the base of the retaining wall over large rocks and ascends steeply over a rock ledge to the road at 4.95 mi. The trail then climbs through scrub conifers up the ridge above the road and rounds off in an open spot at 5.09 mi. where the summit is in sight. Starting the final pitch at 5.25 mi. the trail passes a rain gauge, leads L around base of the weather station observation tower, climbs the steps and reaches the PBM on the summit of Whiteface at 5.34 mi.

Distances: Memorial Highway to Wilmington Reservoir, 0.27 mi.; to ski trail near top of ski lift on Marble Mt., 2.41 mi.; to trail over Lookout to Esther, 3.65 mi.; to Whiteface lean-to, 4.72 mi.; to summit of Whiteface, 5.34 mi. Ascent from highway, 3670 ft. Elevation, 4867 ft. Order of height, 5.

Trail to McLenathan Bay and Whiteface Landing

This is an SOA trail connecting the Connery Pond Trail with the trail around Lake Placid and provides access to the dock at McLenathan Bay. To reach the start of this trail, take Connery Pond–Whiteface Trail to junction at 1.11 mi. (See above.)

Leaving red DEC trail (0 mi.) and following blue SOA markers, the trail climbs gradually, veering away from the DEC trail and swinging toward the W. At 0.18 mi. it follows up the R bank of a brook, soon crosses it, comes to a pitch up and levels off at 0.28 mi., followed by a slight downgrade. Climbing gradually again at 0.59 mi., a brook is crossed at 0.72 mi. in a blowdown area, and a trail fork is reached at 0.76 mi. (Old trail took R branch.) Turning L the present trail joins a tractor road at a height of land at 0.79 mi. The present trail soon turns R away from the road. Care is required for some distance as the foot trail has been crossed and recrossed by a tractor making the trail muddy and wet. Going L on an old tote road at 0.86 mi. and again crossing a tractor road at 0.98 mi., the junction with the red SOA trail around Lake Placid is reached at 1.24 mi. Turning L with red and blue markers, the blue trail branches R at 1.26 mi. and reaches McLenathan Bay dock at 1.30 mi.

Starting (0 mi.) from the above junction at 1.24 mi., the red trail may be followed N along the lake, passing two private camps at about 0.55 mi. and coming to Whiteface Landing at 2.02 mi. where it joins the red DEC trail to Whiteface. This makes a nice circuit, returning by the tote road.

Distances: From Route 86 to start of blue SOA trail, 1.11 mi.; to junction with red SOA trail, 2.35 mi.; to McLenathan Bay dock, 2.41 mi.; to Whiteface Landing, 4.37 mi. (4.49 mi. if also going to McLenathan Bay dock).

Sunrise Notch Trail

This trail connects the Connery Pond–Whiteface as well as the Whiteface Landing section of Lake Placid with High Falls on the Wilmington Notch Road, Route 86, about 4.5 mi. from Wilmington. It leaves the Connery Pond–Whiteface trail 0.77 mi. NE from Whiteface Landing and 3.81 mi. from the start of the trail on Route 86 (see above). This trail climbs 450 ft. to Sunrise Notch and descends 900 ft. in a little over a mile to High Falls. The trail is no longer regularly maintained, somewhat difficult to follow, and a fee will be charged for use of the bridge at High Falls, above which fording the river is difficult.

Distance: Whiteface Trail to High Falls, about 3.25 mi.

Owen and Copperas Ponds

These two ponds and their small neighbor, Winch Pond, offer a satisfactory short walk with very little climbing. The easier of two approaches is via Owen Pond from Highway 86, and the trail is described in this direction, returning to the highway 1 mi. NE from the starting point. The start is located on E side of the highway about 5 mi. NE of the traffic light at the intersection of Route 86 and 73 in Lake Placid Village, and 2 mi. NE of where the river road from Route 73 at the ski jump joins Route 86. It is marked on the roadside with a DEC sign, as is also the N end of the trail.

Leaving the highway (0 mi.) and following blue markers, the trail enters the woods on a tote road and turns L away from it at 0.08 mi. Heading in a general easterly direction, the trail follows up the R bank of Owen Pond Brook, pretty much on the level. After climbing an easy grade through a hemlock grove, the trail levels off at 0.36 mi. and reaches the NW corner of Owen Pond at 0.55 mi.

Following along the N shore, the NE corner of the pond is reached at 0.72 mi. where the trail veers away, heading about 60°, and starts climbing at an easy grade. After easy ups and downs the grade becomes steeper just before the trail swings to the N at 1.00 mi. Easing off again at 1.08 mi., the trail swings R and descends a steep pitch at 1.16 mi. and then levels off. Continuing straight ahead the trail passes behind the Copperas Pond lean-to (1958) at 1.28 mi. This lean-to faces the pond with an excellent view of Whiteface to the N. A second lean-to (Copperas Pond No. 2) is located on the N shore. Copperas Pond has also been known as Sentinel Lake.

Following counterclockwise around the pond, the trail crosses the outlet just past the lean-to. At 1.43 mi. an inlet and marshy area is crossed on a bridge, and a trail junction is reached at 1.44 mi. (Trail R with yellow markers leads 0.44 mi. to Winch Pond. See below.) Continuing along the shore, a trail junction is reached at 1.56 mi. just after crossing a small inlet. Trail straight ahead along the shoreline reaches the N shore lean-to in 0.1 mi. About half way to the lean-to there is a nice picnic spot at some large rocks on the shore.

The blue trail leaves the pond at the 1.56 mi. junction and climbs to a height of land at 1.64 mi. Descending three steep pitches between easy stretches, another trail junction is reached at 1.79 mi. (Trail R with red markers leads 0.51 mi. to Winch Pond. See below.) Going L with the blue markers, the trail becomes very rocky and eroded as it descends a fairly steep grade, easing off at 1.96 mi. and reaching Route 86 at 2.01 mi., having descended about 300 ft. from the height of land near Copperas Pond.

Distances: From S starting point on Route 86 to Owen Pond, 0.55 mi.; to new Copperas Pond lean-to, 1.28 mi.; to yellow trail to Winch Pond, 1.44 mi.; to side trail to picnic rocks, 1.56 mi.; to red trail to Winch Pond, 1.79 mi.; to N end of trail on Route 86, 2.01 mi. This is 1.0 mi. by highway from S end of the trail.

Winch Pond

This little pond lies ENE from Copperas Pond. The shortest approach is from Route 86 via the N end of the Owen Pond–Copperas Pond Trail. (See above.) Leaving the highway (0 mi.), the trail climbs gradually at first and then fairly steeply on a rocky and eroded trail to the junction with the red trail on L at 0.22 mi. Turning L with red markers over a trail with easy ups and downs, another junction is reached at a tote road at 0.60 mi. Going L on tote road following yellow markers, with little change in elevation, the end of the tote road is reached at 0.70 mi. where the trail turns R and reaches the shore of Winch Pond at 0.73 mi.

Distances: From N end of blue trail on Route 86 to red trail to Winch Pond, 0.22 mi.; to junction with yellow trail, 0.60 mi.; to Winch Pond, 0.73 mi.

If approaching from the S end of the Owen Pond–Copperas Pond Trail, take this trail from the highway (0 mi.) to the junction with the yellow trail just past the Copperas Pond outlet at 1.44 mi. (See above.) Turning R with yellow markers, the trail heads E and reaches a widened spot in a tote road at 1.69 mi. Going L on the tote road the red trail mentioned above enters on the L at 1.75 mi. Continuing straight ahead with yellow markers, the shore of Winch Pond is reached at 1.88 mi.

Distances: From S end of blue trail on Route 86 to yellow trail to Winch Pond, 1.44 mi.; to junction with red trail, 1.75 mi.; to Winch Pond, 1.88 mi.

The Sentinel Range

The Sentinel Range, running NE and SW, lies SE of the Wilmington Notch Road. Its highest summit, Kilburn Mt., falls a bit short of being a major peak, rising to an elevation of 3893 ft., but its interesting summits offer challenge and unusual views to the trailless climbers. Approach to the range may be made by either the North Notch or South Notch Trail, the former coming closer to the higher summits. Both of these trails are primarily ski trails, being old tote roads; they are both also good foot trails in the summer. The trails start from the river road connecting Route 73 and 86 and climb into the notches from the W. The ski trails used to continue through the notches and descend the slopes on the E, but these sections are no longer maintained and are difficult to follow. There is a lean-to at about 0.5 mi. below the height of land in the South Notch. Another lean-to, much newer, is located only 0.35 mi. from the river road on the South Notch Trail.

North Notch Trail

This trail starts on the river road 3.0 mi. N of its junction with Route 73, and 1.0 mi. S of its junction with Route 86, at a point where a fair-sized brook flows into the river. It is marked with a DEC sign and red markers. The road widens out at this point providing ample room to park cars.

Leaving the road (0 mi.), the trail follows a tote road on the N side (R bank) of the brook. At 0.06 mi. the trail turns sharp L away from the tote toad which tends to be wet beyond this point. Climbing moderately up the side of a ridge, a height of land is reached at 0.23 mi. Descending and circling back, Holcomb Pond outlet is reached and crossed on a log bridge at 0.41 m. The trail crosses the tote road on the L bank and continues on the higher ground. At 0.74 mi. a stream is crossed on a log bridge and the trail rejoins the tote road following up the R bank. A small waterfall is heard at 0.96 mi., and the grade gets a little steeper at 1.03 mi. Continuing with an occasional breather at short, level stretches, the trail meets the R bank of a small brook at 1.19 mi. and soon crosses it. After traversing a level, but very wet section from 1.23 to 1.28 mi., the grade becomes moderate at 1.33 mi. An interesting boulder is visible in the woods on the R at 1.48 mi., shortly before crossing a brook from its R bank at 1.52 mi. where the grade gets steeper. A soggy section is crossed at 1.75 mi. as the climbing continues at a fair grade with some easy stretches and moderate pitch-ups. The overgrown site of the North Notch campsite is reached at 2.41 mi.

Straight ahead about 65 yds. the old tote road meets the R bank of a good-sized brook where the old corduroy bridge has long since collapsed. This nonmaintained and ummarked section of the old ski trail continues to the height of land just beyond the campsite and then continues along the course of Clifford Brook. It reaches a dirt road near Clifford Falls in about 3.0 mi.

Distance: River road to end of maintained trail at old North Notch campsite, 2.41 mi. Ascent from river road, 1400 ft.

South Notch Trail

This trail starts on the river road 2.0 mi. N of its junction with Route 73, and 2.0 mi. S of its junction with Route 86. It is 1.0 mi. S of the North Notch Trail. A few yards N of the trailhead there is a clearing on the E side of the road where cars may be parked.

Leaving the road (0 mi.) the red marked trail follows a dirt road up the R bank of a brook. A chain near the main road prevents vehicular traffic on the dirt road. At 0.15 mi. the trail swings L away from the brook and starts to climb. The going gets easier at 0.21 mi., the general direction being SE. A lean-to is located on a rise above the trail on the L at 0.35 mi. At 0.45 mi. the trail swings L as another tote road enters like a trailing switch from the R. (Note that on returning the marked trail does not go straight ahead at this point, but swings R.)

The trail comes close to the R bank of the main brook at 0.58 mi. and follows up the brook, periodically being close to the bank. This companionship of the brook makes this section most enjoyable. A tributary is crossed from its R bank on an old corduroy at 0.91 mi. as the trail starts up an easy grade. The main brook is crossed on an old corduroy at 1.10 mi. and the grade becomes moderate up the L bank. After the grade slackens the main brook is recrossed at 1.26 mi. and an interesting large boulder is passed on R at 1.29 mi. Again crossing the main brook at 1.37 mi., the trail climbs up the L bank and swings R away from the brook, following up a small tributary at easy to moderate grades. The climbing is steeper from 1.71 mi. to 1.79 mi. and is then periodically easy to moderate, becoming very easy at 2.23 mi. and reaching a height of land at

2.34 mi. Descending slightly, the trail becomes fairly level and makes a moderate pitch up at 2.47 mi. After this the grade is easy and the South Notch lean-to is reached at 2.72 mi.

The height of land in the S notch is approximately 0.5 mi. and 200 ft. elevation above the lean-to with no maintained trail. Beyond the height of land, the non-maintained trail descends steeply down the E side of the notch and joins the Old Military Road in back of Pitchoff Mt. in about 1.30 mi. at a point 0.92 mi. from the end of the Alstead Mill Road leading up from Keene. (See Cascade–Keene–Hurricane Region, Sect. B7.)

Distances: River road to end of maintained trail at South Notch lean-to 2.72 mi., to height of land in South Notch 3.2 mi. Ascent from river road 1200 ft.

Haystack from Marcy
Photo by H. Hammond

SECTION B10

SARANAC LAKE REGION

Saranac Lake is one of the popular summer vacation spots of the northern Adirondacks. Located on Route 86 the village is 9 mi. W of Lake Placid and lies directly N of the western part of the high peak area. Coming from the direction of Keene on Route 73, Lake Placid Village may be avoided by bearing L on hard-surfaced road at fork shortly after crossing iron bridge over W branch of Ausable River. From the summits of the nearby mountains one can enjoy excellent views of the high peaks to the S and SE, with the lake country extending to the W and SW.

With the exception of the Ampersand Mt. Trail, which is maintained by DEC, all of the marked trails described in this section are maintained by several chapters of the ADK.

Trail Described	Year Measured	Total Miles
Baker Mt.	1956	0.89
Haystack Mt.	1956	2.44
McKenzie Mt. from DEC Headquarters	1956	4.40
McKenzie Mt. from Whiteface Inn	1956	3.55
Scarface Mt.	1966	2.39
Ampersand Mt.	1961	2.71

Baker Mt.

This little mountain probably affords a lake and mountain view unsurpassed in the Adirondacks for the length of climb. From its partially wooded summit, lookouts provide views from Moose and McKenzie Mts. over McKenzie Pond to the E, around to the Great Range to the SE, the MacIntyre Range, Sewards and the lake country to the SW around the Saranacs.

To reach the start of the trail at the N end of Moody Pond just E of Saranac Lake Village, turn R at the information booth coming in from Lake Placid on Route 86, cross the RR and turn L on Pine St. Recross RR and turn R on E Pine St. over RR. Follow E Pine St. to N end of Moody Pond. By turning R on hard-surfaced road just beyond DEC headquarters at Ray Brook, one will come out at Pine St. at the first RR crossing mentioned above, thereby avoiding village traffic by Lake Flower.

Leaving the road (0 mi.) the trail, marked with ADK markers, starts in an old tote road heading NE and immediately turns R upgrade to another tote road at 0.02 mi., which it follows to the L. Entering a small clearing at 0.06 mi. the trail bears R to an old stone quarry at 0.12 mi. Climbing to the R it swings L past the quarry and enters the woods, the grade being moderate with an occasional steeper stretch, leveling off and becoming easy at 0.38 mi. The grade becomes steep at 0.59 mi. as the trail climbs up over rock ledges and through red pine with several lookouts to the S. Turning sharp L at 0.77 mi., the trail continues its steep ascent to the summit at 0.89 mi.

Distance: Moody Pond to summit of Baker, 0.89 mi. Ascent, 900 ft. Elevation, 2452 ft.

Haystack Mt.

This little peak, not to be confused with the 4960 ft. peak of the same name in the Great Range, is just SW of McKenzie, and offers a maximum outlook for a short, steep, rocky climb. The trail starts behind the Adirondack Regional Headquarters of the DEC at Ray Brook on Route 86 between Lake Placid and Saranac Lake. There is a parking lot at the rear of the building. The adjacent log building is now occupied by the Adirondack Park Agency. From the parking lot behind the new DEC building, proceed N about 150 ft. to a picnic area in a grove of large trees. A red ADK marker together with direction signs will be found at the entrance to the picnic area. Starting at this point (0 mi.), proceed along the wooded trail through the picnic area and woods, coming to a power line clearing at 0.08 mi. A dirt road is crossed diagonally to the L at 0.16 mi., after which the trail runs near a sand pit on the L. Care should be exercised here since there is danger of cave-ins. The trail has been re-routed slightly at 0.25 mi. to avoid a cave-in section. After crossing another dirt road proceed across a meadow with a good view of Haystack ahead and slightly L. Enter woods at 0.35 mi. and cross another dirt road diagonally to the R at 0.51 mi. At 0.62 mi. turn L on a grassy woods road which becomes a footpath at 0.67 mi., following the water supply brook of the former State Sanatorium up a wooded gorge with beautiful spruce timber and recurrent waterfalls. Small tributaries are crossed at 0.71 mi. and 0.92 mi., and the main stream is reached at 1.04 mi. The trail has been level all the way, but starts up an easy to moderate grade at about 1.25 mi. near an old camp foundation and reaches a junction at 1.50 mi. (Trail R leads to McKenzie. See below.)

Going L the Haystack Trail crosses a tributary and then the main brook at the water supply dam at 1.57 mi. (last water). Now climbing at a moderate grade the trail starts up the mountain, soon reaching alternate steep and easy sections. The trail becomes quite steep at 2.24 mi., breaks out into the open at 2.31 mi. where there are good views and an easier grade. Entering the woods again at 2.34 mi. at a short, level stretch, the trail climbs steeply up a rocky section, comes out on another open area at 2.39 mi. with less grade and reaches the summit at 2.44 mi. Here there are views of the mountains to the E and S, and over the Saranac Lakes to the W. A. short trail leads about 40 yards to the N lookout where one can see McKenzie Mt. to the NE and McKenzie Pond slightly N of W with Baker Mt. beyond.

Distances: DEC Headquarters to junction with trail to McKenzie, 1.50 mi.; to water supply dam, 1.57 mi.; to summit of Haystack, 2.44 mi. Ascent, 1275 ft. Elevation, 2878 ft.

McKenzie Mt. from DEC Headquarters

Leaving DEC headquarters (0 mi.) follow same trail as for Haystack to trail junction at 1.50 mi. (See above.) Going R at the junction the trail climbs at an easy grade up old tote road, crosses a brook flowing from R near old shack at 1.93 mi., bears L past the shack and crosses a larger brook from R at 1.95 mi. After crossing a small tributary at 2.35 the trail soon comes near the L bank of the main brook and crosses it at 2.51 mi. Continuing on old tote road following the brook (last water) the trail crosses the DEC Whiteface Inn–Saranac Lake horse trail at 2.76 mi., here just an overgrown tote road.

Turning sharp L at 2.79 mi. (tote road straight ahead is an old route to the summit of McKenzie via Bartlett Pond which is no longer maintained) the trail climbs moderately and then goes steeply straight up the mountain at 3.01 mi. A lookout is reached at 3.42 mi. and a better lookout off trail on R at 3.47 mi. shortly before the trail rounds off at a height of land at the S end of the ridge at 3.50 mi. The trail descends slightly and then makes its way among the ferns and conifers along the ridge. A steep pitch is reached at 3.62 mi. followed by steady climbing at 3.79 mi. After climbing between large rocks at 3.86 mi. the trail rounds off, passes a lookout to the N at 3.90 mi. and reaches the summit of the S peak at 4.01 mi.

Descending sharply, the trail levels off, then starts down again, reaching the bottom of the col at 4.13 mi. Climbing again, steep pitches are ascended at 4.24 mi. and 4.36 mi., reaching the summit of the N peak at 4.40 mi. While the N summit is heavily wooded, side trails shortly before the summit lead L and R to overlooks giving unobstructed views from Scarface in the S, westerly around to Moose Mt. in the NE, and from Scarface easterly overlooking Lake Placid around to Whiteface in the ENE.

Distances: DEC headquarters to junction with trail to Haystack, 1.50 mi.; to DEC horse trail, 2.76 mi.: to top of steep climb at S end of ridge, 3.50 mi.; to S peak of McKenzie, 4.01 mi.; to N peak, 4.40 mi. Ascent, 2250 ft. Elevation, 3861 ft.

McKenzie Mt. from Whiteface Inn

This is a shorter route to the summit than from the DEC headquarters described above and requires less climbing. The trail leaves the Whiteface Inn Road 1.40 mi. from Route 86 and 0.10 mi. before reaching the Whiteface Inn tennis courts. At the start this horse trail is a good gravel road with a barway to exclude vehicular traffic, but there is room to park a car or two off the paved road. While there are no trail markers, it is marked with a DEC sign at its beginning and is used as a ski trail.

Leaving the paved road (0 mi.) the gravel road heads NW climbing at a moderate grade, crosses a yellow property line at 0.38 mi. and passes a side road on L at 0.47 mi. leading to a water supply dam and reservoir. At 0.63 mi. a small brook rises out of the ground on the L side of the road, and the grade becomes easier. This may be the last water. Many log loading stations for hurricane timber are passed, and the gravel road gives way to a grassy tote road at about 0.83 mi. The forest becomes denser at about 1.00 mi. and the grade fairly easy. Near the height of land at a brook crossing (may be dry) the Placid lean-to on the L is reached at 1.51 mi. W of the lean-to the tote road is more over-grown and meets the ADK trail from DEC headquarters at 1.91 mi. From here, turning R on the ADK trail, the route to McKenzie is the same as that described above.

Distances: Whiteface Inn Road to Placid lean-to, 1.51 mi.; to ADK trail, 1.91 mi.; to top of steep climb at S end of ridge, 2.65 mi.; to S peak of McKenzie, 3.16 mi.; to N peak, 3.55 mi. Ascent, 1940 ft. Elevation, 3861 ft.

Scarface Mt.

This mountain offers very rewarding views from the open ledges below the wooded summit. However, the approach to the trail is under re-routing because of new Olympic construction and those interested in climbing this peak should check with DEC in Ray Brook for the latest information. The present description is being left in the guide so that when another access is ready, the hiker can easily key into it at the proper point.

Leaving gravel road junction at parking lot (0 mi.) follow dirt road (road not maintained) S up slight hill. The grade soon becomes level as the road leads through hardwoods and then a white pine forest, passing a small clearing on L at 0.66 mi. and reaching a larger clearing on L, dotted with white pines, at 0.85 mi. where one looks SE directly at Scarface. Here the trail turns L along the near edge of the clearing following ADK markers and enters the woods heading E at 0.97 mi. Soon swinging R and climbing a gradual grade the trail crosses a small tributary at 1.10 mi. and then reaches the R bank of a brook at 1.13 mi. Following up the R bank the trail crosses the brook at 1.20 mi. (last sure water) and follows up the L bank. Veering away from the brook at 1.25 mi., the grade gets a little steeper, eases off, then climbs almost to the col between Scarface and the top of the ridge extending toward Oseetah Lake. After crossing a brook bed at 1.84 mi. the trail makes a steep pitch at 2.04 mi. up to an open ledge at 2.13 mi., reaching the upper corner of the ledge on the R at 2.15 mi. (By bushwhacking to the R a better lookout can be reached.) The trail continues up the ridge at an easy grade in and out of scrub. At 2.39 mi., it ends at a bare spot on the summit ridge. There is no trail from here to the viewless summit. Ledges near the end of the trail offer an 180° vista to the W from the Sawteeth and Seward Mts. in the S to Ampersand and Lower Saranac, Kiwassa and Oseeth Lakes in the W to Baker and McKenzie in the N. Lake Placid and Whiteface can also be seen.

Distances: Parking lot to start of foot trail at second clearing, 0.85 mi.; to brook crossing, 1.20 mi.; to top of ledge, 2.15 mi.; to summit of Scarface, 2.39 mi. Ascent, 1475 ft.; Elevation, 3088 ft.

Ampersand Mt.

The trail to this fire tower peak commences on Route 3 about 8.1 mi. SW of the traffic light at the bridge in Saranac Lake Village. There is a parking space for cars on the R side of the highway and a DEC sign marks the start of the trail on the L side. A trail leads N from the parking space and then swings W to the lean-to on the S shore of Middle Saranac Lake, distance about 0.5 mi.

Leaving the road (0 mi.) the Ampersand Trail enters the woods at a locked barway. Heading S it follows a good jeep road and soon swings SE and ESE. Being a well defined trail, markers are not needed and few are provided. The grade is practically level through a beautiful hardwood forest with some conifers. A fair-sized brook with a steel pipe culvert is crossed from its L bank at 0.17 mi. Smaller brooks, also flowing from the R, are crossed at 0.38 mi. and 0.43 mi., and another large brook is crossed at 0.50 mi. The jeep road ends at 0.63 mi. where there is a small space for the DEC truck to park. Now becoming a footpath the trail passes through a fine hemlock grove and then crosses a swampy section on a long corduroy from 0.78 mi. to 0.83 mi. Two more brooks are crossed at 0.97 mi. and 1.29 mi., after which the trail swings R and starts to climb steadily at a fair grade, heading 120°. The grade rounds off just before reaching the site once occupied by a fire observer's cabin at 1.64 mi. where there is good water from Dutton Brook.

Now the trail turns R and follows up the L bank of the brook on an easy to moderate grade. Gradually veering away from the brook the trail becomes quite steep at 1.90 mi. The climbing continues with occasional breathers on one of the worst trails in the mountains. The grade varies from the steep to very steep and the footpath is very badly eroded, necessitating climbing over many roots and around boulders. The grade finally becomes relatively easy at 2.38 mi. and levels off through a small col with bare rock visible through the trees on the L at 2.46 mi. Starting up a moderate grade a large, overhanging rock on R is passed at 2.54 mi. Descending slightly the trail swings R at a steep and eroded spot. Here the trail originally climbed between two large boulders at 2.60 mi., but the preferred route detours around the boulders to the L. Finally emerging from the woods on bare rock at 2.64 mi. the trail circles to the L following the tree line and then heads up over the bare rock to the PBM on the summit at 2.71 mi. The fire tower, scheduled in 1976 for removal in the near future, lies a little beyond and below the summit. On rock face near the tower is a memorial tablet to Walter Channing Rice, 1852–1924, the "Hermit of Ampersand, who kept Vigil from this Peak, 1915–1923."

The view is excellent, with little Ampersand Lake close by to the S and high peaks to the SE. To the N and NW lie the Saranacs and the countless ponds beyond. This summit used to be wooded, but Verplanck Colvin in his survey had the trees on the summit removed so as to use this peak as a triangulation station. Erosion set in, washing away all the soil, and now nothing but bare rock remains.

Distances: Route 3 to observer's cabin site, 1.64 mi.; to summit of Ampersand, 2.71 mi. Ascent, 1775 ft. Elevation, 3352 ft.

Cold River from Rondeau Lean-to
Photo by Tom Dunn

SECTION C

PEAKS WITHOUT MAINTAINED TRAILS—
THE TRAILLESS PEAKS

The Sixth, Seventh and Eighth editions of this guide called this section "The Trailless Peaks." And indeed through the 1940s and 1950s that term "Trailless Peaks" that has become a treasured part of Adirondack folklore was an apt title for this chapter, which gives instructions for climbing those mountains of the High Peak Region that do not have formal trails.

Until the last decade or so, this was still a wilderness in which there were few hikers from year to year on either the marked trails or the paths beaten out by climbers on the Trailless Peaks which have become known as "herd paths." However, the increased recreational use of this area brought about a proliferation of herd paths that was destroying precious Adirondack conifer and alpine vegetation and the wilderness flavor of the mountains. To help preserve the plant life and character of this great natural resource of the Eastern United States, we are asked to *follow one herd path in climbing one of these peaks.* This is the official philosophy of the Adirondack Forty-Sixers, described further on, and this practice has the approval of the Department of Environmental Conservation.

Because there are these herd paths or informal trails on all of the so-called Trailless Peaks, we have changed the heading of this section to "Peaks without Maintained Trails—The Trailless Peaks." Thus we keep the expression "Trailless Peaks" which has become so meaningful to generations of hikers while giving a more precise description of the type of climbing that is involved here.

In his preface to the Trailless Peaks section of the Seventh Edition of this guide, published in 1962, the former editor, the late L. Morgan Porter, wrote: "To stand practically alone on some peak like Phelps, Macomb, East Dix or Rocky Peak, to name only a few, and realize that you are one of the comparatively few people who have ever reached that secluded spot in the wilderness is a thrill experienced only by those who have bushwhacked their way with map and compass."

Today, one's chances of standing practically alone on the summit of a trailless peak are considerably less likely than they were in Porter's day. Phelps and Rocky and many of the others are no longer trailless. The herd paths beaten by countless climbers following the same route have made climbing faster and easier than it was only a couple of decades ago.

Perhaps, to get the experience of feeling what it means to be alone in the wilderness *a la* Daniel Boone and David Crockett, we can no longer go the way of the so-called trailless peaks but instead must look elsewhere. Indeed it is possible to find areas in the Adirondacks without trails where the hiker would be in a wilderness setting.

Of the forty-six peaks of the Adirondacks determined to be 4000 ft. or more in elevation above sea level by the United States Geological Survey, twenty of them lack formal trails. Though all of them now possess rough paths beaten out by many climbers, these herd paths are not marked, and ascents of these peaks still call for considerable route-finding and tracking skills.

Trailless climbing is fun and full of adventure, but a few words of caution and advice should be heeded by all who go into this region. We do not recommend winter ascents, which may vary from being easy to impossible, of these peaks. A person without winter mountaineering experience should not attempt them, and then only with others with similar training. As noted in the Preface Page for the Hiker, temperatures above the tree line are often as low as those at the Arctic Circle.

Do not climb trailless peaks alone. If you are not worried about the consequences of a mishap to yourself, think of the many people who may have to comb the mountainside looking for you. Be sure that your group stays together. Inform someone of your destination and possible routes. Where possible, register in the DEC registers found at trailheads, giving details of your planned trip. Upon return, write "Out" on your entry listing. If at a lean-to, leave a note.

Know the location of all trails in the vicinity of a climb. Know your mountain peaks and be able to recognize them from any viewpoint. *Before* you make your trip, learn to read a topographic map and use a compass. Magnetic N is about 15′ W of true N in this area. Carry with you a guidebook, USGS topographic map, compass, flashlight with extra batteries, first-aid kit, insect repellant, matches, extra food, and clothing designed to keep you as dry and warm as possible in case bad weather sets in and you are forced to bivouac for the night.

As noted earlier, climbers should be aware of the problem of overuse. There is no formal program of maintaining these herd paths. To avoid further erosion, climbers are asked to *follow the present herd paths* where erosion is now pretty well stabilized. They should do everything they can to leave the summits and bivouac areas clean and free from signs of man's presence. During recent years, cooperation by hikers in preserving the natural condition of the trailless peaks has made them much more attractive than they were in the days when climbers were less aware of the overuse problems.

The present interest in trailless climbing dates back to Robert and George Marshall, who in 1924 with their friend and guide, Herbert Clark, completed climbing the forty-six peaks over 4000 ft. as indicated on the USGS maps available at that time. Since then, following completed ascents of the same mountains nine years later by Fay Loope, thousands of recreationists have sought out this special outdoor activity. These mountaineers have organized a unique climbing society known as The Adirondack Forty-Sixers. They have their own articles of organization, by-laws, and a distinctive shoulder patch. The Forty-Sixers meet twice a year at places like Adirondak Loj or Johns Brook Lodge and publish a newsletter known as *Adirondack Peeks.*

In deciding what constituted an individual peak, the Marshalls set an arbitrary rule that it should rise 300 ft. on all sides or be at the end of a long ridge at least 0.75 mi. from the nearest peak. Since then more recent surveys, with better equipment and aided by aerial photography, have indicated that four of the peaks— Blake, Cliff, Nye and Couchsachraga—are under 4000 ft. and that some peaks fail to qualify if the above rule is strictly applied to the new survey data. Conversely, the new survey has revealed that MacNaughton, originally indicated as being 3976 ft., is now considered to be a 4000-footer. However, since The Adirondack Forty-Sixers was founded to bring together those who had climbed the same forty-six peaks climbed by the Marshalls and Herb Clark, it has been resolved that the climbing of these same forty-six peaks, regardless of their corrected elevations, still shall be considered a prerequisite for membership in that organization. If you seriously intend to become a Forty-Sixer, write to The Adirondack Forty-Sixers, Adirondack, New York 12808. It is not necessary to belong to the ADK to become a Forty-Sixer, but most Forty-Sixers are also ADKers.

It has been the position of the Adirondack Mountain Club for many years that a considerable number of the Adirondack peaks should be left trailless. The Temporary Study Commission on the Future of the Adirondacks in its report of January 2, 1971 described the damage to trailless peaks from overuse and recommended that the trailless conditions of the certain major peaks should be perpetuated by whatever means necessary. The Club supports this recommendation.

The editor of this guide, in following the philosophy of the Adirondack Forty-Sixers of using one herd path, offers instructions on following one herd path in the following descriptions.

Cold River Region

Seymour. This peak was named for Horatio Seymour, several times Governor of New York. The popular route ascends the first brook 0.10 mi. SE of Ward Brook lean-to. The most westerly branch leads to an easily ascended slide, above which the going is easy to the top of the ridge. Follow the ridge SW to the summit. Ascent from the SW by way of Ouluska Pass Brook is more difficult because of blowdown. Descent into Ouluska Pass, the col between Seymour and Seward, is complicated because of blowdown and cliffs.

Seward, Donaldson and Emmons. Seward was named for William Henry Seward, who succeeded William L. Marcy as Governor. He was one of the founders of the Republican Party and Secretary of State in Lincoln's cabinet. Donaldson, the first Adirondack peak to be named during the Twentieth Century, stands as a monument to Alfred Lee Donaldson, who wrote the first and most complete history of the Adirondacks. The southernmost peak in the Seward Range honors the memory of Ebenezer Emmons, state geologist and leader of the 1837 expedition which made the first ascent of Mt. Marcy, and the man who gave the name "Adirondacks" to this mountain region.

The usual route to Seward begins at the bridge 0.23 mi. SE of the clearing where the red foot trail from Coreys-Axton joins the fire truck trail. This is the third bridge NW of Ward Brook lean-to. After starting on the E side of the brook, follow old tote roads on the W side to the end of the second growth where blow-down begins. Avoid the ridge to the W. For easier going, climb part way up the ridge to the E, eventually striking the NE ridge of Seward which leads to the summit. Present herd paths descend to the S flanks of the western Seward ridge, reaching Donaldson more or less on a compass line from Seward's summit. For Emmons from Donaldson, stay on the ridge to the col, then drop to the W to avoid blowdown, returning to the Emmons ridge as soon as practical.

Today, most people reaching Emmons over Seward and Donaldson from the Ward Brook lean-to area find it easier to return by retracing their steps over the latter two peaks. There are other alternatives. The return through Ouluska Pass is complicated by blowdown. The descent via the Calkins Brook has some difficult sections. The return via the Northville–Placid Trail and the Duck Hole truck road takes about the same time as returning over Donaldson and Seward, but this route, formerly the usual route chosen, is now more difficult to find because once-open lumber roads are now badly overgrown.

To descend to the Northville–Placid Trail, find a herd path leaving the ridge about 0.25 mi. N of the Emmons summit. This route descends through blowdown into the valley leading SE to a brook from Ouluska Pass (which is located between Seward and Seymour). About 0.25 mi. up Ouluska Brook from its junction with the brook from Emmons, find a large lumber clearing. (A R turn will lead down Ouluska Pass Brook to the Northville–Placid Trail and Ouluska Pass lean-to on the Cold River about 0.5 mi. S of the Rondeau hermitage site.) From the SE edge of this clearing, an overgrown lumber road heads SE and E in about a mile to the Northville–Placid Trail at a point 0.9 mi. NE of the former Noah John Rondeau hermitage.

A more difficult route to the Seward Range is from the W by way of Calkins Brook. This stream is reached from Coreys and Axton by way of the trail to the Ward Brook area and the Calkins Brook truck trail. (See Sanford Lake Region, Section B5.) Avoid striking directly for Emmons from the head of the Calkins Brook. It is easier to cross over the summit of Donaldson.

Couchsachraga. Pronounced "Kook-sa-kra-ga," this term is an ancient Algonquin name for the Adirondacks, which means the "dismal wilderness." Most people today reach Couchsachraga by way of the herd paths following the ridge westerly to Couchsachraga from the N-S Panther–Santanoni ridge. The route leaves the latter ridge about 0.25 mi. S of the summit of Panther.

However, because easy access to Panther and Santanoni from the E is now technically illegal, mention should be made of the once popular route to Couchsachraga from Cold River. Approach is made via a bridge on the horse trail from Shattuck Clearing to the Northville–Placid Trail NW of the Duck Hole. (See Section B5.) It is about 5.50 mi. from Shattuck Clearing, 4.00 mi from the Northville–Placid Trail near the Duck Hole, and 15.70 mi. from the gatehouse to the Santanoni Preserve on a recently constructed trail (see Section B5). Follow the latter-mentioned trail to the top of the first hill, then head N to the brook, which drains the area N of Couchsachraga and NW of Panther, following it past a beaver swamp and up the grade beyond. Avoid the first tributary from the SW near the top of this grade. It comes from the wrong side of Little Couchsachraga. A short distance up the main stream beyond this first tributary, turn R and follow the second tributary, which joins the main stream about 1.00 mi. from the horse trail. Follow the R branches of this second tributary to near the Little Couchsachraga–Couchsachraga col, where striking upwards SE leads to the summit. The register is at the Panther end of the summit ridge.

Santanoni. The name of this highest peak W of the Hudson

River and the dominating one in the range is derived from the name Saint Anthony; it filtered down through the French Canadians to the Abenaki Indians who adopted their own pronunciation of the word. The traditional approach was a herd path starting 3.41 mi. from the old Tahawus Club road on the trail to the Duck Hole via Bradley Pond. But now the beginning of this herd path lies on private land where hiking has been banned. Using the trail map which accompanies this guidebook, a legal approach to Santanoni can be plotted from N of Bradley Pond by way of State land, but the blowdown on this route is extreme and there are no herd paths. Approaches from the Santanoni Preserve to Santanoni's summit have not yet been scouted by the guidebook editors, but they offer interesting possibilities.

Panther. As with Santanoni, the traditional approach to Panther from the trail to the Duck Hole via Bradley Pond crosses private land which has been closed to the public. This once-popular route followed the brook descending from S of Panther's summit to a point near Bradley Pond where it turns S to pick up the outlet from the pond. Using the map that accompanies this guidebook, a legal route to this brook may be plotted from N of Bradley Pond, as noted above in the description for the approach for Santanoni. The route connecting Panther and Santanoni along the ridge between these two peaks is relatively easy.

Approaches to Panther's summit from the Cold River area are long but relatively free of blowdown. The herd path between the summits of Santanoni and Panther has a fork about 0.25 mi. S of the summit of Panther that leads to Couchsachraga (see above).

MacNaughton. MacNaughton is named after James MacNaughton, grandson of Archibald McIntyre, who headed the original Adirondack Iron Works. Though not officially one of the forty-six peaks, it is the one mountain to be raised to the 4000 ft. status on the 1953 USGS map. The upper reaches of the mountain are almost completely covered with blowdown. Leave the Henderson Lake–Duck Hole Trail at the brook crossing beyond the beaver pond about 0.60 mi. NW of Hunter Pond. (See Section B5.) Follow the SE side of the brook valley nearly to the summit ridge. Climb N to the summit, which is the southernmost of three peaks all of which are about the same height. Ascent from the Wallface Ponds is also feasible, though blowdown is bad. The distance is about a mile.

Heart Lake Region

Table Top. The popular routes up Table Top leave Marcy Brook either just above Indian Falls on the Van Hoevenberg Trail to Marcy from Adirondak Loj, or from a point about 0.30 mi. further up the brook. Head E or NE from the starting points to the summit. Detour the summit blowdown (though a herd path of sorts now cuts straight through it) by skirting it to the NW.

Street and Nye. Colvin named the first peak in honor of Alfred Billings Street, New York State Law Librarian and author of the book, *The Indian Pass.* The latter peak bears the name of William B. Nye, the well-known North Elba guide, best known for having carried Matilda across Hitch-Up-Matilda ford on Avalanche Lake. Leaving the Indian Pass Trail at the W corner of Heart Lake (see Section B6), follow the old Nye ski trail to Indian Pass Brook. Descend Indian Pass Brook to the first tributary entering from the L(W). Follow the herd paths along this brook into the basin E of, and separated by a ridge from, the summit of Nye. The best herd path as of 1979 leads to a col on the ridge S of this basin. It then turns W, climbs steeply to the ridge top extending NE from Street, follows it towards Street a short distance, and then descends westerly to join the herd path between Street and Nye. Turn N for Nye; S for Street on a herd path descending to an attractive vlei and then reaching Street by staying W of the Street–Nye ridge top.

The easiest routes from Rocky Falls involve flanking the base of Street away from Indian Pass Brook to join the regular herd paths, though Street may also be climbed by various "direct assault" routes above the lean-to.

A beautiful but longer approach to Street and Nye lies up the valley above Wanika Falls, reached from Lake Placid via the Northville–Placid Trail. The northern terminus of the Northville–Placid trail may be reached by going S on the Averyville Road from Lake Placid 1.2 mi. from the DEC sign at its junction with

Old Military Road. Follow the larger, more easterly branch and stick to the flanks of Nye in the brook's upper reaches.

Esther Mountain

This major peak N of Whiteface has in the past been listed as a peak with a trail in the Lake Placid section of the guidebook. However, the ski trails once cut to its summit are now so overgrown that they are presently somewhat difficult to follow—showing that nature "reclaims its own" rapidly when man does not interfere by maintaining trails.

This most northern of the major Adirondack peaks was named for Esther McComb, who in 1839 at the age of 15, while trying to climb Whiteface from the N, became lost and made the first recorded ascent of this mountain instead. A tablet to her memory was placed on the summit in 1939 by the Forty-Sixers.

Take the Wilmington–Whiteface Trail (see Section B9) to the junction at 3.65 mi. where the latter trail begins to flank the sides of the hump known as Lookout Mountain. Leaving the red-marked trail where an old illegible sign points NW, a herd path to Esther ascends to the summit of Lookout Mountain where a ski lodge once stood. From here, the route to Esther descends into a col and continues N along the ridge to Esther's summit at 1.24 mi. from the Whiteface Trail.

Elk Lake Region

Macomb, South Dix, East Dix, Hough. Macomb honors the memory of Alexander Macomb, who defeated the British in the Battle of Plattsburgh on September 11, 1814. Hough bears the name of one of the early Adirondack conservationists, Franklin B. Hough (pronounced "Huff").

The most popular route up Macomb follows the great slide of 1947. Take the Elk Lake–Dix Trail (see Section B4) to Slide Brook, divided at this point into two channels some 100 yds. apart, beyond which there is a lean-to. Follow the brook eastwardly for about 0.60 mi. to the first tributary of significance which comes in from the SE. Ignoring a false herd path and secondary tributary joining the key tributary from the S, follow the key tributary about 0.75 mi. to the first major slide descending from the NE. Above the brook, it is steep and covered with loose rock and dirt. Beyond the first pitch, however, the going is less steep and the footing improves. The slide leads to the base of the cliffs below the summit of Macomb's South Peak. A fine herd path bypasses these cliffs on the north side, leading to the ridge connecting the South Peak and Macomb's summit. (Be sure to walk a few yds. south to the top of the South Peak for an excellent view.) The summit of Macomb is about 0.50 mi. N over a well-worn herd path.

Macomb may also be climbed by following the main valley of Slide Brook to the ridge N of Macomb's summit. A large slide descending to the upper reaches of the brook offers a feasible route half way up the summit ridge, above which a herd path leads to the ridge top N of the summit.

Still another route follows the valley of West Mill Brook from Route 9 crossing under the Northway, Interstate 87, through the brook culvert.

From Macomb to South Dix, the going is easy, following the height of land and up spectacular open rocks below South Dix's summit. From South Dix to East Dix is likewise an easy walk of about an hour over a good herd path. Going from South Dix to Hough, skirt the blowdown just N of the South Dix summit on its W side and then climb the hogback between South Dix and Hough. There is a bivouac site in the col between the hogback and Hough (with wet-weather water available). From Hough to Dix, continue along the ridge to the Beckhorn of Dix.

Good descent routes to the Elk Lake–Dix Trail lead from the col between Macomb and South Dix, and from the col between the S side of Hough and the hogback. Herd paths lead along Lillian Brook and then follow an old lumber road to the height of land on the Elk Lake–Dix Trail between the Slide and Lillian Brook valleys (0.70 mi. N of Slide Brook lean-to).

The Dixes may also be climbed from the NE via the North and South Forks of the Bouquet River (see Bouquet Valley Region, Section B8). Another very interesting approach to East Dix is from the E via Lindsay Brook. The start is at a tote road just S of the highway (Route 9) crossing the Schroon River near the Sharp's

Bridge campsite, about 5 mi. S of the junction of Routes 9 and 73.

Sanford Lake Region

Marshall (Clinton or Herbert). Colvin named this peak in honor of Governor DeWitt Clinton. He at first attached the name to the peak we now call Iroquois, but later transferred it to the southernmost peak of the MacIntyre Range. ADKers have called it Herbert in honor of Herbert Clark, and the Adirondack Forty-Sixers call it Marshall for Robert Marshall, who died in 1939. The latter name is now officially approved by the New York State Board of Geographic Names, but it is labeled "Clinton" on the regular USGS maps.

The lean-tos around Lake Colden and Flowed Lands make good bases for climbing this mountain. The map would suggest that the best route to Marshall is via the yellow DEC trail from Lake Colden to the Indian Pass Trail. However, bad blowdown on the small peak between Algonquin Pass and Marshall makes Herbert Brook the best approach to the peak. This brook crosses the red trail 0.74 mi. NE of the Calamity lean-tos and 0.32 mi. from the Lake Colden dam. This is the only brook to flow directly into Flowed Lands between the Calamity lean-tos and Lake Colden dam. Follow the brook through the blowdown. Avoid following a tributary entering from the R about 0.50 mi. up the brook. Open rock slides make the ascent attractive for part of the way. At the head of the brook, near the col, one valley SW of Algonquin Pass, head SW for Marshall, staying close to the ridge line.

Another route more practical for a day trip from Heart Lake leaves the yellow Lake Colden–Indian Pass Trail a short distance NW of the height of land in Algonquin Pass between Marshall and Iroquois. Flank the small peak between Algonquin Pass and Marshall on its NW side, avoiding the top of the ridge where there is blowdown. Descend to the col between this peak and Marshall and climb SW to the summit.

Gray Peak. This mountain, the highest of the trailless peaks, was named by Colvin for Professor Asa Gray, one of the most noted botanists of his day. Climb from the Sanford Lake–Marcy

Trail at the outlet of Lake Tear of the Clouds over a ridge into a valley. The route then heads N from the summit ridge striking it about 200 yds. W of the summit. Another route leads from the lowest extension of timberline on the westerly side of Marcy, dipping to the S of the ridgeline at times to avoid cliffs.

Redfield. This peak was named by Colvin for Professor William C. Redfield, meteorologist and organizer of the first expedition to Marcy. It was Redfield who first described Marcy as the "High Peak of Essex" after a reconnaissance up the Opalescent River above Lake Colden before the first ascent in 1837.

Because blowdowns in 1970 made the approach to Redfield from the Cliff–Redfield col very difficult, the best route to Redfield's summit follows Uphill Brook from Uphill lean-to (see Section B5) to a point about 0.25 mi. above a high waterfall on the main stream where a tributary comes in from the R(S). After following the tributary's L fork for about 0.25 mi., bear to the R(S) straight for the summit to avoid bad blowdown on the NE section of the summit ridge.

Another route to Redfield leads from Lake Tear of the Clouds SW to the summit. Stay below the summit ridge until directly under the top of the mountain.

Cliff. This self-explanatory name was bestowed by Colvin. Start from the height of land between Cliff and Redfield on the Sanford Lake–Marcy Trail (see Section B5). Head W, in general keeping to the R of the higher cliffs. Reaching the northeastern summit, follow the broad ridge SW about 0.5 mi. to the true summit which rises steeply beyond a col.

Another interesting approach to Cliff summit is from the Yellow Trail near the height of land in the pass between Cliff and Redfield. Enter Upper Twin Brook, walk upstream to the slide and thence up the slide to its end, and it is only a short distance to the summit.

Allen. This mountain was named by Reverend Joseph Twichell for his close friend, Reverend Frederick B. Allen, who became Superintendent of the Episcopal City Mission in Boston. The naming took place on a camping trip to the Upper Ausable Lake with Charles Dudley Warner and Dr. Horace Bushnell when they were caught in the great cloudburst of August 20, 1869. This was the same storm that caused the great avalanche on Mt. Colden.

The formerly popular approach to Allen from the Sanford Lake–Marcy Trail—crossing the Opalescent River below the South Branch confluence and following lumber roads to Skylight Brook and Allen Brook which flows from an area near Allen's summit—crosses private land and has been closed to the public. Hence, routes to Allen's summit involve fighting cripple brush and blow-down along the ridge from Skylight or climbing from the Elk Lake–Marcy Trail (see Section B4). The latter approach is best made from the flat area N of the Adirondack Mountain Reserve boundary line, descending to Marcy Brook and heading along the slopes of Allen to the upper reaches of Sand Brook where a route leads to the summit through relatively little blowdown. Heading for Allen lower down on the Marcy Trail leads one into lumber slash. There are no herd paths on the east side of Allen.

Along the Northville-Placid Trail (Shattuck Clearing to Duck Hole)
Photo by Bruce Wadsworth

SECTION D

THE NORTHVILLE–PLACID TRAIL

INTRODUCTION

The Northville–Placid Trail is a trunk line footpath that traverses the heart of the Adirondack wilderness as a lowland route. Starting from Northville, the first two-thirds of its length provides an undulating gradual ascent to a plateau area, following streams from lake to lake. Once past Long Lake, the largest body of water encountered on the route, the northern third is a valley route between several trailless high peaks. The trail does not traverse ridges or peaks. The highest point reached is a saddle at 3008 ft., involving a climb of 1165 ft. from Tirrell Pond. At the Northville bridgehead, the elevation is 760 ft., at the Upper Benson roadhead 1300 ft., and at the Averyville roadhead near Lake Placid, 2000 ft. At 2377 ft., Spruce Lake is the highest in elevation, close to West Canada Lake which is only a few feet lower.

The area through which the trail passes is not solid wilderness. There are four road crossings, and the trail passes near or through three villages. At both ends, there are road approaches. In between there are two stretches of blacktop, ¾ and 3 mi. in length, and one gravel road, 6¾ mi. in length. There are two major roadless areas which take several days to cover on foot. The trail is used by backpackers, snowshoers, ski tourists, fishermen and some hardy hunters. The entire length is closed to motorized vehicles during all seasons. The N-P Trail intercepts side trails to four mountains with fire observation towers: Cathead Mt. (2427 ft.), Wakeley Mt. (3617 ft.), Blue Mt. (3759 ft.) and Kempshall (3366 ft.). Bushwhack access may be had to the following trailless peaks: Couchsachraga (3820 ft.) and Panther (4442 ft.) in the Santanoni Range; Emmons

(4040 ft.), Donaldson (4140 ft.) and Seward (4361 ft.) in the Seward Range; Seymour (4120 ft.), Street (4166 ft.) and Nye (3895 ft.).

Only the last two sections of the trail, from Shattuck Clearing to Duck Hole and from Duck Hole to Averyville and Lake Placid, will be included here. For a detailed description of the entire trail, see *Guide to the Northville–Placid Trail* published by the Adirondack Mountain Club.

SHATTUCK CLEARING TO DUCK HOLE

(USGS Maps: Long Lake and Santanoni)

This section of the Northville–Placid trail follows the Cold River Valley into the wild and rugged High Peak Region. The route goes up the Cold River past the natural big dam at Miller's Falls to the site of the old hermitage of Noah John Rondeau. At that point it leaves the river and follows an old tote road to Mountain Pond. Soon after rejoining the Cold River at its confluence with Moose Creek, it follows the river most of the remaining distance to Duck Hole, a dammed mountain pond.

The view ENE up the Cold River Valley from the former Shattuck Clearing ranger's station is most impressive with the Seward Range on the L and the Santanoni Range on the R. The gravel road heading S of E is a so-called fire truck trail (Wolf Lake Road) which leads about 9.5 mi. to Rt. 28N (Newcomb–Long Lake Highway) at a point 3.8 mi. W of Newcomb. For most of its distance, it is in the Huntington Wildlife Forest operated by the College of Forestry, Syracuse University and is not open to public vehicles.

There are alternate routes from the ranger's station to the Latham Pond lean-to (Cold River No. 4).

The N-P Trail follows the gravel road straight ahead past the ranger's station 0.2 mi. and then turns N into the woods. A campsite, fireplace and privy are located at this point. After crossing Moose Creek on a bridge, it returns to the L(S) bank of Cold River and crosses to the R bank on a suspension bridge at 0.7 mi. where the Latham Pond (Cold River No. 4) lean-to is now located on the L of the bridge. Turning R the trail meets a tote road and the newly marked trail on the R bank of the river in 60 yds.

The alternate route from the clearing (0 mi.) turns L sharply to the N and descends on a gravel road to cross Cold River on a bridge at 0.1 mi. Turning R the trail follows a gravel lumber road up the R bank and comes to a junction at 0.2 mi. The tote road branches L and leads 0.7 mi. via another tote road to Latham Pond. This is also the yellow-marked horse trail route via the Calkins Brook fire truck trail which leads 9.5 mi. to the Ward Brook Trail at 1.4 mi. E of its beginning at the parking area. (See Sanford Lake Region, Section B5.)

Continuing up the river, this route reaches Cold River No. 3 lean-to on a high point above the river at 0.6 mi. This is a beautiful spot looking up the river toward the mountains and the suspension bridge. At 0.7 mi. a footpath branches R and leads 55 yds. to the Cold River No. 4 lean-to. Eighty yds. on the road beyond the fork the preferred route from the suspension bridge joins the tote road.

The trail continues to follow the same tote road with ever-changing views of the river and the mountains ahead. Because of the 1950 hurricane damage and the clean up, most of the trail up to the Seward lean-to is pretty much in the open, making its way through patches of second growth, sometimes near the river and sometimes at a distance from it. Descending gradually through a pebbly stretch, the trail continues to follow the tote road and crosses a small brook at 1.5 mi., then climbs back to grade. At 1.6 mi. there is a good view of the Santanoni Range. The trail crosses a culvert at 1.8 mi. At 2.0 mi. there is a large pool (Big Eddy) with some interesting falls in the river. Coming to the brink of the river at 2.1 mi., the trail follows the tote road up the R bank and crosses a large brook on a bridge at 3.1 mi. Pitching up at 3.5 mi. the trail bears R from the tote road at 3.6 mi. where there is a view of Mt. Seymour to the L and then descends abruptly and enters the woods at 3.7 mi. Then the trail passes through a small blowdown area and comes to the Seward lean-to at 4.0 mi. Located here is Miller's Falls where large rock outcrops have formed a natural dam in the river. There is a good spring beside the trail on the L, 105 yds. beyond the lean-to.

Continuing past the spring, the trail follows the old footpath along the river, climbing to an open spot at 4.2 mi. where there is a good view over the stream below. Here the trail veers away from the river and continues through the woods high above it, descending to it again at 4.4 mi. Now, following the river fairly closely, the trail reaches a grassy, muddy stretch at 5.3 mi., followed by a small brook crossing at 5.4 mi. A PBM 1876 ft. is indicated by a painted tree at 5.7 mi. (bronze marker on boulder 25 ft. E of trail). After crossing another small brook at 5.8 mi., the trail reaches Ouluska Pass Brook at 6.1 mi. In times of high water it may be necessary to ford this stream. The trail crosses this brook and reaches Ouluska lean-to on the bank of Cold River at 6.2 mi.

Beyond the Ouluska lean-to the trail follows the cold River and joins a tote road entering on the L at 6.6 mi. It follows this tote road all the way to the junction with the Ward Brook Trail near Mountain Pond. At 6.6 mi. the trail branches R and leads 140 yds. to the site of the hermitage of Noah John Rondeau.

From this site one can continue NE on an old tote road to open Cold River Flow and on the other side, the horse trail returning from Shattuck Clearing. Following this trail E toward Duck Hole provides views of Cold River Canyon mentioned in early Colvin reports.

Swinging L with the tote road from the Rondeau turnoff, the N-P Trail heads N and temporarily leaves the Cold River Valley. After crossing a small brook and a grassy, lumbered area, it crosses another small brook just before crossing from Essex into Franklin County. (The county line is marked by a yellow pole at L.) Climbing further away from the river, the trail crosses a large brook on stones from the R bank at 7.5 mi. Then an old tote road enters from the L where the main tote road swings sharply R to the E with little change in elevation. A large boulder is passed on the E at 7.9 mi. Descending on the trail, you can see a pond through the trees on the L at 8.0 mi. Climbing to 8.1 mi., the trail levels off and then starts down at about 8.3 mi. Following an easy descent, the grade steepens a bit at 8.6 mi. as the trail descends to cross a large brook on stones at 8.7 mi. Descending gradually, the trail, still on the tote road, swings NNE, leveling off at about 9.0 mi. and descending again to cross another large brook from the R bank at 9.3 mi., and enters a clearing. Now heading E across the clearing the trail ascends an easy grade as it approaches the R bank of Mountain Pond outlet which it crosses on a bridge at 9.6

mi. The pond comes into view at 9.7 mi., and the trail soon swings around to the N over easy ups and downs with views of the pond through the trees on the L and reaches a junction with the red-marked Ward Brook truck trail and horse trail going W to the Stony Creek parking area. (See Sanford Lake Region, Section B5.) Turning R with red and blue markers, the N-P Trail follows the fire truck road to 10.5 mi. and then descends to Cold River lean-tos Nos. 1 and 2 at 10.7 mi. Crossing Moose Creek on a truss bridge at 10.8 mi. at its confluence with the Cold River, the trail climbs the far bank at a fair grade, easing off and descending with a veiw of MacNaughton Mt. ahead. The N-P Trail soon meets a horse trail on the E side of Cold River. Continuing pretty much on the level at some distance from the river, the trail (on a truck road) again comes close to the bank at 11.5 mi. At 11.6 mi. there is a sharp bend in the river where the trail climbs over a low ridge and, descending abruptly, comes to the trail junction at Duck Hole at 12.0 mi. This is the end of the truck road. The original lean-to (Duck Hole No. 1) is about 45 yds. past the trail junction on the R on a grassy knoll. The second lean-to (Duck Hole No. 2 built 1960) is hidden on a point 100 yds. SE of the old lean-to. This is one of the most beautiful camping spots in the mountains. (Blue trail across the dam leads 8.5 mi. via Bradley Pond to Tahawus Club road 2.0 mi. N of Sanford Lake bridge. (See Sanford Lake Region, Section B5.)

Distances: Shattuck Clearing to Cold River lean-to No. 4, 0.6 mi.; to Latham Pond lean-to (Cold River No. 3) on the side trail, 0.7 mi.; to Big Eddy, 2.0 mi.; to Seward lean-to at Miller's Falls, 4.0 mi.; to Ouluska lean-to, 6.2 mi.; to site of Rondeau's hermitage, 6.7 mi.; to Ward Brook fire trail, 10.3 mi.; to Cold River lean-tos Nos. 1 and 2, 10.7 mi.; to Duck Hole, 12.0 mi. (109.4 mi. from Upper Benson; 119.0 mi. from bridge at Northville).

DUCK HOLE TO AVERYVILLE AND LAKE PLACID

(USGS Maps: Santanoni, Saranac Lake, Lake Placid)

Originally the Northville–Placid Trail followed up the valley of Moose Creek from Cold River lean-tos Nos. 1 and 2, but the

1950 hurricane forced the present relocation via Duck Hole. This part of the trail is through wild forest country until it reaches Wanika Falls. There are lean-tos at Moose Pond and Wanika Falls. Originally the N-P Trail ended at the Lake Placid railroad station, but the elimination of passenger service made this rather pointless. The official end of the trail is now the large DEC sign where the Averyville Road crosses Old Military Road which bypasses Lake Placid Village.

Leaving the trail junction at Duck Hole (0 mi.) and following red and blue markers, the trail heads NE over a slight rise and descends over a small tributary brook at 0.3 mi. After ascending again the trail descends and comes to a junction on the R (W) bank of Roaring Brook at 0.5 mi. Here the red trail crosses the brook on a bridge and leads to either Indian Pass or Tahawus Upper Works via Preston Ponds and Henderson Lake. (See Sanford Lake Region, Section B5.)

Continuing straight ahead with blue markers, the N-P Trail crosses back into Essex County in about 0.3 mi. It remains in Essex County for the remainder of the distance to Lake Placid. The N-P Trail follows up the R bank of the brook which is generally on the level on easy grades and crosses a tributary brook at 1.3 mi. There is a moderate pitch up at 1.5 mi., followed by a steep pitch down at 1.6 mi. The trail is now some distance back from Roaring Brook. After reaching the R bank of another brook at 1.8 mi., the trail starts down at about 2.0 mi. along the L bank of a small brook, crossing it at 2.1 mi. and another brook from the R at 2.3 mi. The trail climbs gradually from 2.5 mi. to 2.6 mi. and crosses a brook at 3.1 mi. where it turns E along the S side of an old beaver flow at about 3.3 mi. It then heads N and NE and crosses a beaver dam at 3.4 mi. The trail reaches the L bank of Moose Creek at 3.7 mi. Swinging away from the stream, the trail climbs to Moose Pond lean-to at 3.9 mi.

The N-P Trail goes around the rear of the lean-to and heads NE on easy to moderate ups and downs. It crosses two branches of a brook with cascades at approximately 4.1 mi. A fair-sized brook from the R is crossed at 4.6 mi., followed by a gradual climb to another brook crossing at 4.8 mi. Climbing moderately at 5.0 mi. and descending a fair grade at 5.2 mi., the trail comes to a steep down pitch at 5.3 mi. and passes PBM 2311 ft. at 5.4 mi. The side trail on R leading to Wanika Falls lean-to is reached at 5.5 mi. This trail climbs steeply 0.1 mi. to a log bridge above the falls where it crosses to the lean-to on the R bank of the brook. There are higher falls about 100 yds. or so above the lean-to. This brook, the headwaters of the Chubb River, offers a bushwhack route to Street and Nye.

The N-P Trail now follows the L bank of the Chubb River below the falls on a gradual grade, then turns off the former trail to Averyville at 6.1 mi. to the R. This new section opened in 1978. It crosses the Chubb River on a narrow log bridge and then crosses Hemlock Brook at 6.9 mi. on a small bridge, alongside a large evergreen tree to the R. Just to the R of the trail, water also bubbles out from under a rock in the brook and appears much like a spring. The trail, having been traversing the side of a hill since the Chubb River, now moves out onto a plateau-like area. At 8.0 mi. a dry brook is seen on the L that has almost perfect steps of small rocks for some 30 or 40 feet. At 7.4 mi. the trail crosses Nason Brook and after coming to Lost Cabin Brook at 7.5 mi., turns sharply to the L at 7.6 mi. and descends steadily to a beaver pond on the L at 8.1 mi.

At 8.2 mi. the trail reaches a tote road with Tote Road Brook to the L, then turns R at 8.17 mi., the overgrown tote road continuing straight ahead. At 9.1 mi. a sign on a tree marks a side trail to the east where a tenting site has been established. Peacock Brook is just past this point. This trail then continues over easy upgrades and downgrades, is crossed by a hunters' dim trail at 11.0 mi. and comes to a junction at 12.1 mi. with the carry described by Dr. Paul Jamieson that leads to attractive canoeing on the Chubb River above the rapids heard to the L. (See his *Adirondack Canoe Waters: North Flow*).

The Averyville Road is reached at 12.3 mi. Just up the hill to the L is a parking lot for cars of hikers. To the R it is 1.2 mi. to the official end of the N-P Trail and the DEC Northville–Lake Placid Trail sign, on Old Military Road in Lake Placid.

Distances: Duck Hole to Preston Ponds Trail, 0.5 mi.; to Moose Pond lean-to, 3.9 mi.; to side trail to Wanika Falls lean-to, 5.5 mi.; to crossing of the Chubb River, 6.2 mi.; to junction with the Averyville Road, 12.3 mi.; to DEC sign at Old Military Road, 13.5 mi. (122.9 mi. from Upper Benson; 132.2 mi. from the bridge at North-ville).

Editor's note: The ADK wheel measurement of the distance from the Averyville Road to Wanika Falls lean-to is 6.78 mi. An independent DEC figure, obtained from Ranger Gary Hodgson, was 6.73 mi. for the same distance, a difference of less than 1%.

SECTION E1

ADIRONDACK ONE HUNDRED HIGHEST MOUNTAIN PEAKS

In order to stimulate greater interest in this very substantial outlying mountainous area, a list of the highest 100 mountains in the Adirondacks has been prepared. It is not presented with the idea of climbing them all or of forming a club. Forty of the new listings are presently trailless. Indeed, some are privately owned for which permission is needed to pass.

Heading the list are the original 46 high peaks. These were all originally thought to be at least 4000 ft. high by early surveys. The criteria for the additional 54 peaks, simply stated, are a 300 ft. rise all around and ¾ mi. distance to any other qualified summit. (This is a refinement of the 46 criteria which, again simply stated, were 300 ft. or ¾ mi.)

This selection of 46 to head the list is prompted by the fact that for 40 years, since the organizaton was formed in 1937, 46 has helped popularize hiking and climbing among the high peaks. Almost as well known among hikers and climbers is the roster of the 46 high peaks. To abridge this roster would serve no useful purpose but would create controversy and confusion. By retaining the 46 we offer the visitor to the Adirondacks a single, contiguous climber's list, shared for the present by the two foremost organizations in the region, The Adirondack Mountain Club, Inc. and The Adirondack Forty-Sixers.

An asterisk on the roster indicates that there is a footnote; the number of the footnote will correspond to the number on the roster. Under "Remarks" a "c" following elevation indicates that the elevation shown is that of the highest contour line. The symbol "Tr" indicates that there is presently a standard, maintained trail to the summit. An extra "T" means that there is a fire tower on the summit. A "P" indicates private ownership or private land-locking.

No.	Name	Elev.	Remarks	Topographical Map and Sector
1	Mt. Marcy	5344	Tr	Mt. Marcy (W)
2	Algonquin Peak	5114	Tr	Mt. Marcy (W)
3	Mt. Haystack	4960	Tr	Mt. Marcy (C)
4	Mt. Skylight	4926	Tr	Mt. Marcy (W)
5	Whiteface Mt.	4867	Tr	Lake Placid (C)
6	Dix Mt.	4857	Tr	Mt. Marcy (SE)
7	Gray Peak	4840c		Mt. Marcy (W)
8	Iroquois Peak	4840c		Mt. Marcy (W)
9	Basin Mt.	4827	Tr	Mt. Marcy (C)
10	Gothics	4736	Tr	Mt. Marcy (C)
11	Mt. Colden	4714	Tr	Mt. Marcy (W)
12	Giant Mt.	4627	Tr	Elizabethtown (W)
13	Nipple Top	4620c	Tr	Mt. Marcy (E)
14	Santanoni Peak	4607		Santanoni (C)
15	Mt. Redfield	4606		Mt. Marcy (W)
16	Wright Peak	4580	Tr	Mt. Marcy (W)
17	Saddleback Mt.	4515	Tr	Mt. Marcy (C)
18	Panther Peak	4442		Santanoni (C)
19	Table Top Mt.	4427		Mt. Marcy (C)
20	Rocky Peak Ridge	4420c	Tr	Elizabethtown (W)
21	Macomb Mt.	4405		Mt. Marcy (SE)
22	Armstrong Mt.	4400c	Tr	Mt. Marcy (C)
23	Hough Peak	4400c		Mt. Marcy (SE)
24	Seward Mt.	4361		Santanoni (W)
25*	Mt. Marshall	4360		Santanoni (E)
26	Allen Mt.	4340c		Mt. Marcy (SW)
27	Big Slide Mt.	4240c	Tr	Mt. Marcy (N)
28	Esther Mt.	4240		Lake Placid (C)
29*	Upper Wolf Jaw Mt.	4185	Tr	Mt. Marcy (C)
30*	Lower Wolf Jaw Mt.	4175	Tr	Mt. Marcy (C)
31	Street Mt.	4166		Santanoni (NE)
32	Phelps Mt.	4161	Tr	Mt. Marcy (W)
33	Mt. Donaldson	4140		Santanoni (W)
34	Seymour Mt.	4120		Santanoni (W)
35*	Sawteeth	4100c	Tr	Mt. Marcy (C)

No.	Name	Elev.	Remarks	Topographical Map and Sector
36	Cascade Mt.	4098	Tr	Mt. Marcy (N)
37	South Dix	4060		Mt. Marcy (SE)
38	Porter Mt.	4059	Tr	Mt. Marcy (N)
39	Mt. Colvin	4057	Tr	Mt. Marcy (C)
40	Mt. Emmons	4040		Santanoni (W)
41	Dial Mt.	4020	Tr	Mt. Marcy (E)
42	East Dix	4012		Mt. Marcy (SE)
43*	Blake Peak	3960c	Tr	Mt. Marcy (S)
44	Cliff Mt.	3960c		Mt. Marcy (W)
45	Nye Mt.	3895		Santanoni (NE)
46	Couchsachraga Peak	3820		Santanoni (C)
47	McNaughton Mt.	4000		Santanoni (E)
48	Green Mt.	3980c		Elizabethtown (NW)
49*	Peak, Unnamed (Lost Pond)	3900c		Santanoni (E)
50*	Moose Mt.	3899		Saranac Lake (E)
51	Snowy Mt.	3899	TrT	Indian Lake (N)
52	Kilburn Mt.	3892		Lake Placid (S)
53*	Sawtooth Mts. (No. 1)	3877		Santanoni (W)
54	Panther Mt.	3865		Indian Lake (N)
55	McKenzie Mt.	3861	Tr	Saranac Lake (E)
56	Blue Ridge	3860c		Indian Lake (W)
57	North River Mt.	3860c		Mt. Marcy (SW)
58	Sentinel Mt.	3838		Lake Placid (S)
59	Lyon Mt.	3830	Tr	Lyon Mt. (N)
60*	Sawtooth Mts. (No. 2)	3820c		Santanoni (N)
61*	Peak, Unnamed (Indian Falls)	3820c		Mt. Marcy (W)
62	Averill Peak	3810		Lyon Mt. (N)
63	Avalanche Mt.	3800c		Mt. Marcy (W)
64	Buell Mt.	3786		Indian Lake (N)
65	Boreas Mt.	3776	TrT	Mt. Marcy (S)
66	Blue Mt.	3760c	TrT	Blue Mt. (C)

No.	Name	Elev.	Remarks	Topographical Map and Sector
67	Wakely Mt.	3760c	TrT	W. Canada Lakes (NE)
68	Henderson Mt.	3752		Santanoni (C)
69	Lewey Mt.	3742		Indian Lake (W)
70*	Sawtooth Mts. (No. 3)	3700c		Santanoni (N)
71	Wallface Mt.	3700c		Santanoni (E)
72	Hurricane Mt.	3694	TrT	Elizabethtown (NW)
73	Hoffman Mt.	3693		Schroon Lake (E)
74	Cheney Cobble	3683		Mt. Marcy (SW)
75	Calamity Mt.	3620c		Santanoni (E)
76	Little Moose Mt.	3620c		W. Canada Lakes (NE)
77	Sunrise Mt.	3614	Tr	Mt. Marcy (SE)
78	Stewart Mt.	3602		Lake Placid (S)
79*	Jay Mts.	3600		Ausable Forks (SW)
80	Pitchoff Mt.	3600c	Tr	Mt. Marcy (N)
81	Saddleback Mt.	3600c		Ausable Forks (SW)
82	Pillsbury Mt.	3597	TrT	W. Canada Lakes (SE)
83	Slide Mt.	3584		Lake Placid (S)
84	Gore Mt.	3583	TrT	Thirteenth Lake (NE)
85	Dun Brook Mt.	3580c		Blue Mt. (E)
86	Noonmark Mt.	3556	Tr	Mt. Marcy (E)
87	Mt. Adams	3540c	T	Santanoni (E)
88	Fishing Brook Mt.	3540c		Blue Mt. (NE)
89	Little Santanoni Mt.	3500c		Santanoni (SW)
90	Blue Ridge	3497		Blue Mt. (SW)
91*	Peak (Fishing Brook Range)	3480c		Blue Mt. (NE)
92	Puffer Mt.	3472		Thirteenth Lake (W)
93*	Sawtooth Mts. (No. 4)	3460c		Santanoni (N)
94*	Sawtooth Mts. (No. 5)	3460c		Santanoni (N)
95	Wolf Pond Mt.	3460c		Schroon Lake (N)
96	Cellar Mt.	3447		W. Canada Lakes (NE)
97*	Blue Ridge Mt.	3440c		Schroon Lake (NE)
98	Morgan Mt.	3440c		Lake Placid (N)

No.	Name	Elev.	Remarks	Topographical Map and Sector
99	Blue Ridge	3436		Raquette Lake (SE)
100	Peak, Unnamed (Brown Pond)	3425		Indian Lake (N)

* *25. Mt. Marshall.* This is shown as Mt. Clinton on the 1953 map. Formerly known as Herbert Mt., Mt. Clinton was officially named Mt. Marshall for Robert Marshall in 1942.

29 and *30. The Wolf Jaws.* The map reads Wolfjaw. Since frog leg is two words, it is assumed that wolf jaw is too. Early mountaineers used a singly hyphenated word.

35. Sawteeth. This mountain was named for the profile of its several summit nubbles which were said to resemble the teeth of a great saw. Sawtooth is incorrect.

43. Blake Peak. Blake Peak rather than Blake Mt. is the name in common use.

49. Peak, Unnamed (Lost Pond). This mountain is easily located since Lost Pond lies practically on its summit. The coordinates are 44°10′N × 70°02′W.

50. Moose Mt. (St. Armand Mt. on sign boards.) A trail leads up this mountain from a point 0.50 mi. up Lake Placid from Whiteface Inn. Another leads from the summit of McKenzie Mt.

53. Sawtooth Mts. The Sawtooths comprise a large, completely wild area southeast of Ampersand Mountain. It is a region of many knobs, five of which qualify for this list. These have been numbered from one to five in order of descending altitude. Numbers 4 and 5 are the same height but No. 4 is much more massive. The highest peak, elevation 3877 ft., is central to the region. The coordinates are 44°11′N × 70°07′W.

60. Sawtooth Mts. (No. 2). The 3800 ft. twin knobs of this summit mark the N end of a three step ridge which lies W of the main 3877 ft. peak. The coordinates are 44°11′N × 74°08′W.

61. Peak, Unnamed (Indian Falls). Lying to the NW of Indian Falls on the trail from Marcy Dam to Mt. Marcy the coordinates are 44°08′N × 73°56′W.

70. Sawtooth Mts. (No. 3). Lying ½ mi. W of the Essex County line, this 3700 ft. peak marks the SE threshold of the Sawtooths. The coordinates are 44°10'N × 74°07'W.

79. Jay Mts. The 1953 map shows a 3340 ft. peak W of Grassy Notch for Jay Mt. This is believed to be an error.

91. Peak (Fishing Brook Range). This 3480 ft. unnamed peak marks the end of a long ridge leading SW from Fishing Brook Mt. 43°55'N × 74°19'W.

93. Sawtooth Mts. (No. 4). This 3460 ft. peak at the NW end of the Sawtooths lies about a mile SSE of Beaver pond. Coordinates, 44°12'N × 74°10'W.

94. Sawtooth Mts. (No. 5). Also 3460 ft., this summit is found at about 1 mi. NE of the pass between Ward Brook and Cold River country. Coordinates, 44°11'N × 74°03'W.

97. Blue Ridge Mt. (Schroon Lake Map). The 2825 ft. elevation shown for this mountain on the 1953 map is incorrect.

100. Peak, Unnamed (Brown Pond). This 3425 ft. peak is found at about 3½ mi. ENE of Wakely Dam. Brown Pond lies in a slight depression on its westerly slope. The coordinates are 43°44'N × 74°25'W.

SECTION E2

WINTER HIKING

Anyone of sound wind and limb capable of enjoying the dazzling beauty of a clear, crisp winter day will soon discover that the Adirondacks have as much to offer in winter as they do in summer. The sparkling snow surface, the long, blue shadows and the utter hush of the snow-stilled forest all add up to an unforgettable experience.

In discussing winter hiking in the Adirondacks, it is important to distinguish between short ski or snowshoe rambles in the valleys or on one of the more gentle slopes of the lower mountains, and winter ascents of the major peaks. Winter mountaineering requires great stamina and special knowledge of snowcraft, mountain weather and winter survival techniques. Special training and equipment is required before one should venture into these high regions. Winter hiking in the valleys is far less demanding and can serve as an introduction to the challenge and rewards of the winter outdoor experience.

This section of the guidebook does not intend to discuss the proper techniques for the use of skis, snowshoes or other methods of winter forest travel but attempts to set forth some features of the Adirondack terrain as they affect the winter recreationist.

Forest Patterns

The Adirondacks are covered with irregularly shaped holdings of state land interspersed with privately owned parcels. Under the "forever wild" policy, large portions of the state lands have remained undisturbed for perhaps fifty years and the mature forest thus resulting is extremely open, as the shade of the larger trees suppresses the undergrowth.

The implication of this, for the winter outdoorsman, lies in the fact that trails in forests containing a high portion of undergrowth are easily distinguishable under winter conditions whereas in mature forests it may become impossible to distinguish the trail from open forest under heavy snow cover. Trail markers may either be snowed under or covered by snow sticking to the trees and cannot be relied upon. There is no assurance that one can follow a lightly used trail in the Adirondacks for any extended distance in deep winter.

This openness of a mature forest is an advantage as well as disadvantage for when sufficient snow cover has accumulated to cover ground obstacles, a glade-like effect is produced. The snowshoer or ski tourer can wander about at will unrestricted by the need of a trail.

For those who like extensive openness in their outings without the necessity of climbing mountains, swamps, marshes, vleis and beaver meadows become broad, open highways in winter. Some of these penetrate long distances in the mountains as essentially level routes.

In such ramblings, touring skis are more terrain limited than are snowshoes, as ski touring is best on slopes of moderate steepness. Terrain suitable for ski touring is represented on topographic maps by 100 ft. contour lines spaced from $3/16$ to $1/4$ mi. apart.

In planning winter outings, it is emphasized that one should go in and out over the same route and not attempt loop or through trips. At all costs one must avoid circumstances that will cause the parties to be caught out in the woods after dark.

As has been pointed out previously, one cannot rely on being able to follow a trail for any extended distance unless it is well used. On in-and-out trips losing the trail imposes no danger as one can always backtrack on the path made going in. The exception occurs with high wind or blizzard conditions when the backtrack vanishes very quickly. On a through trip the time spent casting about for the trail that cannot be found may represent the time difference between coming out of the woods at dusk and becoming benighted.

It should also be realized that when new powder snow first experiences a thaw it may become wet, heavy and sticky so that large accumulations build up on skis and snowshoes, thus slowing the pace to a fraction of a mile per hour. This effect is far less pronounced on a trail that has been packed down, again pointing out the importance of not being committed to go all the way through in unbroken snow. Other sources of delay can arise which can be accommodated by an earlier time of turnaround on an in-and-out trip but which may cause an overdue party when on a through trip. The hours of daylight are much shorter in winter. One should keep careful track of time so as to be certain of being out of the woods by last light.

The best security against getting lost in the winter woods is the availability of an easily distinquished backtrack.

Firewood Availability

The Adirondack Forest is principally deciduous or deciduous and conifer mixed. The use of dead and down-only wood is the law and these hardwoods make excellent firewood.

As one goes higher in elevation this hardwood forest gives way to one of spruce and balsam. Here firewood is distinctly a problem, and a compact mountain stove is essential for hot meals.

Clothing Considerations

While various individuals have preferences for various styles of winter clothing, there is universal agreement that there must be means to achieve enough ventilation under all conditions so as to prevent any accumulation of perspiration. Clothing that has become saturated with perspiration will chill a person rather than warm him. One should be continuously on guard to prevent over-heating, opening or removing clothing as needed. The point at which ordinary winter outerwear becomes marginally ineffective and specialized Arctic or high altitude mountain gear becomes essential is in the general range of +10°F, depending on circumstances. When the temperature hovers near zero, those equipped with conventional sweaters, wool shirts or jackets will be entirely comfortable as long as they are moving but may rapidly become chilled if they stop. Under this condition of cold, it is inadvisable to stop for lunch. Instead the lunch is broken up into snacks that can be munched as one moves or can be taken in short breaks. One of the best equipment investments that one can make for winter-time use is a good quality, down-filled jacket of the type used by winter mountaineers. Such a jacket packs in a space almost as small as a coffee can, weighs very little and yet affords more protection than any other garment yet developed. With a good down jacket, one is not burdened by a pack full of extra clothing, yet is prepared for almost any eventuality.

Another essential item is a face mask to prevent frostbite when traveling over exposed areas such as frozen lake surfaces.

The foregoing remarks apply to times when the temperature is near the zero mark. On still, sunny days when the thermometer reads in the 20's, it is an entirely different story. Winter outings under these conditions can be extremely pleasant; the party can enjoy a leisure lunch in the sundrenched woods and savor the stillness and beauty of the winter outdoors without any great attention to protection from the cold.

Winter Mountaineering

Up to this point the discussion has centered on winter hiking in the valleys and lower reaches of the Adirondack Mts. With respect to the higher elevations, entirely different conditions prevail. Like the White Mts. of New Hampshire the winter climate in the Adirondacks is far more severe than is found even in the Himalayas. Unlike the White Mts. the distances are greater, the shelters fewer and effective systems for rescue for a lost or injured climber are difficult to carry out. For information on Hypothermia, see Section A, Clothing.

When traveling in deep snow, one is completely dependent on the proper functioning of skis or snowshoes, and any equipment failure can have serious consequences. Equipment failures do occur. Simple tools and repair materials should always be carried so that field repairs can be made as needed. For example, soft wire, rawhide webbing and spare straps should be on hand for snowshoe repair.

The upper slopes of the Adirondack Mts. are frequently steep enough to cause difficulty in climbing with snowshoes (crampons are recommended for icy summits), or are covered with an almost impenetrable tangle of scrub evergreens, are subject to bitter cold, sweeping winds and the possibility of snow cornices, ice falls and spruce holes. This latter hazard forms early in the winter when the snow covers over the branches of scrub evergreens so as to conceal hollows into which a snowshoer can fall.

At timberline, one should be aware that one's tracks can easily and quickly be drifted over so that they disappear.

It cannot be emphasized too strongly that winter mountaineering on the major Adirondack summits is only for strong parties (four or more) of highly experienced people.

A summer hiker who suffers some misadventure so that he is forced to spend the night in the woods with only the contents of his day pack to sustain him may be uncomfortable but seldom is any the worse otherwise because of his adventure. The winter traveler who is overcome by dark is in a much more serious predicament. If he has no flashlight, has exhausted his food, cannot find water, has no extra clothing and no means to get fire, life itself may be in jeopardy.

Sources of Information

All of this may be avoided by sensible precautions, and to assist the public in achieving a safer and more enjoyable winter outdoor experience, the Adirondack Mountain Club has published *Winter Hiking and Camping,* a book written especially for those interested in winter mountaineering. This guide provides practical advice on equipment selection, the effective use of skis, snowshoes, ice axes and crampons, discusses the art of keeping warm in winter and gives much detailed knowledge on winter camping, snow and ice craft and winter outdoor living. A recent edition of this winter guide is available from ADK, 172 Ridge St., Glens Falls, New York 12801 (price on request).

In addition, the club offers training sessions at various times in the year on the subject of winter outdoors. Contact the Club's Executive Director for further details.

On Big Slide (toward Whiteface)

SECTION E3

ADIRONDACK SKI CENTERS

In the Adirondack area, skiers can choose from a dozen or so ski centers. The largest in the area, and one of the largest in the East, is the state-operated Whiteface Mountain Ski Center at Wilmington. With a vertical drop of more than 3000 ft., Whiteface has trails that meet the standards of Olympic competition. Chair lifts to the summit of Little Whiteface are also operated for summer sightseers.

Other centers in or near the High Peak Region are at Jay, Lake Placid, Saranac Lake and Tupper Lake. Further afield in the Adirondack area ski centers are located at Warrensburg, North Creek (Gore Mt.), Wells, Speculator, Old Forge, Turin, Malone and Plattsburgh. For detailed information on these and other ski centers in the state, write to the New York State Department of Commerce, 112 State Street, Albany, New York 12201 for free circular, *Ski New York*.

For the snowshoer and the cross-cross country skier, an extensive trails system exists in a variety of lengths at Adirondak Loj, 9 miles south of Lake Placid. For information about the Loj, the campgrounds and the trails system, write to Reservation Manager, Adirondak Loj, P.O. Box 867, Lake Placid, New York 12946. In addition, a well-maintained cross-country ski development is located nearby on the N side of Mt. Van Hoevenberg near the Bobsled Run.

SECTION E4

CANOE ROUTES

The Adirondack Park has many lakes, large and small, and claims a generous portion of the extensive and famous canoe routes of New York. The route through the Fulton Chain of Lakes begins at Old Forge, where canoes may be rented, and by connected waterways leads all the way to the Saranacs and beyond. From the Lake Flower "putting in" place in Saranac Lake Village, it is easy to canoe to Lower, Middle and Upper Saranac Lake, to Fish Creek Ponds campsite (a good canoe base), and for many miles through a network of small ponds connected by short carries, all the way to Paul Smith's and beyond.

A good portion of the shoreline of the Saranac Lakes is in the State Forest Preserve. Two state lean-tos are located on the S shore of Middle Saranac Lake near the foot trail to Ampersand Mt. There is another lean-to on the NE shore of Hungry Bay and still another at the NW end of Weller Pond. There are also two lean-tos on Upper Saranac, one on Indian Point and one on the N shore of Saginaw Bay while a third lean-to is approximately 1.0 mi. NE of Saginaw Bay. Two lean-tos are located on Lower Saranac, one at Norway Point and one at Tom's Rock, Eagle Island. One lean-to located on the S shore of Kiwassa Lake, and there are two each on Fish Pond and Follensby Clear Pond to the W of Upper Saranac while still another is on St. Regis Pond to the N of Upper Saranac. For canoeing these waters, the Saranac Lake and St. Regis USGS maps will be useful. For a map and description of the Old Forge–Saranac Route, a recreation circular, *Adirondack Canoe Routes,* will be sent free on request by the New York State Department of Environmental Conservation, 50 Wolf Road, Albany, New York 12233. DEC also supplies a free list of canoe liveries along the route. Dr. Paul F. Jamieson has written a guide to many of the canoe waters of the Adirondacks in his work: *Adirondack Canoe Waters: North Flow,* published by the Adirondack Mountain Club. The canoe route from Old Forge to Blue Mountain Lake is covered in Robert J. Redington's *Guide to Trails of the West-Central Adirondacks,* published in 1980 by the Adirondack Mountain Club.

SECTION E5

OVERNIGHT ACCOMMODATIONS

Johns Brook Lodge

Johns Brook Lodge, 5.12 mi. from Keene Valley (3.52 mi. from the Garden) on the trail to Mt. Marcy, is owned and operated by The Adirondack Mountain Club, Inc. The lodge itself is open to all comers for meals and lodging from approximately July 1 to Labor Day each year. The hutmaster in charge will make every effort to accommodate transients but only reservations in advance will guarantee space in one of the two bunk rooms. Available the year around are three lean-tos and two closed camps having cooking facilities, Winter Camp housing twelve and Grace Camp, Six. For further details or reservations, contact Johns Brook Lodge, Keene Valley, New York 12943.

Adirondak Loj

Adirondak Loj on Heart Lake is 9 mi. by car from the village of Lake Placid. The Loj and the square mile of surrounding property, including all of Heart Lake and most of Mt. Jo, are owned by The Adirondack Mountain Club, Inc. The Loj offers accommodations to all comers by the day or week, either in private bedrooms or in bunk rooms. Other accommodations include lean-tos with fireplaces and numerous tent sites for which nominal charges are made. Camping supplies may be purchased from the Campers and Hikers Building located at the entrance to the parking lot at the Loj. A nominal parking charge is made for nonmembers not registered at the Loj or using the lean-tos and tent sites.

The Loj is open year around. Several cross-country ski trails are located on the property and on nearby Forest Preserve land.

This extensive network is a center of much winter-time activity. Snowshoers find much territory in which to enjoy their particular sport.

Of special interest at Adirondak Loj is a Nature Museum where one finds specimens of mosses, lichens, birds' nests, rocks and other Adirondack features. A modest library is available to help those who wish to identify their own samples.

A ranger-naturalist program is available during the summer months. The leader conducts walks along a special nature trail and furnishes talks and slide shows on conservation and natural history topics. The latter are generally conducted in a scenic outdoor amphitheatre especially constructed for this purpose.

For full information about reservations, rates, or activities, one should address the Manager at Adirondak Loj, P.O. Box 867, Lake Placid, New York 12946 (telephone: 518-523-3441).

State Campsites in the Adirondack Park

Public campsites have been established by DEC at many attractive spots throughout the state. Thirty-seven of these are within the bounds of the Adirondack Park or close to it. These campsites are maintained by DEC for the use of the public. Each is supervised by a caretaker who assigns parties to campsites, issues permits, supervises sanitation, patrols the camp and maintains order. Recreation Circular, *Guide to Outdoor Recreation in New York State*, will be sent on request by the New York State Department of Environmental Conservation, 50 Wolf Road, Albany, New York 12233. The campsites in or near the Adirondack Park are:

Northeastern Section

Poke-o-Moonshine: On Route 9, 12 mi. N of Elizabethtown at the foot of Poke-o-Moonshine Mt.

Wilmington Notch: On Route 86 between Lake Placid and Wilmington on the bank of the W branch of the Ausable River in a picturesque setting, trout fishing.

Meadowbrook: Located on Route 86 between Lake Placid and Saranac Lake. A convenient stopping place for the region.

Cumberland Bay: Route 9, 1 mi. N of Plattsburgh on Cumberland Bay, Lake Champlain. Outside NE corner of park.

Macomb Reservation: 3 mi. W of Route 22B at Schuyler Falls. Outside NE corner of park.

Northwestern Section

Eel Weir: On outlet Black Lake near Ogdensburg. Fishing, camping. Outside corner of park.

Fish Creek Ponds: On Route 30 between Tupper Lake and Saranac Lake, largest in the Adirondacks. Lake front sites. A canoeing center.

Rollins Pond: Just W of Fish Creek Ponds.

Meacham Lake: On Route 30, 19 mi. N of Lake Clear Junction on road to Malone. Fine beach, hiking and trails.

Cranberry Lake: Entrance by dirt road from Route 3 at sign just E of Cranberry Lake Village. On edge of virgin timber. Hiking trails, fishing.

Higley Flow: Cold Brook Drive, South Colton, 1½ mi. W of Route 56.

Central Section

Lake Eaton: On Route 30, 2 mi. W of Long Lake. Riding, boating, fishing. An excellent place to camp.

Golden Beach: On Route 28, 3 mi. E of Raquette Lake Village. On Fulton Chain canoe route. Fishing, boating, hay fever retreat.

Eighth Lake: On Route 28 between Raquette Lake and Inlet. Good place to camp. Hiking trails. On Fulton Chain canoe route.

Lewey Lake: On Route 30 between Speculator and Indian Lake Village. A wilderness camp. Hiking trails, boating, fishing.

Lake Harris: 2 mi. N of Route 28N, 14 mi. N of Speculator. Access by boat.

Brown Tract Ponds: Access via Route 28, 7 mi. E of Eagle Bay on Uncas Road. No motor boats permitted.

Lake Durant: On Route 28, 3 mi. E of Blue Mt. Lake on N-P Trail.

Forked Lake: 8 mi. SW of Long Lake Village. Access from

Route 30 at Deerland. Campsites on lake can be reached only by boat.

Western Section

Pixleys Falls: 6 mi. S of Boonville on Route 46. Outside the western park boundary.

Whetstone Gulf: 6 mi. S of Lowville near Route 12D. Outside the western park boundary.

Eastern Section

Paradox Lake: Entered from Route 73 which meets Route 9, 2 mi. N of Schroon Lake Village. Hiking trails, boating, fishing. A small campsite.

Eagle Point: On Route 9, 2 mi. N of Pottersville on the shore of Schroon Lake.

Hearthstone Point: On Route 9N, 2 mi. N of Lake George Village on the shore of the lake. This is one of the larger campsites.

Rogers Rock: On Route 9N, 3 mi. N of Hague on the shore of Lake George.

Lake George Battleground: On Route 9 just S of Lake George Village.

Crown Point Reservation: On Route 8, 9 mi. N of Crown Point Village. Lake Champlain bridge crosses here.

Sharp Bridge: On Route 9, 16 mi. N of Schroon Lake Village. A fine place to camp. Bathing and trout fishing in Schroon River.

Putnam Pond: W of Ticonderoga, 3 mi. S of Route 73 at Chilson.

Lake George Islands: Island Headquarters at Glen Island, Long Island and Narrow Island. Access by boat.

Sacandaga: At the forks of the Sacandaga River, 4 mi. S of Wells on Route 30.

Moffitt Beach: On Sacandaga Lake, 2 mi. W of Speculator on Route 8. A good place to camp. Boating, fishing, hiking, fine sandy beach.

Poplar Point: On Piseco Lake. Access from Route 8, 2 mi. W of Piseco. Lake fishing.

Little Sand Point: On Piseco Lake. Access from Route 8, 3 mi. W of Piseco.

Point Comfort: On Piseco Lake. Access from Route 8, 4 mi. W of Piseco.

Caroga Lake: On Route 29A, 9 mi. NW of Gloversville on shore of East Caroga Lake. Popular locally for water sports.

Northampton Beach: Just off Route 30, 2.5 mi. S of Northville on shore of Sacandaga Reservoir.

LISTING OF ADIRONDACK LEAN-TOS

In view of the rising interest in camping areas outside the High Peaks Region, a list of all lean-tos in the Adirondacks is presented below. The shelters are listed by region and by USGS map to aid in trip planning.

Shelter	*USGS Map*	*Location*
Benson Region		
Hamilton Lake Stream	Lake Pleasant	¼ mi. N suspension bridge crossing Hamilton Lake Stream.
Silver Lake	Lake Pleasant	S end of Silver Lake.
Big Moose Region		
Russian Lake	Big Moose	W end of Russian Lake.
Queer Lake	Big Moose	Queer Lake.
Gull Lake	Big Moose	Southern tip of Gull Lake.
Andy's Creek	Big Moose	"The Rocks," Andy's Creek, ¾ mi. N of inlet, Big Moose Lake.
Trout Pond	Big Moose	N shore of Stillwater Reservoir.
Salmon Lake	Big Moose	S end of Salmon Lake.
Lower Sisters	Big Moose	S shore of Lower Sisters Lake.
Big Otter Lake Region		
Cedar Lake	McKeever	N shore of Cedar Lake.
Middle Branch Lake	McKeever	N end near inlet of Middle Branch Lake.

Shelter	*USGS Map*	*Location*
Middle Settlement Lake	McKeever	1500 ft. SW of Middle Settlement Lake.

Blue Mt. Region

Wilson Pond	Blue Mt.	N shore of Wilson Pond.
Utowana Lake	Blue Mt.	NW end of Utowana Lake.
Tirrell Pond No. 2	Blue Mt.	S end of Tirrell Pond.
Walker Clearing	Blue Mt.	S end of Tirrell Pond.
Tirrell Pond	Blue Mt.	N end of Tirrell Pond.
Stephens Pond	Blue Mt.	SW end of Stephens Pond.
Cascade Pond	Blue Mt.	E shore Cascade Pond.

Bouquet Valley Region

Bouquet River	Mt. Marcy	At trail crossing ½ mi. S of Dial Pond, N branch Bouquet River.

Cascade–Keene–Hurricane Region

Hurricane Mt. No. 1	Elizabethtown	SE slope of Hurricane Mt. near observer's cabin.
Hurricane Mt. No. 2	Elizabethtown	N side of Hurricane Mt. at junction of mountain trail and trail to Lost Pond.

Cold River Region

Number 4—No. 1	Santanoni	On Ward Brook Truck Trail.
Number 4—No. 2	Santanoni	On Ward Brook Truck Trail.
Ward Brook	Santanoni	Between Blueberry Pond and Cold River.
Blueberry	Santanoni	On Blueberry Trail, 1000 ft. W of Duck Hole Truck Trail.
Wanika Falls	Santanoni	N-P Trail, Wanika Falls on Chubb River.
Moose Pond	Santanoni	At Moose Pond.
Cold River No. 2	Santanoni	Cold River at Moose Pond outlet.

Shelter	USGS Map	Location
Moose Pond Outlet Stream No. 1	Long Lake	Near Moose Creek where it crosses Road No. 16.
Moose Pond Outlet Stream No. 2	Long Lake	Near Moose Creek where it crosses Road No. 16.
Santanoni	Santanoni	¾ mi. N of Bradley Pond.
Duck Hole No. 1	Santanoni	Duck Hole Dam.
Duck Hole No. 2	Santanoni	NW shore of Duck Hole near ranger headquarters.
Seward	Santanoni	Between Big Eddy and Big Dam on Cold River.
Ouluska	Santanoni	¼ mi. below Big Dam (Rondeau).
Newcomb Lake No. 1	Santanoni	N shore Newcomb Lake ½ mi. W of Santanoni Brook.
Newcomb Lake No. 2	Santanoni	S shore of Newcomb Lake.
Cold River Flow No. 1	Santanoni	S side of Cold River near head of Flow.
Cold River Flow No. 2	Santanoni	Near head of Flow, S side of river.

Cranberry Lake Region

Cage Lake	Oswegatchie	E end of Cranberry Lake.
Little Shallow	Cranberry Lake	S shore of Little Shallow Pond.
Big Shallow	Cranberry Lake	E end of Big Shallow Pond.
Sand Lake	Oswegatchie	E end of Big Sand Lake.
Wolf Pond	Cranberry Lake	NE shore of Cranberry Lake.

Elk Lake Region

Slide Brook	Mt. Marcy	Where Slide Brook crosses the Dix Mt. Trail.
Lillian Brook	Mt. Marcy	At Dix Pond inlet along trail from Elk Lake to Dix Mt.

Shelter	*USGS Map*	*Location*
Panther Gorge	Mt. Marcy	At entrance to Panther Gorge on Elk Lake Trail to Marcy.

Fulton Chain Region

*Alger Island No. 1	Old Forge	Alger (Big) Island, Fourth Lake.
Alger Island No. 2	Old Forge	Alger (Big) Island, Fourth Lake.
Alger Island No. 3	Old Forge	Alger (Big) Island, Fourth Lake.
Alger Island No. 4	Old Forge	Alger (Big) Island, Fourth Lake.
Alger Island No. 5	Old Forge	Alger (Big) Island, Fourth Lake.
Alger Island No. 6	Old Forge	Alger (Big) Island, Fourth Lake.
Alger Island No. 7	Old Forge	Alger (Big) Island, Fourth Lake.
Alger Island No. 8	Old Forge	Alger (Big) Island, Fourth Lake.
Alger Island No. 9	Old Forge	Alger (Big) Island, Fourth Lake.
Alger Island No. 10	Old Forge	Alger (Big) Island, Fourth Lake.
Alger Island No. 11	Old Forge	Alger (Big) Island, Fourth Lake.
Alger Island No. 12	Old Forge	Alger (Big) Island, Fourth Lake.
Alger Island No. 13	Old Forge	Alger (Big) Island, Fourth Lake.
Alger Island No. 14	Old Forge	Alger (Big) Island, Fourth Lake.
Alger Island No. 15	Old Forge	Alger (Big) Island, Fourth Lake.

* New Alger Island Campsites–Service charge imposed during the camping season.

Shelter	*USGS Map*	*Location*
Seventh Lake Island	Raquette Lake	Island in Seventh Lake opposite carry to Eighth Lake.
Seventh Lake	Raquette Lake	N shore of Seventh Lake.
Dunning	Raquette Lake	N end of Eighth Lake.
Eighth Lake	Raquette Lake	N shore of Eighth Lake.
Eighth Lake Island	Raquette Lake	Island in Eighth Lake.
Arnolds Rock	Raquette Lake	N shore of Seventh Lake.

Heart Lake Region

South Meadow Brook	Mt. Marcy	On South Meadow Brook where the ski trail crosses.
Klondike	Mt. Marcy	On Klondike Brook near summit of notch.
Rocky Falls	Mt. Marcy	At Rocky Falls on W Branch Ausable River Trail from Adirondak Loj to Indian Pass
Marcy Dam No. 1	Mt. Marcy	At Marcy Dam on Van Hoevenberg Trail.
Marcy Dam No. 2	Mt. Marcy	At Marcy Dam, N shore.
Marcy Dam No. 3	Mt. Marcy	At Marcy Dam on Van Hoevenberg Trail.
Marcy Dam No. 4	Mt. Marcy	N shore of pond at Marcy Dam.
Marcy Dam No. 5	Mt. Marcy	At Marcy Dam 500 ft. in from Avalanche Trail, W side of pond.
Marcy Dam No. 6	Mt. Marcy	At Marcy Dam ranger station E of dam.
Hudowalski	Mt. Marcy	S shore of pond at Marcy Dam.
Phelps	Mt. Marcy	0.65 mi. S of Marcy Dam on Van Hoevenberg Trail at junction with ski trail.
Marcy Brook (Kagel)	Mt. Marcy	On trail from Marcy Dam to Avalanche Lake.

Shelter	*USGS Map*	*Location*
Marcy Brook	Mt. Marcy	On trail from Marcy Dam to Avalanche Lake.
Avalanche No. 1	Mt. Marcy	On trail from Marcy Dam to Avalanche Lake.
Avalanche No. 2	Mt. Marcy	On trail from Marcy Dam to Avalanche Lake.
Caribou	Mt. Marcy	At junction of yellow and blue trails between Lakes Colden and Avalanche.

Hope Falls Region

Murphy Lake	Harrisburg	E shore of Murphy Lake.

Keene Valley Region

Bear Brook	Mt. Marcy	1 mi. W of Garden where Bear Brook crosses trail.
Deer Brook	Mt. Marcy	N side of Johns Brook Trail, 3 mi. from Keene Valley.
Wm. G. Howard	Mt. Marcy	On Johns Brook Trail to Marcy near ranger cabin.
Wolf Jaw	Mt. Marcy	At headwaters Wolf Jaw Brook on trail to Wolf Jaw.
Orebed Brook	Mt. Marcy	2 mi. S of Johns Brook ranger station.
Johns Brook Lodge	Mt. Marcy	1000 ft. W of Johns Brook Lodge.
Hogback	Mt. Marcy	On Johns Brook Trail by Hogback Brook.
Bushnell Falls No. 1	Mt. Marcy	At Bushnell Falls on Johns Brook Trail.
Bushnell Falls No. 2	Mt. Marcy	On Johns Brook Trail on ridge above falls at junction of red and yellow trails.

Shelter	*USGS Map*	*Location*
Bushnell Falls No. 3	Mt. Marcy	S bank of Johns Brook at Bushnell Falls, junction Hopkins Trail and Phelps Trail.
Slant Rock	Mt. Marcy	At Slant Rock on Phelps Trail.

Lake Champlain Region

Crown Point	Port Henry	At small point N of Coffin Point.
Poke-o-Moon-shine	Ausable Forks	100 yds. from tower on Poke-o-Moonshine Mt.
Lost Pond	Ausable Forks	NE end of Lost Pond.

Lake George Region

Black Pond	Bolton Landing	N shore of Black Pond.
Five Mile Mt.	Bolton Landing	N of the summit of Five Mile Mt.
Fifth Peak	Bolton Landing	Fifth Peak, Tongue Mt. Range.
Fishbrook Pond No. 1	Bolton Landing	NE shore Fishbrook Pond.
Fishbrook Pond No. 2	Bolton Landing	S end Fishbrook Pond.
Lapland Pond	Bolton Landing	E shore Lapland Pond.
Milman Pond	Bolton Landing	E shore of Milman Pond.

Lake Placid Region

Taylor Pond No. 1	Lake Placid	SE bay of Taylor Pond.
Taylor Pond No. 2	Lake Placid	SE bay of Taylor Pond.
Taylor Pond No. 3	Lake Placid	SW bay of Taylor Pond.
Cooperskill Pond	Lake Placie	E side Cooperskill Pond.

Shelter	*USGS Map*	*Location*
Moose Island No. 1	Lake Placid	Quad on Moose Island.
Moose Island No. 2	Lake Placid	Quad on Moose Island.
Whiteface Brook	Lake Placid	R side of trail from Lake Placid (Barrel Bay Landing) to Whiteface Mt., ¾ mi. from Landing.
Loch Bonnie	Lake Placid	On Loch Bonnie (in beaver swamp).
Whiteface Mt.	Lake Placid	N slope Whiteface Mt. near observer's cabin.
South Notch	Lake Placid	S notch of Sentinel Range.
Copperas Pond No. 1	Lake Placid	S shore Copperas (Sentinel) Pond.
Copperas Pond No. 2	Lake Placid	N shore of Copperas Pond.

Long Lake Region

Catlin Bay No. 1	Long Lake	E shore Long Lake at Catlin Bay, ½ mi. S of Round Lake.
Catlin Bay No. 2	Long Lake	E shore Long Lake at Catlin Bay.
Kelly's Point No. 1	Long Lake	E shore of Long Lake at Kelly's Point.
Kelly's Point No. 2	Long Lake	E shore of Long Lake at Kelly's Point.
Plumley's No. 1	Long Lake	E side of Long Lake, Plumley's Landing.
Plumley's No. 2	Long Lake	E side of Long Lake, Plumley's Landing.
Rodney Point No. 1	Long Lake	S of Camp Islands, E shore of Long Lake.
Rodney Point No. 2	Long Lake	S of Camp Islands, E shore of Long Lake.

Shelter	*USGS Map*	*Location*
Round Island	Long Lake	½ mi. S of Round Island on E shore of Long Lake.

Meacham Lake Region

Hays Brook No. 1	Santa Clara	Northern edge of old sheep meadow S of Star Mt. on Meacham Lake Horse Trail.
Hays Brook No. 2	Santa Clara	Northern edge of old sheep meadow S of Star Mt. on Meacham Lake Horse Trail.
DeBar Mt.	Loon Lake	On fire tower trail S of tower.

Minerva Region

Minerva Stream	Schroon Lake	Junction of Minerva Stream and Hewitt Pond Brook.
Stony Pond	Schroon Lake	Outlet of Stony Pond.

Piseco Lake Region

T-Lake	Piseco Lake	S shore of T-Lake.
Chase's Lake	Gloversville	S end of Chase's Lake.

Raquette Lake Region

Forked Lake	Raquette Lake	On Forked Lake near the outlet.
Big Island No. 1	Raquette Lake	W end of Big Island, Raquette Lake.
Big Island No. 2	Raquette Lake	W end of Big Island, Raquette Lake.
Big Island No. 3	Raquette Lake	W end of Big Island, Raquette Lake.
Boucher Point No. 1	Raquette Lake	N shore of Outlet Bay, Raquette Lake.
Boucher Point No. 2	Raquette Lake	Northern part of Boucher Point, Outlet Bay, Raquette Lake.

Shelter	USGS Map	Location
Boucher Point No. 3	Raquette Lake	N shore of Outlet Bay, Boucher Point.
Clarks Point No. 2	Raquette Lake	Clarks Point, Beaver Bay, W side Raquette Lake.
Clarks Point No. 3	Raquette Lake	Clarks Point, Beaver Bay, W side Raquette Lake.
Outlet Bay	Raquette Lake	N shore of Outlet Bay.

Raquette Lake–Lower

Shelter	USGS Map	Location
Lost Channel No. 2	Long Lake	W bank of Raquette River below foot of Long Lake.
Calkins Creek	Long Lake	Junction Cold River and Calkins Creek.
Calkins Creek No. 1	Long Lake	N side Calkins Creek Trail near junction Calkins Creek.
Calkins Creek No. 2	Long Lake	N side Calkins Creek Trail near junction Calkins Creek.
Latham Pond No. 1	Long Lake	N side Cold River near outlet Latham Pond.
Latham Pond No. 2	Long Lake	On Cold River N end of Cold River bridge above clearing.
Cold River No. 1	Long Lake	Where N-P Trail meets Cold River.
Raquette Falls No. 1	Long Lake	E bank Raquette River, ½ mi. below Raquette Falls.
Raquette Falls No. 2	Long Lake	E bank Raquette River below Raquette Falls.
Stony Creek	Long Lake	Raquette River E of Stony Creek Pond outlet.
Trombley Clearing	Long Lake	Raquette River at Trombley Clearing between Axton and Tupper Lake.
Raquette Falls	Long Lake	Raquette Falls Carry.

Shelter	*USGS Map*	*Location*

Raquette Lake–Upper

Forked Lake Carry	Raquette Lake	Raquette River, 1½ mi. below Forked Lake.
Raquette River No. 1	Blue Mt.	Buttermilk Falls on Raquette River.
Raquette River No. 2	Blue Mt.	Buttermilk Falls on E bank.

St. Huberts Region

Roaring Brook (Giant Mt.)	Elizabethtown	On headwaters of Roaring Brook, Elizabethtown–Giant Mt. Trail.

Sanford Lake Region

Henderson	Santanoni	Indian Pass Trail between head of Lake Henderson and Calamity Brook Trail.
Wallface	Santanoni	Indian Pass Trail S of Indian Pass.
Scott Clearing	Santanoni	Indian Pass Trail E of Scott Pond outlet.
Twin Brook	Santanoni	Junction of red and yellow trails on Upper Twin Brook.
Gorge	Santanoni	Mouth of gorge on Opalescent River (or East River) on trail to Colden.
Calamity No. 1	Mt. Marcy	W side of Flowed Lands at Calamity Landing.
Calamity No. 2	Mt. Marcy	W side of Flowed Lands near Calamity Dam.
Flowed Lands	Mt. Marcy	W side of Flowed Lands between dam and Calamity Landing.
Livingston Point	Mt. Marcy	At Livingston Point on E shore of Flowed Land.

Shelter	USGS Map	Location
Flowed Lands (Griffin)	Mt. Marcy	Westerly side of Flowed Lands near Opalescent Dam.
Opalescent	Mt. Marcy	On Opalescent River Between Lake Colden and Flowed Lands.
Colden	Mt. Marcy	Midway between Opalescent and McMartin lean-tos.
McMartin	Mt. Marcy	E side of Lake Colden outlet between Colden and Flowed Lands.
Cedar Point	Mt. Marcy	Between dam and Beaver Point lean-to.
Beaver Point	Mt. Marcy	At point on W side of Lake Colden between ranger cabin and dam.
Cold Brook	Mt. Marcy	W of ranger cabin on W side of Lake Colden.
Colden No. 1	Mt. Marcy	At foot of Lake Colden on E side of trail to Marcy.
Colden No. 2	Mt. Marcy	At foot of Lake Colden on E side of trail to Marcy.
Colden No. 3	Mt. Marcy	Above Colden No. 2 upstream towards old swing bridge E side on trail to Marcy.
IOAC Memorial	Mt. Marcy	S bank of Opalescent River.
Colden Outlet	Mt. Marcy	W bank of Opalescent River (red trail) near Lake Colden outlet.
Feldspar	Mt. Marcy	At mouth of Feldspar Brook on Opalescent River, junction of Colden–Marcy Trail and Lake Arnold Trail.
Uphill	Mt. Marcy	At mouth of Uphill Brook on Opalescent River, Colden Trail to Marcy.

Shelter	*USGS Map*	*Location*
Saranac Lake Region		
Norway Point	Saranac Lake	At Norway Point, N shore Lower Saranac Lake.
Tom's Rock	Saranac Lake	At Eagle Island, Lower Saranac Lake.
Saranac River	Saranac Lake	On N shore of Saranac River opposite Cold Brook.
Placid	Saranac Lake	1¼ mi. from Whiteface Inn on trail to Saranac.
St. Regis	St. Regis	S shore of St. Regis Pond approximately ¼ mi. from outlet.
Fish Pond No. 1	St. Regis	NW shore Fish Pond.
Fish Pond No. 2	St. Regis	Near end of truck trail.
Kiwassa Lake	Saranac Lake	Outlet of Kiwassa Lake.
Weller Pond	St. Regis	N shore of Weller Pond.
Middle Saranac No. 1	Saranac Lake	Middle Saranac at foot of trail to Ampersand Mt.
Middle Saranac No. 2	Saranac Lake	Middle Saranac Lake at foot of trail to Ampersand Mt.
Rice's Point	St. Regis	E shore of Hungry Bay, Middle Saranac Lake, Rice's Point.
Saginaw Bay No. 2	St. Regis	N shore of Saginaw Bay, Upper Saranac Lake.
Indian Point	Long Lake	At Indian Point ¾ mi. from Indian Carry Landing, Upper Saranac.
Middle Saranac Lake	Saranac Lake	Bull Rush Bay.
Schroon Lake Region		
Rock Pond	Paradox Lake	E side of Rock Pond.
Mud Pond	Paradox Lake	300 ft. off trail to Crab Pond.
Tub Hill Marsh	Paradox Lake	Along Crab Pond Trail near Tub Hill Marsh.

Shelter	*USGS Map*	*Location*
Grizzle Ocean	Paradox Lake	N shore of Grizzle Ocean.
Oxshoe Pond	Paradox Lake	S end Oxshoe Pond.
Lillypad Pond	Paradox Lake	N shore of Lillypad Pond.
Clear Pond	Paradox Lake	S side of Clear Pond.
Eagle Lake	Paradox Lake	At Crown Point Bay, Eagle Lake.
Berrymill Pond No. 1	Paradox Lake	S side of Berrymill Pond.
Berrymill Pond No. 2	Paradox Lake	S side of Berrymill Pond, 800 ft. W of No. 1.
Lost Pond	Paradox Lake	W side of Lost Pond.
Pharaoh Lake No. 1	Paradox Lake	SE shore of Pharaoh Lake Horse Trail system, about 1 mi. NE of caretaker's cabin.
Pharaoh Lake No. 2	Paradox Lake	SE shore of Pharaoh Lake, about 1 mi. NE of caretaker's cabin.
Pharaoh Lake	Paradox Lake	N shore of lake.
Pharaoh Lake	Paradox Lake	Pharaoh Lake, E shore, .3 mi. from outlet.
Pharaoh Lake	Paradox Lake	S side of Pharaoh Lake, .5 mi. above Outlet Dam.
Pharaoh Lake	Paradox Lake	W shore Pharaoh Lake

Thirteenth Lake Region

Siamese Brook	Thirteenth Lake	Sacandaga River Crossing Trail to Siamese Ponds.
Johns Pond	Thirteenth Lake	S of Johns Pond on Puffer Pond Trail.
Lixard Pond	Thirteenth Lake	E end of Lixard Pond.
Puffer Pond No. 1	Thirteenth Lake	E end of Puffer Pond.
Puffer Pond No. 2	Thirteenth Lake	NW corner of Puffer Pond.
Wilcox Lake	Harrisburg	S shore of Wilcox Lake.

Shelter	*USGS Map*	*Location*
West Canada Lakes Region		
Colvin Brook	Indian Lake	S side of Cedar River, junction of Colvin Brook.
Miami River	Indian Lake	2 mi. from Perkins Clearing at Miami River.
West Canada Creek	West Canada Lakes	W side of West Canada Creek at Mud Lake.
West Canada No. 1	West Canada Lakes	E end of West Lake.
West Canada No. 2	West Canada Lakes	Clearing near the ranger's cabin.
Third Lake	West Canada Lakes	W shore of most westerly lake.
Spruce Lake No. 1	West Canada Lakes	E shore of Spruce Lake.
Spruce Lake No. 2	West Canada Lakes	S of outlet from Balsam Lake.
Spruce Lake No. 3	West Canada Lakes	SE shore of Spruce Lake.
South Lake	West Canada Lakes	S shore of South Lake.
Sampson Lake	West Canada Lakes	N shore of Sampson Lake.
Pillsbury Lake	West Canada Lakes	NE shore of large bay on S side.
Cedar Lakes	West Canada Lakes	N end, W shore of Cedar Lakes.
Mud Lake	West Canada Lakes	E end of Mud Lake.
Cedar River Flow	Indian Lake	1¾ mi. from Flow on inlet.
Brook Trout Lake	West Canada Lakes	E end of Brook Trout Lake.
Woodhull Lake Region		
Remsen Falls	McKeever	N bank of S branch of Moose River.

Shelter	USGS Map	Location
Gull Lake	McKeever	N shore of Gull Lake.
Chubb Pond	McKeever	SE shore of Chubb Pond.
Four Mile Brook	Ohio	200 ft. S of Four Mile Brook.
Big Woodhull	McKeever	S shore of Big Woodhull Lake.
Sand Lake Falls	McKeever	Outlet of Sand Lake.

SECTION E7

TRAILS MAINTAINED BY ADK

The following is a listing of trails located in the Forest Preserve that are maintained by the Adirondack Mountain Club.

Southside Trail	2.31 mi.	North Jersey Chapter
Crossover Trail (To Southside Trail)	0.24 mi.	North Jersey Chapter
Woodsfall Trail to Lower Wolf Jaws	2.20 mi.	Trails Committee
Trail to Woodsfall Trail from Southside Trail	0.88 mi.	Trails Committee
Short Job Trail	0.42 mi.	Trails Committee
Range Trail over Upper Wolf Jaws, Armstrong and Gothics	3.35 mi.	Trails Committee
Range Trail over Rooster Comb and Hedgeheg to W. A. White Trail Jct.	3.50 mi.	Keene Valley Chapter
Rooster Comb Trail from Hwy. 73	1.60 mi.	Keene Valley Chapter
Big Slide Mt. via Klondike Notch Trail	2.70 mi.	Trails Committee
Big Slide Mt. via Slide Mt. Brook Trail	2.35 mi.	Trails Committee
The Brothers Trail	3.55 mi.	Long Island Chapter
Porter Mt. Trail from K. V. Airport	4.54 mi.	Schenectady Chapter
Porter Mt. Trail from road near Garden	3.40 mi.	Schenectady Chapter
Baxter Mt. Trail from Beede Farm	1.45 mi.	Algonquin Chapter

Baxter Mt. Trail from Upham Road	1.70 mi.	Algonquin Chapter
Baxter Mt. Trail from Spruce Hill	0.67 mi.	Algonquin Chapter
Spread Eagle Trail	1.32 mi.	Genesee Valley Chapter
Hopkins Trail	2.65 mi.	Genesee Valley Chapter
Ranney Trail	1.52 mi.	Keene Valley Chapter
Mt. Jo Long Trail (Adirondak Loj Prop.)	1.10 mi.	Loj Operating Comm.
Mt. Jo Short Trail (Adirondak Loj Prop.)	0.38 mi.	Loj Operating Comm.
Heart Lake Trail (Adirondak Loj Prop.)	0.50 mi.	Loj Operating Comm.
Kelsey Trail (Adirondak Loj Prop.)	0.90 mi.	Loj Operating Comm.
Hicks Trail (Adirondak Loj Prop.)	0.40 mi.	Loj Operating Comm.
Nature Trail to SW Corner and return via W property line (Adirondak Loj Prop.)	1.30 mi.	Loj Operating Comm.
The Crows Trail	2.08 mi.	Hurricane Chapter
Lost Pond Trail	3.02 mi.	Hurricane Chapter
Hurricane Mt. Trail	2.29 mi.	Hurricane Chapter
Scarface Mt. Trail	2.15 mi.	Laurentian Chapter
McKenzie Mt. Trail from Ray Brook	4.40 mi.	Albany Chapter
Haystack Mt. Trail from Ray Brook	0.94 mi.	Albany Chapter
Baker Mt. Trail	0.89 mi.	North Woods Chapter
Mt. Marcy–Van Hoevenberg Bypass Trail	1.92 mi.	Glens Falls Chapter
Total Miles	62.61 mi.	

INDEX

The abbreviation "Mt." is used only where needed to avoid confusion with lakes, brooks, etc. bearing similar names. Lakes are listed under their names instead of under "Lake."

Other Publications
of
The Adirondack Mountain Club, Inc.
172 Ridge Street
Glens Falls, N.Y. 12801
(518) 793-7737

Guidebooks

AN ADIRONDACK SAMPLER, Day Hikes for All Seasons
  50 hikes throughout the Adirondack Park; includes winter hikes for the snowshoer

GUIDE TO THE NORTHVILLE–PLACID TRAIL
  Detailed description and guide to 133-mile trail

GUIDE TO TRAILS OF THE WEST–CENTRAL ADIRONDACKS
  Hiking trails and canoe route from Old Forge area to Blue Mountain Lake

OLD ROADS AND OPEN PEAKS
  Walks, climbs, canoe routes, bushwhacks in Great Sacandaga Lake–Johnsburg area

ADIRONDACK CANOE WATERS—NORTH FLOW
  Definitive guide to 700 miles of canoe routes in St. Lawrence/ Lake Champlain drainage basins

Natural History

THE ADIRONDACK LANDSCAPE
  Complete hiker's guide to common High Peak land forms

TREES OF THE ADIRONDACK HIGH PEAK REGION
  Hiker's identification guide to trees in the Forest Preserve

ROCK SCENERY OF THE HUDSON HIGHLANDS AND PALISADES
  Guide to the geology of southern New York State

BIRDLIFE OF THE ADIRONDACK PARK
  Complete text for researcher, describing 261 species accounts

How-to

WINTER HIKING AND CAMPING
Authoritative basic manual on winter wilderness excursions

General Reading

PEAKS AND PEOPLE OF THE ADIRONDACKS
Geography and lore of the Adirondack High Peaks

Maps

Trails of the Adirondack High Peak Region
USGS quads of Marcy, Santanoni, half of Elizabethtown

Old Roads and Open Peaks of the Sacandaga Region
*Portions of USGS quads of Indian Lake, 13th Lake, North Creek,
Lake Pleasant, Harrisburg, Lake Luzerne*

Trails of the West-Central Adirondacks
Old Forge area to Blue Mountain Lake

Price List available on request